TRANSFER OF LEARNING AND THE CULTURAL MATRIX

Culture, Beliefs and Learning in Thailand Higher Education

Dr. Jonathan H. Green
University of Southern Queensland

Deep University Press
Blue Mounds, Wisconsin, USA

Deep University Online!

For updates and more resources
Visit the Deep University Website:
www.deepuniversity.net

Copyright © 2015 by Poiesis Creations Ltd - *Deep University Press*
Member of Independent Book Publishers Association (IBPA)

All rights reserved. Permission is granted to copy or reprint portions up to 5% of the book for noncommercial use. Excerpts may not be posted online without written permission from the publisher.
For permissions, contact: publisher@deepuniversity.net

ISBN 978-1-939755-18-6 (pb)

Library of Congress Cataloging-in-Publication Data
1. Higher Education. 2. Thailand. 3. Transfer of Learning. 4. Culture and beliefs. 5. Thailand. 6. Jonathan H. Green

Keywords: Higher Education, Cultural Matrix, Culture and Belief Systems, Transfer of Learning, Social Science Research

Target audience: Collegiate language instructors – English education instructors – second language acquisition – field researchers – cultural studies students –graduate students - university researchers

Topics: transfer of learning, culture, belief systems, international education, national identity, higher education

Version 2
Cover photos: Isabelle C. Druc, Poiesis Creations LLC, Wisconsin

WHAT OTHERS ARE SAYING...

The field of quality teaching and learning is a complex and dynamic one. Jonathan Green's book on the transfer of learning makes an original contribution to this field in that it adds value to the discourse on influences and forces impacting on quality student learning. Learning is not a one-directed process, characterised by teacher-centeredness, but one where students are at the centre. Understanding how students perceive and experience their own learning is a key to unlocking their potential. This is a long-overdue publication.

—Professor Arend E. Carl, Vice-Dean: Teaching, Stellenbosch University, South Africa

Through this research, Jonathan Green has contributed to the body of knowledge about transfer of learning. His rigorous research investigates transfer in the context of learners' personal epistemology and culture, yielding a culturally relative understanding of transfer that is highly relevant in today's increasingly diverse classrooms. The findings, which have implications for educators in a wide range of educational contexts, will be of particular interest to those who teach in internationalized and multicultural institutions.

—Alexander Nanni, Director, Preparation Center for Languages and Mathematics at Mahidol University International College, Thailand

Original thought provoking, high quality research that extends our knowledge of transfer of learning in relation to multicultural tertiary students in international education settings. Deep insights are gained, through use of the researcher's Measure of Academic Literacy (MALT), a new tool that explored issues of context and cultural values and beliefs, and metacognitive knowledge in transfer of learning.

—Associate Professor Shirley O'Neill, Applied Linguistics Discipline Coordinator, School of Linguistics, Adult and Specialist Education, University of Southern Queensland

At a time when the debate on education prioritizes the transfer of learning as the focus of teaching models in advanced societies, Jonathan Green's research offers a sophisticated analysis of empirical data to move forward in understanding the belief systems of the learners and their relation to learning transfer reviewing the rooted cultural matrix model, and incorporating the perceptions of students with international and intercultural educational background. This research work is brilliantly illustrated by narrative episodes.

—Dr. Manuel Fernandez Cruz, Professor, University of Granada, Spain

This research is nuanced, addresses learning transfer its complexity, and is as such outstanding. Jonathan H. Green did an excellent job in the mixed study, which is unusually thorough in so many respects: it complements parametric measures with non-parametric appreciations, uses sophisticated factorial analyses of correspondences based on chi square clusters, and explores fascinating interviews in Thailand that not only illustrate the cultural matrix but furthermore contribute to its theorising.

—Dr. François Victor Tochon, Professor and head, World Language Education, University of Wisconsin-Madison, USA

As a foreign language education researcher, teacher, learner, and user, I fully and deeply realize the value of Dr. Jonathan Green's gorgeous work in his mixed study of transfer of learning and the interrelationship of culture, beliefs, and learning and the improvement that the fascinating cultural matrix will bring to language education. This book is innovative, insightful and an invaluable resource for students and teachers engaged in world languages education.

—Dr. Jianfang Xiao, Associate Professor, Guangdong University of Foreign Studies, China

Jonathan Green has produced a detailed and relevant contribution to the discussion on the topic of the transfer of learning. His study sheds new light on the issue of transference and highlights the importance of this issue in relation to course outcomes and syllabus design, especially with regard to EAP (English for Academic Purposes) curricula at pathways schools and international colleges. The future applications of this research are enormous and promise to have a long lasting influence on this field of study.

—Rhys William Tyers, Subject Leader, English for Academic Purposes, Trinity College, The University of Melbourne

This study should be required reading for high school teachers, who are still overly concerned with the process of instruction. This work makes it clear that the context and the individual student are just as worthy of our attention. In encouraging a "culturally pluralistic" paradigm, it nudges the reader towards a more egalitarian way of perceiving new learning.

—Charles Kusner, High School English Teacher, The Kenmont School, South Africa

With a focus on the context of an English for General Academic Purposes Program at a Thai University, Green presents a comprehensive analysis of learners' personal epistemologies. Educational leaders, language program developers, researchers, and instructors would find this text useful. A strong contribution to studies on learners' beliefs.

—Dr. A. Cendel Karaman, Assoc. Prof., Middle East Technical University, Turkey

Acknowledgements

I owe a debt of gratitude to Associate Professors Shirley O'Neill, PhD, and Peter McIlveen, PhD, both of the University of Southern Queensland, for their encouragement, patience, and insights along the way.

I am also indebted to Karen Coe, PhD, and Aimee Provost in helping me avoid an ethical quandary by conducting the semi-structured interviews.

I should be remiss, too, in not thanking the administration at Mahidol University International College for their support, and my colleagues, who have given me encouragement and advice over the years.

I am especially grateful to my wife, Orie, who has shared much of my academic journey with me over the years, and to my sons, Joshua and Nathan, both born after I had embarked.

Contents

Abstract	11
Chapter 1: Introduction to the Study	13
1.1 Background	13
1.1.2. Mahidol University International College	14
1.1.3. The English Communication Programme	15
1.1.4. Students' Cultural Backgrounds	18
1.2. Overview of the Study	26
Chapter 2: Conceptual Development	31
2.1. Methods	31
2.2. Transfer of Learning	32
2.2.1. Definitions	32
2.2.2. Conceptual Development	33
2.2.3. The Failure of Transfer of Learning	38
2.2.4. Strategies for Transfer of Learning	39
2.3. Learners' Beliefs about Knowledge, Knowing, and Learning	48
2.3.1. Definitions	49
2.3.2. Conceptual Development	50
2.3.3. Beliefs and Learning	64
2.3.4. Beliefs and Cross-Cultural Studies	74
2.4. Culture	78
2.4.1. Definitions of Culture	78
2.4.2. Societal Culture	81
2.4.3. Organisational Culture	92
2.4.4. Culture and Learning	98
2.4.5. Culture and Learners' Beliefs	103
2.5. The Cultural Matrix of Social Psychology	106
2.5.1. Enculturation	110
2.5.2. The Cultural Matrix and the Present Study	112
Chapter 3: Research Methods	113
3.1. Research Purpose and Questions	113

3.2. Conceptual Framework	113
3.3. Participants	115
3.4. Piloting the Study	115
3.5. Data Collection	116
3.5.1. The Questionnaire	119
3.5.2. Semi-Structured Interviews	124
3.6. Ethical Considerations	128
3.7. Expected Outcomes and Significance	106
3.8. Projected Data Analysis - Pilot Study	130
Chapter 4: Results	**145**
4.1. Pilot Study	145
4.2. Stage 1: Questionnaire	146
4.2.1. Initial Data Screening	146
4.2.2. The Epistemic Beliefs Inventory (EBI)	147
4.2.3. The Measure of Academic Literacy Transfer (MALT)	160
4.3. Stage 2: Semi-Structured Interviews	164
4.3.1. Deductive Themes	164
4.3.2. Inductive Themes	165
4.3.3. Participants: "Cast of Characters"	171
4.4. Addressing the Research Questions	175
4.4.1. Research Question 1: What is the Nature of Students' Perceptions of the Transfer of Learning from the Academic-Literacy-Based English Communication Programme to the Courses in the Disciplines?	175
4.4.2. Research Question 2: What is the Nature of the Relationship Between Students' Perceptions of the Transfer of Learning from the EC Programme and their Personal Beliefs About Knowledge and Learning?	193
4.4.3. Research Question 3: What is the nature of the relationship between students' beliefs about knowledge and learning and their secondary school background ("culture")?	217
Chapter 5: Discussion and Recommendations	**231**
5.1. Discussion	231

5.1.1. The Validation of the Questionnaire	231
5.1.2. Transfer of Learning to the Disciplines	236
5.1.3. Relationship between Transfer of Learning and Students' Beliefs about Knowledge and Learning	240
5.1.4. Relationship between Students' Beliefs about Knowledge and Learning and their Secondary School Backgrounds	243
5.2. Limitations	250
5.3. Conclusions: Transfer of Learning and the Cultural Matrix	253
5.3.1. Implications for Theory	255
5.3.2. Implications for Practice	256
5.4. Recommendations	257
References	259
Appendices	276
Appendix A: Excerpt from Outcomes Statement for First-Year Composition from Council of Writing Program Administrators (2008)	276
Appendix B: Part One of Questionnaire	278
Appendix C: Part Two of Questionnaire	282
Appendix D: Part Three of Questionnaire	284
Appendix E: Matrix for Semi-Structured Interviews	285
Deep University Press: Scientific Board Members	286
Guide to Authors	294
Correspondence	295

List of Tables

Table 1. Research Questions and Corresponding Methods	118
Table 2. Descriptive Statistics of Typical Cases for Each "Secondary School Background"	135
Table 3. Factor Loadings for Principal Components Analysis with Oblimin Rotation of EBI Scales (N=177)	152
Table 4. Descriptive Statistics of Skew and Kurtosis for EBI Factor Scores	154
Table 5. Good Fit Indices, Critical Values and Values for EBI and MALT	157
Table 6. Factor Loadings for Principal Components Analysis with Oblimin Rotation of MALT Scales	162
Table 7. Descriptive Statistics of Skew and Kurtosis of MALT Factor Scores	161
Table 8a. Themes Developed A Priori Relating to Students' Beliefs about Knowledge and Learning	165
Table 8b. Themes Developed A Priori Relating to Students' Beliefs about Knowledge and Learning	166
Table 9. Themes Developed A Priori Relating to Students' Perceptions of Transfer of Learning	167
Table 10a. Deductive Themes Derived From Template Juxtaposed to Inductive, Data-driven Themes	168
Table 10b. Deductive Themes Derived From Template Juxtaposed to Inductive, Data-driven Themes	169
Table 11. Descriptive Statistics for MALT Summed Subscales and Individual Items	177
Table 12. Pearson Correlations for EBI and MALT Scale and Subscale Variables	194
Table 13. Spearman Correlations for EBI and MALT Scale and Subscale Variables	195
Table 14. Measures of Central Tendencies for Analyses of Variance between Cultural Factors (Secondary School Background and Nationality), and EBI and MALT Scores	219
Table 15. Results of t-tests and Descriptive Statistics for EBI & MALT Scores by Secondary School Background	224
Table 16. Results of Mann-Whitney U Tests and Descriptive Statistics for EBI and MALT Scores by Revised Secondary School Background	224

Table 17. Results of Mann-Whitney U Tests and Descriptive Statistics for EBI and MALT Scores by Revised Nationality 226

List of Figures

Figure 1. The cultural matrix of social psychology 114
Figure 2. Stages undertaken by Fereday and Muir-Cochrane (2006) in coding the data 138
Figure 3. Stages of hybrid approach as adapted to this study 139
Figure 4. Scree plot showing initial extraction of Epistemic Beliefs Inventory (EBI) factors with related eigenvalues 151
Figure 5. Graph showing eigenvalues of raw data (rawdata) from initial extraction of Epistemic Beliefs Inventory factors compared to means ("means") and percentile ("percentile") eigenvalues 152
Figure 6. Confirmatory factor analysis model of three extracted factors from Epistemic Beliefs Inventory 158
Figure 7. Scree plot showing initial extraction of Measure of Academic Literacy Transfer (MALT) factors with related eigenvalues 160
Figure 8. Graph showing eigenvalues of raw data from initial extraction of Measure of Academic Literacy Transfer (MALT) factors compared to means ("means") and percentile ("percntyl") eigenvalues 160
Figure 9. Confirmatory factor analysis model of two extracted factors from Measure of Academic Literacy 163
Figure 10. Scores of interview participants in Epistemic Beliefs Inventory, overall, and for the three dimensions extracted by the principal components analysis of the questionnaire data 173
Figure 11. College-wide enrolment, by percentage, in various Majors 179
Figure 12. Scatter plot displaying linear regression of EBISUM as a predictor of MALTSUM 197

Abstract

This study, conducted in an international college in Thailand, aimed to understand the transfer of learning from an undergraduate academic literacy programme to the disciplines. In so doing, it adopted a cultural matrix to investigate the interrelationship among students' perceptions of transfer of learning, their personal beliefs about knowledge, knowing and learning, and their secondary school backgrounds. A three-part questionnaire, supplemented by purposive semi-structured interviews, was used to collect data from all consenting students from the final course in a four-trimester programme. The first part of the questionnaire employed the Epistemic Beliefs Inventory (EBI) in gauging students' beliefs about knowing and learning, the second part comprised the Measure of Academic Literacy (MALT), which measure students' perceptions of transfer of learning from the academic literacy programme to the disciplines, and the third part of the questionnaire surveyed students' demographic details, specifically with regard to their secondary school context. Data were then analysed to establish the interrelationship between these data sets. Open-ended questions to the MALT section of the questionnaire were analysed, and, in order to illustrate and further understand the data analysis from the questionnaire, trained interviewers conducted semi-structured interviews.

Initial, factorial analysis of the EBI indicated a factor structure that differed from that of the US origins of the instrument, suggesting a relationship between culture and beliefs. While analysis indicated a significant low-moderate relationship between students' beliefs about knowledge and learning and the transfer of learning, no such association was detected between the beliefs and students' secondary school background. The students' multicultural backgrounds, coupled with ambivalent beliefs, may provide an explanation for this. The findings, thus, give partial support for the application of the cultural matrix to transfer of learning.

The study makes an original contribution by applying the cultural matrix to learning in a previously unexplored way. In so doing, it aims to generate a general theory of transfer of learning while fostering a culturally pluralistic understanding of learners' beliefs about knowledge and learning and the implications for such transfer. It also advocates an approach that supplements existing classroom-specific pedagogical methods with school-wide cultural management initiatives in order to better effect transfer of learning.

Chapter 1
Introduction to the Study

1.1 Background

Transfer of learning is widely proclaimed as one of education's main aims. However, despite a long and eminent history of discussion in education and training (since Thorndike & Woodworth, 1901a, 1901b), a general theory of transfer remains elusive. Since the 1980s, cognitive-based instructional frameworks, such as that of Salomon and Perkins (1989), have predominated in attempting to address the failure of certain types of transfer, but the question remains as to whether these strategies alone are sufficient in promoting the long-term goals of transfer. An argument can be made that successful transfer is predicated on elements relating to the learners themselves, especially concerning their beliefs about the nature of learning, knowing, and knowledge. Hence, any efforts to address the learning environment and improve pedagogy without addressing this dimension may, at best, produce only short-term success or, at worst, failure. Learners may continue to perceive learning as context- or task-dependent or as merely "jumping through hoops" in response to instructors' demands. They may thus disregard long-term proficiency goals. For these reasons, any strategies aimed at addressing learning transfer may depend on a personal belief system, on the part of the learner, that values autonomy, elements of metacognition, such as abstraction and decontextualisation, and what Dweck and others (e.g., Diener & Dweck, 1978) refer to as *mastery-orientedness*.

Orientations in learners such as independence, decontextualisation and personal mastery, however, may not reflect the universal educational values that they once appeared to do. A growing corpus of criticism argues that they are frequently premised on Western cultural assumptions (e.g., Fiske, Kitayama, Markus, & Nisbett, 1998; Hofer, 2008). East Asian and Southeast Asian cultures, especially, value interdependence above independence (Hofstede, 2001), reflect a perceptual preference for interconnectedness and context (Ventura, Pattamadilok, Fernandes, Klein, Morais, & Kolinsky, 2008) and are more concerned with communal harmony than personal mastery (Fiske et al., 1998). As Vygotsky (1978), Lave (1988), and others have convincingly argued, these external, interpersonal social values may find *intra*personal, psychological form; cultural values may thus find inner manifestation in the belief systems of individuals, including their beliefs about knowledge and learning.

Transfer of learning, then, may be closely associated with learners' beliefs about knowledge and knowing, while these beliefs are themselves largely related to culture. This broad assertion, developed below against a cultural psychology matrix, provides the framework for this particular study.

1.1.2. Mahidol University International College

Mahidol University International College (MUIC) provides English-medium instruction in all its subject areas. At the time of data collection, its 2,728 enrolled students ("Facts and figures," 2011) presented a relatively culturally diverse population. Although most students were Thai nationals, a significant number were foreign, many Western. The diversity was reflected in the students' different secondary school backgrounds, including attendance at regular Thai state schools, bilingual schools, international schools in Thailand, and schools abroad.

The college requires all students, at the start of their studies, to be enrolled for least four trimesters (three for native or near-native speakers of English) in the English Communication programme as part of their general education requirements. The English Communication classes aim to develop students' academic literacy and communication knowledge; the purpose is that this knowledge is then transferable by the students to their further disciplinary studies in their majors.

Unfortunately, at the time that the study was conceived, the extent to which the programme successfully fulfilled its support aim was not known. Indeed, providing the initial impetus for this study, anecdotal evidence from instructors in the target disciplines, in addition to personal observation by this researcher, indicated that many students were not transferring much of the knowledge from the English Communication classes to the disciplines.

1.1.3. The English Communication Programme

The English Communication (EC) programme at MUIC is what Jordan (1997) would term an English-for-General-Academic-Purposes (EGAP) programme. EGAP programmes are distinguished from English-for-Specific-Academic-Purposes (ESAP) programmes by their aim, which is to develop university students' academic literacy skills for general transfer to all or any of the disciplines in the tertiary context. ESAP, on the other hand, targets transfer to particular academic disciplines, such as Engineering or Sociology, based on the dominant discourse on those disciplines.

At MUIC, the EGAP model is adopted from necessity, as the students, when they start the EC programme, have not yet begun to engage in their respective majors. This is a function of the American-style liberal arts model to which the college adheres; in this model, students complete general education (GE) courses that are intended to be of wide application to the students' future studies, regardless of discipline. The notion of general transfer is thus inherent to the liberal arts model and thus to MUIC. This is more explicitly so for the EC programme.

The fact that students have not yet begun their major studies at the time that they complete their first courses in the EC programme presents a challenge to instructors. As Carroll (2002) has identified in her study of first-year composition, to which the EC programme is akin, the *what* and the *how* need to be integrated for successful development of academic literacy skills. The *how*, general academic literacy knowledge, such as that related to identifying and acknowledging sources and composing essays, cannot be meaningfully developed in the classroom without the *what*, the content that acts as both a medium and a source of engagement for the development of such knowledge.

The EC programme meets this challenge of integrating content and literacy knowledge by adopting a theme-based approach. Ideally, the theme-based approach allows content to act as an engaging vehicle for the meaningful development of the relevant *know-how*. It can be distinguished from content-based instruction (CBI) in that the focus remains on this *know-how* and not on the content itself. Although, in the theme-based approach that the EC programme has adopted, students are expected to engage in the content, their assessment is based on their competence in demonstrating the academic literacy skills.

In a typical lower-level class in the EC programme, students and instructors might negotiate a broad social theme, such as Gender Inequality or Human Rights. The instructor might initially provide the texts and other impetus materials on this theme, but as the programme progresses, much of this scaffolding is gradually removed and the responsibility for locating and evaluating materials for engagement shifts to the students. Students, with the instructor's assistance, decode and discuss the texts (or other media, such as film), identify issues and stances, and then compose supported essays (or, in one of the courses, speeches) communicating their respective stance.

In reading, researching and composing, students are expected to demonstrate academic literacy knowledge in a number of areas. During a curriculum review conducted in 2011, these areas were adopted retrospectively from the outcomes statement for first-year composition issued by the US-based Council of Writing Program Administrators (2008) because these outcomes were considered to be aligned with the EC programme's actual practice and ideal outcomes at the time. The five areas are: *rhetorical knowledge*, such as the ability to compose a structured essay or speech; *critical, thinking, reading and writing*, which emphasises, particularly, the relationship between reading and writing; *knowledge of processes*, such as the steps involved in composing an essay; *knowledge of conventions*, such as those related to the formats of different texts, or to referencing; and *knowledge of composing in electronic environments* (see Appendix A for the specific items listed by the WPA in each of these five domains).

While the adoption of these areas from the WPA suggests that the EC programme is a writing programme, it is not exclusively so, which is the reason that, in most of this discussion, it is referred to as an academic literacy class (not to be confused with the research orientation of Academic Literacies, which, in the Marxist tradition, incorporates an agenda critical of dominant social and academic discourse (see Coffin & Donahue, 2012).

For most MUIC students, the EC programme commences with enrolment in their first trimester in Intermediate English Communication I (known as EC1), which, similarly to a traditional first-year composition class in the US, focuses on reading and on writing essays according to various rhetorical patterns, such as comparison-contrast, or cause-effect. The students are exposed to thematic texts in a variety of genres, such as literary, non-fiction—or literary non-fiction.

Students then progress to Intermediate English Communication II (EC2), which focuses on their engagement, both through traditional texts and other media, in the social issues comprising the themes and their responses to these issues. Students are expected to develop their own stance on these issues, and to support this stance by means of cogent reasoning and appropriate evidence from secondary sources. In evaluating the sources used for these purposes, moreover, students are encouraged to develop knowledge related to locating and identifying reliable, relevant, and accurate sources, and competence in assessing reasoning and evidence. They are expected to demonstrate these knowledge sets through classroom engagement and by means of conventional written academic arguments.

The next course in the progression, Intermediate English Communication III (EC3), anticipates that students will transfer the academic literacy knowledge they have developed in EC1 and EC2 to public speaking. Other than the oral presentation format, the knowledge sets are similar to those employed in EC2: students further develop their rhetorical and critical knowledge, such as that related to effective persuasion or required for identifying logical fallacies. In addition, however, they focus on the knowledge required for effective speech delivery: verbal aspects, such as voice projection and cadence; and non-verbal, such as eye-contact and posture.

The final EC course, English Communication IV (EC4) is somewhat different from the progression thus far in that, firstly, students have a choice in the subject matter of the course, and that, secondly, the focus, for most of the available options, is much more content-orientated. The electives for fulfilling the EC4 requirements include: Introduction to Literary Analysis; Introduction to Linguistics; Global Realities; Creative Writing; Film into Literature; and others. The notion here is that students will transfer the knowledge from the earlier courses in the progression to a content or skills area that interests them and will be of use to them either in their studies or extracurricularly. In addition, unlike the other courses in the progression, in which students enrol in a continuous succession, the EC4 elective may be taken at any time during the student's undergraduate career, provided he or she has already completed the other courses in the EC programme.

By the time that students enrol in the EC4 course, they will have started in their major studies. This is significant in that the students, at this stage, have developed, in principle, general academic literacy skills to support their disciplinary studies. However, as mentioned in the previous section, the extent to which students transfer this knowledge, or perceive the usefulness of the EC programme to their other courses, was unknown at the time of the study and, thus, subject to anecdote and conjecture.

1.1.4. Students' Cultural Backgrounds

At MUIC, the student population is less homogeneous than in most Thai higher education institutions. Students' cultural backgrounds, which can be considered from the perspective of societal or national culture, on the one hand, or from secondary school background, on the other, are relatively diverse. Often, students can claim membership of more than one cultural background; their home background, for example, may be Thai while they have attended Western-orientated international schools for most of their primary and secondary education careers. In addition, even in their home background, students may experience some plurality: it is common, for example, for students to have a Thai mother and, perhaps, an American father. One may argue, therefore, that MUIC has inter- and intracultural diversity represented in its student population. This diversity applies equally to the faculty members employed at the college.

Nationalities. Because MUIC is an English-medium institution that is modelled on liberal arts colleges in the US, it attracts a more diverse student population, in terms of nationalities, than do conventional tertiary institutions in Thailand. The majority of students are Thai, but many of these have had exposure to other, particularly Western, cultures, whether through attending international schools, travelling abroad, or engaging in exchange programmes, particularly to English-speaking countries, such as the US, Australia and New Zealand. Of these Thai students, many have dual nationalities; one parent is a Thai national and the other a foreign national. This duality is also well represented in the large number of third-, fourth- or even fifth-generation Thai students of Indian, particularly Sikh, descent. While the Sikh community has been present in Thailand for over a century (Wyatt, 2003), it has retained a number of cultural practices and values from its country of origin, particularly in terms of religion and language.

In addition, a number of students are admitted from neighbouring countries in Southeast Asia, such as Myanmar, Vietnam, and Malaysia, with many also coming from further afield in Asia: MUIC has seen a steady increase in the number of Korean, Japanese, Taiwanese, and Mainland Chinese students.

A certain number of students from Western countries, particularly the US, Canada, Australia, the UK, and Germany, also study at MUIC. Some of these students, as the sons and daughters of expatriate parents, are enrolled full-time, while others, because MUIC operates a system of partnerships and MOUs with other institutions globally, are visiting or exchange students.

Secondary school background. Culture may be defined not only in terms of broader national and societal groups, but also of organisational membership. In particular, and of relevance to this study, MUIC students are admitted from a number of types of secondary schools that may differ somewhat in their respective institutional cultures.

Thai state schools. Because standard-programme students from these schools are often not as well equipped in English communicative proficiency as students from international schools or bilingual programmes, they are not as well represented in the MUIC student population as are students from these other schools and programmes.

State schools in Thailand are administered either by the Ministry of Education or provincial schooling authorities, such as the Bangkok Metropolitan Administration. Often these schools are nominally affiliated with local Buddhist temples that serve a rural or urban community. These schools serve the greater majority of the Thai population and provide the basic education (a minimum of nine years is mandated) required by the various education acts governing compulsory education in Thailand. The centralisation of schooling administration has been acknowledged by Ministry of Education officials to have produced a "compliance culture" (Hallinger & Kantamara, 2001), which reflects the traditional adherence to hierarchical authority in Thai culture.

In relation to the other types of schools discussed in this section, the state schools, which are funded by the authorities and charge no tuition fees (they do, however, levy some peripheral fees towards, for example, meals) are relatively impoverished in terms of standards and resources. Teachers are recruited from state-run teaching colleges (known as Rajaphat Universities) that provide only the most elemental preparation programmes for primary and lower-secondary teachers (a two-year teaching certificate), although upper-secondary teachers require a four-year degree.

In general, the students who attend state schools, especially in rural areas, are from relatively lower socio-economic backgrounds; their parents are often labourers, farmers, or small-scale vendors. For this reason, these households have had comparatively less exposure to the forces of internationalisation or Westernisation; and Thai cultural mores are more pronounced. This researcher, during his prior three-year experience as a "foreign teaching expert" in a typical Bangkok state school, observed a strong Thai cultural (and nationalistic) imperative in this school; daily institutional practices will be reflective of this. Typically, learners in these schools will start the day with the raising of the national flag and the singing of the national anthem, followed by a period of Buddhist meditation. Collectivity and uniformity are symbolised through the adoption of a common school uniform throughout all schools, and activities that foster *esprit-de-corps* are emphasised.

While various policies by the Thai Ministry of Education have impelled a trend towards more international practices in the classroom such as learner-centeredness, many of the vestiges of traditional Thai schooling remain. These are, in turn, reflective of Thai societal culture and are characterised thus by Hallinger and Kantamara in terms of Hofstede's cultural dimensions theory (discussed in Section 2.4.2.) as a point of departure for their research into change initiatives in Thai schools.

Hallinger et al. (2001) conclude, through their research and the literature at large, that in Thai public schools, as in broader Thai culture, there exists a high power distance: the highly hierarchical and bureaucratic nature of Thai society is evident in schools in the relationship of school administrators to subordinates. This is also evident in the classroom: students regard the teacher as the ultimate authority in the classroom (at least ostensibly) and seldom question him or her. Lessons are typically teacher-centred and knowledge-transmission based, often employing rote-learning, rather than engendering creativity or critical thinking (Pagram & Pagram, 2006)

Collectivism is also the norm: in the classroom, harmony prevails through the lack of opinion-based discussion, student interdependence—and dependence on the teacher—is encouraged. Individual students seldom attract attention to themselves by asking questions or raising objections and curricular or extracurricular group activities that promote group spirit are strongly promoted.

Thai government schools also evince the Thai societal tendency towards high uncertainty avoidance, according to Hallinger et al. (2001), which is indicated by a "high level of discomfort with uncertainty, ambiguity, and complexity" (p. 396). These last three characteristics, by contrast, mark the more Western-orientated constructivist classroom. Moreover, Thai public schools are impelled by a collectivist inclination, Hallinger et al. observe. They add that, for this reason, creativity and "'being different' are regarded as undesirable and disruptive"; tradition is strongly encouraged, and teachers often focus on order in the classroom. Moreover, the certainty provided by frequent summative assessment is the *de facto* focus of the curriculum.

Lastly, in terms of Hofstede's *masculinity-femininity* dimension, Hallinger et al. remark that Thai schools, similarly to Thai society at large, tend towards what Hofstede characterises as *femininity*—a concern for nurturing and relationships rather than the task-based orientation that would characterise a more *masculine* orientation. As this researcher has learnt from through years of observation, interviews, and informal conversations with Thai students, "good" teachers are often characterised as those that demonstrate nurturing, caring characteristics towards their students. When many students are asked to consider the characteristics of a "good" teacher, they seldom mention the teacher's pedagogical effectiveness as evinced through instructional methods.

The foregoing characteristics are, of necessity, broad generalisations (as in all the forthcoming school classifications in this discussion), but they are ones supported by the literature and this researcher's fifteen-year involvement with the Thai education system. While Thai state schools are homogeneous in their student population—seldom will students from non-Thai backgrounds attend—individual students may, of course, diverge from the characterisations that have been described in this section. State schools also differ from each other. Nevertheless, the characteristics are presented here as a point of departure that should provide the reader with a conceptual means of comparison between types of feeder schools to MUIC.

It should be noted, moreover, that many of the students that are admitted to MUIC from public schools in Thailand have had a somewhat "moderated" school experience. Because an important admissions criterion for MUIC is English proficiency, many students, even if they have attended Thai state schools, would have been enrolled in the English programme of such schools. Unlike regular-programme students at these schools, they would have attended intensive English language classes, and other classes in other subjects, such as Geography and Physics, that were conducted in English, frequently by Western teachers. As a result, these students are likely to have been exposed to more learner-centred, task-based, and constructivist pedagogical approaches in these classes, conducted in parallel to their regular, Thai-orientated classes.

Bilingual, Catholic and other private schools in Thailand. MUIC admits, because of its English-language requirements, a greater number of students from private "bilingual" schools than from the state schools. Bilingual schools in Thailand are characterised as dual language immersion schools that divide the overall curriculum between Thai and a minority language. The aim of the dual language policy of these schools is to maintain the learners' competence in the native language while fostering equivalent or near-equivalent proficiency in the minority language (Thomas & Collier, 1997). In a typical English programme in a bilingual school, instruction is divided by subject or content area; in the primary years, the ratio may equal, while, in the secondary years, the proportion of English-medium instruction may be increased to 60% (see, for example "Kasintorn Academy," 2014). The English medium instruction is usually conducted by native English speakers from countries such as the US, UK, Australia, Canada, Ireland, New Zealand and South Africa.

Of the bilingual schools in Thailand, the (at least nominally) Catholic schools form the most significant proportion. Over 300 Catholic schools, most having bilingual programmes, operate within the Archdiocese of Bangkok (Kowitwanij, 2008). While these schools are populated mostly by Buddhist and Muslim students, with Catholic students a minority, the institutions retain an ethos that distinguishes them from the Thai public schools. They also have a history that dates back over 300 years to the Catholic missionaries who were active in proselytising in Southeast Asia during the Ayutthaya period (Kowitwanij), whence Siam and modern Thailand draws its origins as a nation state. This influence by Western missionaries in the past, and by Western-inspired policies and teachers up to the present, has had, arguably, a moderating influence on the Thai cultural norms and values that would operate in Thai state schools.

Prathumarach (2011) asserts that the administrative and management structures in Catholic schools are different from those of the common Thai educational institution: "Catholic education aims to develop human beings in all dimensions, physical and spiritual, intellectual, emotional, and social" (p. 4). Furthermore, the Catholic school, being "based on the teachings of Christ… should promote the dignity of all human beings, giving witness to love, service, and charity." Catholic education has thus emphasised holistic education for longer than it has been espoused by the Thai state schools. Moreover, Catholic schools, being less homogeneous in the composition of their student bodies than are the state schools, have actively encouraged cultural integration, more or less successfully, for a number of years (Kowitwanij, 2008).

In addition, those Catholic schools that are the main feeders for MUIC tend to be prestigious schools that, owing to selective admissions and higher tuition fees, cater to Thai students from relatively affluent backgrounds. These students and their parents, therefore, are more likely to have been exposed to Western-orientated internationalisation trends, often through business and social connections and overseas travel, than are their public school counterparts.

These schools are also far better resourced. Not only do they have a greater number of highly-qualified teachers, they are also likely to have larger cohorts of Western teachers who provide intensive English language instruction and, frequently, English-medium instruction in subjects other than English. It is, thus, probable that students who have attended these schools would have become accustomed to educational practices that are more common in classrooms in, for example, the US and the UK. These practices would include group discussions, student-centeredness, a constructivist learning experience, and an emphasis on individual achievement. As a result, one may assume that these students are somewhat more comfortable that their state school counterparts with the ambiguities of knowledge that the constructivist classroom introduces, more individualistic in their learning styles owing to a greater emphasis on academic excellence, and, correspondingly, more task-orientated.

While the Catholic schools constitute, by far, the largest group of private bilingual schools in Bangkok, MUIC receives students from other Christian and private secular schools in Bangkok. These institutions tend to be similar in their instructional ethos to the Catholic schools—or to the international schools discussed in the next section. In particular, a significant number of students from the Sikh community attend the Thai Sikh International School (TSIS) before enrolling in MUIC. While TSIS positions itself as an international school, it is similar in nature to the Catholic schools in its emphasis on faith values—in this case, those promoted by Sikhism (Stoneham, 2004).

International Schools in Thailand. As MUIC has positioned itself as an international college in both name and curriculum, an accordingly large percentage of MUIC students are admitted from international secondary schools, which are privately administered, similarly to the Catholic schools. These schools adhere to a curriculum other than that of the Thai Ministry of Education, such as the International Baccalaureate (IB) or American or Canadian equivalents. In these schools, the medium of instruction in all subjects (other than in Thai language studies) is a language other than Thai. In Thailand, as is the case globally, English predominates as the language adopted by international schools, although other language communities, such as French, Japanese or Chinese, also have attendant international schools that are based on the curricula in these respective countries.

While the Thai state, bilingual, and Catholic schools are intended primarily for the education of Thai nationals, the purpose of international schools is to attend to the education of foreign nationals (often the children of expatriates). It is, nevertheless, not unusual for a large number of local students who are seeking educational standards beyond those offered on aggregate by the Thai schooling system to enrol in these schools—provided these students' families have the financial means. International schools (there is a wide range of standards and quality, but most MUIC students enter the college from the better-reputed ones that are characterised here) tend to have fees structures that place them beyond the usual local salary range, particularly in developing countries such as Thailand.

International schools have more resources than the other schools described here and they recruit the majority of their teachers from Western countries. Despite a growing body of criticism as to the Western orientation of international schools—one that calls for a more multicultural perspective (e.g., Heyward, 2002; Poore, 2005)—and despite a greater heterogeneity of their population than in the Thai state, bilingual, or Catholic schools, most international schools reflect the ethos of the home environment of the Western students. The assertions of Poore, an experienced international school educator and administrator, are worth reporting at length in this regard:

> [A]ll we have to do is look at the leaders of international education to see that [international] schools themselves are culturally loaded: they are often founded with the assistance of Western governments for the purpose of educating the children of their employees (not to spread multiculturalism); they are largely headed by white educators from the first world who are trained in leadership theories which are culturally biased... they are staffed largely out of necessity by native English speakers; they operate from western liberal humanist curricula often packaged as international; they are more often than not accredited by western agencies which have no real concern with the issue of culture other than the superficial inclusion of the host culture in the curriculum; and they pride themselves on the 'third culture' of the school which is generally rarely more than a variation of the dominant (usually American or British) culture (p. 352).

While Poole's assertion may be at least part polemical, it is clear that international schools, for the most part, engage in practices that reflect values that have been cornerstones of Western education for a number of decades now. Independence, personal mastery, self-efficacy, and individual worth are fostered in a less teacher-centric, more task-based environment that epitomises "best" international practice in Western, developed countries. In contrast to the students in Thai public schools (and, to a lesser extent, in bilingual and Catholic schools), these students, as a result of this exposure, could be expected to display higher levels of independence, a greater tolerance for the ambiguity of knowledge and knowing. They may also have a more individualistic outlook, and, as a result, could be more achievement- and competition-orientated.

Other secondary school backgrounds. In addition to the secondary school types outlined in this section, a number of students at MUIC may have attended schools in other countries, as MUIC's enrolment includes foreign students from a variety of countries. Such students may have attended secondary school in the US or Australia, for example, or, in many cases, may have graduated from schools in neighbouring countries in Southeast Asia (such as Malaysia, Vietnam or Myanmar) or East Asia (particularly Korea, Japan, Mainland China, and Taiwan). Most often, these students will have attended international schools, which tend to retain the Western-orientated ethos described above, along with some local nuances. However, in some cases, the students might have attended schools that are been influenced more by the local culture than by Western values. Many MUIC students, for example, have attended secondary school in India, which may impart values somewhat distinct from those already discussed here.

1.2. Overview of the Study

This study was motivated by an investigation into students' transfer of learning to the disciplines from an undergraduate academic literacy programme in an international college in Thailand. Earlier conceptualisations of the transfer of learning had indicated that certain types of transfer, particularly those related to the application of deeper, abstract principles to new contexts, were bound to fail if students were not provided with explicit instructional strategies that facilitated such transfer.

While Baldwin and Ford (1988), among others, recognised that the successful facilitation of transfer of learning required attention to three essential components—the instruction itself, the learning environment, and the learner—many of the earlier instructional frameworks, such as that of Perkins and Salomon (1988), neglected the latter two components in favour of the former. However, a failure to consider the learning context or the learner may mean that instructional gains are limited. A general model of transfer, therefore, is required that integrates in a meaningful way the three elements of *instruction, learner,* and *context*.

Many earlier studies that focused on the learner—particularly on learner agency—showed that an effective learner was one who was autonomous, motivated, and self-directed. The findings of these studies, while applied to learning in general, found support in the *transfer* of learning. A effective learner, or one who successfully transferred learning, moreover, had certain "theories of intelligence" Diener and Dweck (1983) that were related to certain beliefs as to how learning and knowledge "worked." The learner, in other words, had characteristics that were *availing* of learning (Muis, 2004). The problem that arose, however, was that these characteristics are more valued in certain cultures than in others—independence, mastery-orientedness, and beliefs in learning as process-oriented, for example, are more valued in the US than they would be in Thailand.

It became necessary, thus, to examine students' beliefs in a culturally relative way as they were associated with knowledge and learning. Philosophical and other conceptual arguments for the association between culture and beliefs about knowing and knowledge—epistemic beliefs—in particular, are compelling. Beliefs about learning are, arguably, an extension of epistemic beliefs and strongly related to beliefs about knowledge. Contemporary conceptualisations, such as that of Nisbett (2004, 2009), argue that individuals' "habits of thought," and, therefore, their behaviours, are influenced by their epistemology, which is, in turn, influenced by their sociocultural context—a view that accords with Vygotsky's (1978) view as to the psychological internalisation of the interpersonal to become the *intra*personal.

The cultural matrix of social psychology accounts in a parsimonious way for these interrelated spheres—*sociocultural context, the learners' psychological processes and structures, and individual manifestations*. In terms of the matrix, core cultural values are proximally related, through a culture's institutions, to recurrent events, such as those in school or the home. These recurrent events then have an immediate relationship to psychological structures and processes. This latter relationship, in particular, accords with the thinking of influential theorists, such as Hofstede (2001), who maintained that it was organisation culture, through everyday activities, that had a more immediate, even less permanent, relationship to individual behaviour than did national culture.

Returning to the cultural matrix, an individual's psychological structures and processes have immediate manifestations in perceivable action.

It was, therefore, the cultural matrix—particularly the spheres from recurrent events in a culture's institutions, through individual psychological structures, to individual action—that framed the investigation of the study, as informed by the research questions. The first question, concerning the nature of students' perceptions of the transfer of learning from the academic literacy course to the disciplines, informed the latter sphere of the model, *action*. The second question informed the relationship between such action and *psychological structures*—in the case of this study, the students' beliefs about knowledge and learning. The final question concerned the relationship between the psychological structures and the recurrent events in the cultural context—in this case, the students secondary school contexts.

The cultural matrix thus presents both a comprehensive and parsimonious model for the transfer of learning, one that encompasses much of the relevant theorising in the literature as to the interrelationship among sociocultural factors, individual psychology, and action in the form of transfer of learning.

The three questions that were framed by the cultural matrix were investigated by means of a questionnaire, to give the broad coverage required by model validation, and semi-structured interviews, which would help in illustrating the findings of the questionnaire and in giving deeper insights. The questionnaire, the primary means of data collection, consisted of three components: the Epistemic Beliefs Inventory (EBI), for gauging students' beliefs about knowledge and learning; the Measure of Academic Literacy Transfer (MALT), which examined students' perceptions of the transfer of learning from the academic literacy programme, and the demographic section, which collected, among other demographic data, information concerning students' secondary school backgrounds and their nationalities.

For the sake of validation, the EBI and the MALT were subjected, prior to the analysis demanded by the research questions, to both principal components analysis (PCA) and confirmatory factor analysis (CFA). The factorial analysis of the EBI yielded three dimensions—*innate ability, certain, authoritative knowledge*, and *simple knowledge*—that differed from the five belief dimensions that were hypothesised in the original, US context of the instrument, giving some support for the cultural relativity of beliefs. The factors and scores that emerged from the PCA and the CFA of both the EBI and the MALT were used in the subsequent enquiry.

In terms of the first research question, concerning the nature of students' perceptions of the transfer of learning, descriptive analysis of the MALT revealed that most students agreed that they had used knowledge from the academic literacy programme in their courses in the disciplines. Interview data revealed that this transfer often related to surface features. In addressing the second question as to the relationship between students' beliefs about knowledge and learning and their perceptions of transfer, the Kruskal-Wallis test and a regression model indicated, significantly, that a small-to-moderate association existed between EBI and MALT scores and that the EBI scores predicted the MALT scores, accounting for 6.3% of the variance. The statistical analysis directed towards the third research question, however, detected no significant relationship between the students' beliefs and their reported secondary school backgrounds. Moreover, no significant relationships were detected in subsequent explorations of possible associations between nationality and beliefs, or between either nationality or secondary school background and students' perceptions of transfer.

Possible reasons for the failure to detect the relationship considered in the third research question emerged from reflections on the interview data, which showed the emergence of a theme related to students' ambivalence of beliefs, possibly related to their exposure to multiple cultural contexts. This led to considerations concerning the difficulties in conceptualising and measuring culture as a construct. In terms of conceptual difficulties, it was speculated that concepts of *acculturation*, rather than the *enculturation* assumed by the cultural matrix, was more relevant to the population of students who had been exposed to international education.

The study considers implications of the findings. Theoretical imputations include the partial support of the cultural matrix, which, subject to further investigation, may contribute to a general model for understanding the transfer of learning, particularly with more homogeneous populations. A further theoretical implication may be the need to develop acculturation models that may be more applicable to students in international education who have experienced multiple societal and schooling cultures. Practical implications, if the cultural matrix is accepted, include justifications for school-wide initiatives that address institutional culture, or more narrowly, coaching of students in beliefs as part of a metacognitive "package."

Recommendations are made for further research that includes more objective measures of transfer of learning and takes into account other elements of the cultural matrix, and for studies that: examine causation; consider discrete, homogeneous populations; develop acculturation models; and develop conceptualisations of domain-specificity or -generality, as analogous to theories in disciplinary contexts, in relation to individuals who traverse multiple cultures.

Chapter 2
Conceptual Development

2.1. Methods

The collection of data for this review commenced with a search of all generally accessible electronic databases for literature pertaining to the three main areas covered by the scope of this study: transfer of learning; learners' epistemic beliefs and related beliefs about learning; and culture, both societal and organisational, as it related to learning. The review focuses particularly on relevant literature of the last 20 years. Where possible, print sources are included where they have broad exposure (in the form of multiple citations from one source, or across a number of sources) within the electronically available articles. Articles older than 20 years are also included if they are considered seminal to a particular area of concern, such as culture, personal epistemology, or transfer of learning.

In particular, an effort was made to include relevant literature within the sphere of secondary and tertiary education, moving more specifically towards studies and expositions concerning writing instruction, academic literacy, or English for Academic Purposes (EAP) courses at the university level. However, applicable, seminal articles from other spheres—for example, vocational education—are included.

Although the review aims to be comprehensive, it is not exhaustive. In particular, research and conceptual articles contributing directly to relevant theoretical development; to higher education; or to writing, academic literacy or EAP programmes at the undergraduate level are included, and where principles are duplicated across several similar articles, the most significant is presented as illustrative of these principles.

2.2. Transfer of Learning

2.2.1. Definitions

Although a central, incontrovertible definition of learning transfer is difficult to locate, many writers (e.g., Burke, Jones, & Doherty, 2005; Opfer & Thompson, 2008; Pea, 1987) have agreed that, in essence, such transfer involves the application of previous learning to a new context. In the case of EAP or academic literacy classes, this would entail students applying the knowledge gained in that class, such as that related to structuring an argument or evaluating sources, to any of the other academic disciplines that require these particular kinds of literacy.

Many of the definitions of transfer have made a distinction between transfer of *skills* and transfer of *knowledge*. This account, however, adopts the position of Macaulay and Cree (1999), which recognises that "[r]ecent epistemological debate suggests that traditional ways of conceptualising 'knowledge' (i.e., information) and 'skills' as separate entities have been misleading and this area has been re-conceptualised under the general rubric of knowledge" (p. 188).

In addition, many dichotomies exist between types of transfer or its processes, such as that between *productive* and *reproductive* transfer (Robertson, 2001), knowledge transfer and problem-solving transfer (Mayer & Wittrock, 1996) and high-road and low-road transfer (Salomon & Perkins, 1989). All of these constructions are valuable in understanding transfer; it is, however, the latter that most informs this discussion because of its relative usefulness in developing a serviceable instructional framework. The definition has, moreover, been influential in education in general, and in at least one effort to develop specific instructional strategies in English language teaching (James, 2006).

Another potential area of contention is that, in the last decade, many definitions of transfer have veered away from the traditional position presented above, and many researchers, rather than examining the "direct" application of knowledge, have shifted toward a knowledge construction view. Many of these theorists (e.g., Kozulin, 1998; Rebello, 2007; von Glasersfeld, 1995) reject the perspective that transfer involves the transfer of a unified body of learning; they maintain, rather, that transfer is an active, dynamic process that is mediated by sociocultural factors and is best viewed from the learner's, rather than the researcher's, perspective (Rebello, 2007, p.1). It is the latter view that informs much of the central contention in this discussion: that instructional frameworks based on traditional views that fail to address learners' personal beliefs about knowledge and learning can expect, at best, only minor and temporary gains, and that these beliefs are influenced by sociocultural factors.

2.2.2. Conceptual Development

Because of its centrality to education, transfer of learning has been studied formally for over a century now (see Thorndike & Woodworth, 1901a, 1901b) and has witnessed shifts from classical education to a more utilitarian, specific context-based training, through to a recent re-emergence of concerns for generalisable learning, such as that from numeracy, literacy, and critical thinking. It has traced concomitant changes in concurrent predominant psychological theories, from faculty psychology, behaviourism, and cognitive approaches, to more recent sociocultural perspectives.

Mentalism. Most reviews on the literature of transfer of learning begin with Thorndike and Woodrow's seminal elucidation of the common elements theory, which held "that learning rigorous topics generally disciplines the workings of a young mind" (Pea, 1987, p. 40). Specifically, when certain "elements" between a prior and novel learning context were sufficiently similar, transfer would occur. Thorndike and Woodworth (1901a, 1901b) conceded that their conceptualisation of these elements was loosely formulated (p. 247); subsequent research has been a concerted effort, in fact, to provide definition that is more rigid. The similarity of elements, to Thorndike and Woodworth, referred to the transfer *distance* between the two contexts, *near transfer* being that in which the contexts and performances are similar, while *far transfer* referred to those that were relatively dissimilar. These concepts form the basis for the subsequent evolution of transfer theory (e.g., Butterfield., 1988; Osgood, 1949; Perkins & Salomon, 1988).

Osgood, however, and more recently Butterfield and Nelson (1989), have pointed out that the lack of "specific objective measures between learning and transfer elements" (p. 7), in effect, made this first formulation of the common elements theory "educationally useless"—this despite the significant and formative contribution that the theory made to the study of transfer.

Behaviourism. Subsequent to the formulation of the common elements theory by Thorndike and Woodrow, the dominant school in psychology, and hence in learning theory, was stimulus-response theory. Butterfield and Nelson, who trace much of the development outlined here, comment that much of the early investigations (e.g., McGeoch, 1942; Robinson, 1927; Wylie, 1919) was problematic because "experimenters mixed stimulus and response properties in their measures of transfer distance" (Butterfield & Nelson, 1989, p.8). This resulted in a paradox: although greater proximity is, in fact, more conducive to learning, the failure to separate stimulus from response led these theorists to posit the opposite—that increasing proximity resulted in greater *negative* (undesirable or inappropriate) transfer, because of the increased incidence of interference from the prior learning context.

Osgood (1949), in response to this paradox, generated a theory that recognised the complexity of the transfer equation. He repudiated what he described as the (then-) textbook position that "the greater the similarity, the greater the interference" (p. 132). Osgood's is a three-dimensional representation that separates stimulus similarity, response similarity and degree of effect as "simultaneously interrelated" variables and which resolves the increased proximity–increased interference paradox, and was consequently "more useful" (Butterfield & Nelson, 1989, p. 8) to educators in promoting positive transfer within a stimulus-response framework. General failures within this conceptualisation, however, aside from a gradual falling-out-of-favour of behaviourism, include the gap between the limited number of variables in controlled experimental stimulus-response and the complexity of real-life learning situations; and the individual, internal representations of the learner independent of those of the experimenter. (As will be seen, similar criticisms were later directed at cognitivism.)

Cognitivism. In distinct contrast to behaviourism, cognitivism marked a movement towards a focus on the inner representation of the learner. Rejecting the view of the learner as a mostly passive recipient of environmental cues, theorists such as Piaget saw the learner (in this case, a child) as an active participant, interacting with the world and engaging in problem solving, often through social mediation (Vygotsky, 1962). Inhelder and Piaget (1958) posited a concept that remains current in learning: that of *schemata*, by which previous conceptions of elements were replaced with representational outlines or "scripts" of knowledge. Although Piaget did not explicitly address either learning or transfer, it can be inferred from his writing that in order for learning and, by extension, transfer, to occur, it is necessary to instantiate the necessary schemata—or representations of knowledge—in the target domain.

What became important for the cognitivists was the model of information processing (Butterfield & Nelson, 1989) and the conceptualisation of knowledge not as static and reified, but rather as a product of constructive activation (Bruner, Goodnow, & Austin, 1956). Unlike the behaviourists, cognitivists focused on the "internal" rather than the "external" and posited various models in an effort to explain some of the internal mechanisms of learning and transfer.

Although the focus of this particular discussion is on instructional and socio-cultural strategies rather than the internal representations with which traditional cognitive psychology is concerned, it is worth mentioning here Anderson's (1982) original conceptualisation of his Adaptive Control of Thought (ACT) model. In addressing the acquisition of cognitive skill, Anderson proposes in the ACT a progression from the interpretation of facts about the skill domain through to a stage in which this knowledge is used in the production of procedures for performing the skill. These "productions" are organised into subroutines, each of which is "associated with a goal state that all the productions in the subroutine are trying to achieve" (p. 372). It is the centrality of goals and goal seeking that is interesting here, because goals are also the focus of theories such as that of Dweck & Elliott (1983) in their exploration of goal-orientedness in successful learners. What applies microcosmically for Anderson does so macrocosmically for Dweck and Elliott (and for discussions of personal epistemology) and is germane to conceptualisations of transfer of learning: the internal mechanisms proposed by the ACT may provide an explanation for, and interface between, the internal processes of the mind and the external influences that may either help or hinder transfer of learning.

Concerning pedagogical application, the concepts developed and elucidated by the cognitivists have been influential in the development of many current taxonomies of transfer, such as that of Salomon and Perkins (1989), and concepts such as that of information processing and metacognition remain prominent in many recent studies of transfer (e.g., Billing, 2007; Brand, Reimer, & Opwis, 2007).

Sociocultural and situational approaches to transfer. Ironically, a similar criticism to that levelled against behaviourism can be applied to conventional cognitivism—that it is more reliant on researcher manipulations of representations than on those influences that would occur naturally in the classroom. In other words, as Rogers (1959) early contended, the experiments widely used in cognitive psychology may have lacked ecological validity—results were of dubious value, as the control over variables in the laboratory induced an artificial environment.

Theorists since the time of Vygotsky's *social interactionism* have increasingly recognised the importance of ecological or environmental factors in influencing cognitive processes as they relate to learning. Greeno (1998), for example, advanced a theory on the "situativity" of learning that focuses on the interaction of cognitive agents "with each other and with other subsystems in the environment" (p. 5) and contended that often this interaction is contextually, and more specifically, socially, defined. Earlier, Pea (1987) argued for an interpretative, rather than objective perspective on transfer theory that recognises a concept of transfer that is socioculturally "appropriate." He called, moreover, for the "socialising" of the transfer problem, arguing for an "interpretive" approach in which "common elements" are transferred in accordance with how "appropriate" such transfer is deemed by the learner, which in turn depends on the influence of the learner's culture. In fostering such transfer, Pea emphasised the synergistic learning of skills and knowledge across contexts.

More recent theorising in transfer (e.g., Bransford & Schwartz, 1999; Lobato, 2006; Rebello, 2007) has suggested a fundamental role for these sociocultural factors in the transfer of learning. For example, Bransford and Schwartz (1999), arguing that hitherto conceptualisations of transfer were inadequate, proposed that context, or *field* be more carefully addressed in fostering transfer. Other studies have conclusively shown *field* to be influenced by culture, and even more specifically, by *school* culture (e.g., Ventura et al., 2008). Lobato (2006) drew on the ideas of Lave, (1988) in further addressing the notion of context in transfer of learning by considering it from the perspective of *situated* cognition, which relates strongly to Greeno's (1998) views of the *situatedness* of learning transfer. Rebello (2007), in considering transfer from a knowledge perspective, considered factors that are neglected by the traditional models. In particular, Rebello draws on Vygotsky's social interactionist frame by assimilating the *zone of proximal development* (ZPD) in conceptualising the cognitive process underlying transfer of learning.

The theories mentioned above, while acknowledging to some extent the role of sociocultural factors in transfer of learning, still tend towards a cognitive focus. This cognitive emphasis on individual processing has been criticised by authors such as Greeno (1998), who argued that, particularly in learning, a greater recognition of situational context is needed. In this respect, notable exceptions to the cognitive bent in the literature are articles by Closson (2013) and Larsen-Freeman (2013), which explicitly explore the relationship between context and transfer of learning.

Closson's work, because it draws directly on factors of race and culture, is described in the section "culture and transfer of learning." Larsen-Freeman, within the field of second language education, concurs with authors such as Carroll (2002) that many of the problems in the theory of learning transfer can be accounted for by an erroneous knowledge transmission view. Instead, Larsen-Freeman proposes that knowledge is *transformed*, and in this, she recognises that "transfer is not simply something an individual does in isolation, but rather depends on social and cultural factors" (p. 114), and that the individual has some agency in the transfer scheme. Transfer thus involves the individual actively adapting to different and changing environments. The role of the sociocultural context is thus seen as integral to a dynamic process that involves active transformation on the part of the learner.

2.2.3. The Failure of Transfer of Learning

A large number of studies (e.g., Barrows & Tamblyn, 1980; Bransford, Franks, Vye, & Sherwood, 1986; Scribner & Cole, 1981) have illustrated the problem with transfer: much of the knowledge that learners acquire is not activated in new situations, even where the underlying principles are, upon reflection, similar or identical.

Some authors (e.g., Hirsch, 1987; Opfer & Thompson, 2008) have explained this failure by pointing out that knowledge or skills gained in formal education contexts are often highly localised and, as such do not lend themselves to transfer to other contexts. Others have gone so far as to argue that transfer, in this sense, does not exist. Detterman (1993), for example, found justification for Hegel's belief that "people... simply don't transfer what they learn from one situation to another" (p. 2). He argued, specifically, that knowledge is often restricted to what is taught and learned in specific contexts and thus does not in any significant way transfer beyond the boundaries of these contexts.

These contentions are readily dismissed by an early illustration by Meiklejohn (1908, in Opfer & Thompson, 2008):

> What can we say of a theory that the training of the mind is so specific that each particular act gives facility only for the performing again of that same act just as it was before? (p. 789)

Meiklejohn illustrated this rhetorical barb and his accompanying comments by demonstrating the absurdity of first using a yellow hammer to perform a task, and then being confounded upon being presented with a red hammer to perform the same task.

Meiklejohn's refutation, while it may be intuitive, may also be somewhat conceptually facile; valid objections raised by writers such as Pennington, Nicolich, & Rahm (1995) that some specialist skills are suited only to a particular context—and do not, therefore, lend themselves to transfer—should be acknowledged. However, although some knowledge may indeed be localised, there are certain types of knowledge that have, at least, intermediate applicability (Salomon & Perkins, 1989). In most EAP classes, specifically, the aim is for students to develop cross-disciplinary knowledge, such as that relating to structuring a logical argument, which may be applied as much to the Composition class as to Psychology,

Economics, and Thai History. Although specialist knowledge is highly valued in some disciplines, such as Aeronautical Engineering, EAP, by its definition, is not an end in itself but a means of developing in students with knowledge that they may find useful in other courses throughout their academic careers. Germane to this discussion, of course, is the challenge of fostering this same perspective in the students.

2.2.4. Strategies for Transfer of Learning

While it may not be difficult on an intuitive level to illustrate that transfer does, in fact, exist, the apparent failure of transfer, as demonstrated in the research, persists and cannot be ignored. The literature provides many reasons for the failure of transfer revealed by these studies. One of the reasons for the failure, according to Bransford and Schwartz (1999), is that the initial learning is itself inadequate. They argue that "a number of claims about 'transfer failure' have been traced to inadequate opportunities for people to learn in the first place" (p. 64), and that "the degree to which retrieval of relevant knowledge is 'effortful' or relatively 'effortless' also affects transfer." This observation assumes increased significance later in this discussion when one considers that some cultures may value certain types of effort in learning more than others.

Another possible reason for the apparent failure of transfer is that it is simply not accurately detected owing to the complexity of the knowledge being represented. This pertains particularly to the writing process, as Carroll (2002) has explained. Carroll's four-year longitudinal study of the development of 20 college students is one of two studies that are prominent because of their depth and relevance to the subject of transfer at the undergraduate level (the other being Sternglass's *Time to Know Them,* 1997). Carroll observed that the process of learning to write is a haphazard and continuous one; students are constantly evolving to address the differing expectations of the major disciplines. She challenged "the myth that writing is a stable, unitary skill that can be learned once and then simply applied in new circumstances" (p. 27), a condition that makes it difficult to discern a neat transfer of the skills particular to first-year writing classes.

Writing is, in addition, a complex of "literacy tasks" that "require more much more than the ability to construct correct sentences or compose neatly organised paragraphs with topic sentences" (p. 3). Carroll observed, also, that knowledge developed in first-year writing courses follow an indirect route to students' major areas of studies (p. 9). Moreover, although students may not continue to use certain strategies taught in the first-year composition course (such as outlining and brainstorming) in quite the same way, they do use them selectively, as required, and in a modified, constantly evolving manner (pp. 74-5). However, despite this overall progression, Carroll argues, it is superficial errors, such as those in sentence construction and essay structure, that are far more likely to attract the attention of instructors in the major disciplines, many of whom fail to perceive the successful transfer of other literacy skills involved in the writing process. This is a plausible account for disparities between instructors' and students perceptions of whether transfer is in fact occurring (an issue raised in Green, 2008).

That instructors in the disciplines often perceive a lack of transfer from EAP or writing courses may be, additionally, a result of a mismatch in expectations. As Carroll (2002) wryly commented:

> I share Professor X's fantasy that someone somewhere could teach students to write once and for all, so that ever after one has only to say, 'discuss romanticism, or stock market fluctuations, or world hunger, or the life cycle of tree frogs,' and a stack of well-crafted, cogently argued, eminently readable essays would appear. (p. 2)

It is not only the complexity of the transfer process and these sometimes-unrealistic expectations that may account for the perceived lack of transfer, but the type of transfer that is being sought, and the measures taken—or not taken—to achieve it. Perkins and Salomon (1988) observed that "transfer does not take care of itself, and conventional schooling pays little heed to the problem" (p. 22). This neglect they ascribed to what they called the "Bo Peep" theory of education—the assumption that transfer will take care of itself (as in "leave them alone and they'll come home, wagging their tails behind them"). However, as Perkins and Salomon remarked, "considerable research and everyday experience testify that the Bo Peep theory is inordinately optimistic" (p. 23). Burke et al. (2005), in their investigation of university students' perception of transfer from undergraduate courses, concur with this assumption. They comment that, although a growing body of research has indicated the importance of the process aspects and challenged successfully the assumption that transfer of learning is better effected by increased fidelity, those advocating a high-fidelity skills-based approach have ignored such debate. Burke et al. cite Griffin (1994) in lamenting that "the idea that transfer just 'happens' has been so powerful an assumption as to be deemed beyond discussion" (p. 135).

Low road, high road; hugging and bridging. Perkins and Salomon (1988), in addressing the frequently observed of failure of transfer, pointed out that even though the preponderance of studies did, in fact, reveal such failure, others demonstrated successful abstraction and application of learning from one context to another (e.g., Chase & Simon, 1973; Larkin, 1983; Soloway & Ehrlich, 1984). The key, according to Perkins and Salomon (1988), is in the kind of transfer that is being examined. Furthermore, in developing what they referred to as a "tentative theory" (p. 114), they drew on the studies demonstrating successful transfer. This tentative theory posited two types of transfer, *low road* and *high road*. Low-road transfer refers to that which occurs automatically, as in the studies of successful transfer, when the elements of the learning context are superficially similar to those of the target area (elsewhere referred to as "high-fidelity" transfer). High-road transfer, in contrast, occurs when learners are required to abstract general principles from the learning context to the target (where surface features are not apparently similar; this is also known as "low fidelity" transfer). It is this latter kind of transfer, according to Perkins and Salomon, that is so often in the literature perceived to fail, mainly because no efforts are made actively to invoke it. They argued that the failure of transfer, as has been seen, is often a result of an assumption by educators that transfer will occur automatically and without any instructional intervention. Furthermore, they proposed specific instructional strategies that facilitate both high and low road transfer.

To place the strategies of Perkins and Salomon within a larger context: many contemporary frameworks on teaching for transfer have focused on the need to address structural, pedagogical and learner-centred elements (e.g., Macaulay & Cree, 1999; Marini & Genereux, 1995). Of these, Perkins and Salomon (1988) focused on the first and second as they proposed two instructional strategies to promote both low- and high-road transfer—respectively, *hugging* and *bridging*—in order to gain more effectively the sought-after transfer. The first of these was aimed at inducing low-road transfer by increasing the resemblance between the learning and target domains. In accordance with this, EAP course content and assignments, for example, could "match" those of the target disciplines (Fogarty, Perkins, & Barell, 1992). The second, *bridging*, attended to the metacognitive demands of high road transfer; "one '*mediates*' the needed processes of abstraction and connection making" (Perkins & Salomon, 1988, p. 28) by, for example, directing students' attention explicitly to the general principles underlying certain knowledge, by encouraging a process of generalisation, or by facilitating analogy-making. In EAP, this could involve requiring students to anticipate applications (Fogarty et al., 1992) by prompting them with questions such as "For what kind of subject would this rhetorical pattern be suitable?" or with similar enquiries.

Perkins and Salomon (1988) claimed support for their high-road–low-road, hugging–bridging model from the instances of successful transfer that were reported in the research, which, they argued, "all involved strong bridging activities in the instruction" (p. 29).
The framework (and dependent strategies) advocated by Perkins and Salomon is commendable in its efforts to counter the assumption that transfer occurs automatically. Moreover, it provides concrete, "educationally useful" solutions (in the sense employed by Butterfield and Nelson, 1989) and, thus, it has assumed significance in a number of recent studies, from vocational education and training (e.g., Thomas, Anderson, Getahun, & Cooke, 1992) to at least one conceptual article in the field of English language teaching (James, 2006). As an aid to educators, Fogarty, Perkins, and Barrel (1992) draw on the principles of *hugging* and *bridging* to develop 10 specific teaching strategies for the general education classroom, while James (2006) customises these same strategies to English language teaching. Green (2015) has also found support for a relationship between the hugging-bridging strategies and students' perceptions of transfer of learning from an undergraduate EAP programme to the disciplines.

Limitations to hugging and bridging: Pilot study. Potential limitations in the hugging-bridging concept were revealed in an exploratory study by this researcher (Green, 2008) that, in investigating conditions for transfer, employed the hugging-bridging framework to examine students' perceptions of transfer from the academic literacy programme at MUIC to the disciplines.

While the small-scale study indicated a relationship between hugging and bridging strategies and students' perceptions of transfer of learning, some issues emerged. The first concern was the apparent disparity between the perceptions of instructors and students, with student participants perceiving successful transfer of learning where anecdotal evidence suggested instructors did not. On reflection, this may be because students themselves may be the best evaluators of the transfer of complex literary skills and knowledge (Carroll, 2002), while instructors in the disciplines may not be fully familiar with the intricate and complex transfer that is occurring. Largely because of this consideration, student self-report as to transfer of learning was retained for the present study.

The second question emerged from the observation that although students, in general, perceived that they were transferring knowledge from the EC programme to the disciplines, most did not recognise the presence, in the EC classroom, of many of the hugging and bridging conditions and mechanisms delineated by the theoretical framework of Perkins and Salomon (1988). This apparent incongruence to the theoretical framework, which postulates a positive relationship between the hugging-bridging methods and the transfer of learning, might be explained by arguing that, in fact, the conditions described in hugging and bridging account for only two main constituents of the transfer issue: the instruction design and, to a limited extent, the learning environment (or context). What have been omitted from this consideration are the learners themselves—their motivation, their abilities, and their beliefs—an important element of many other frameworks.

A prominent example of a model that integrates learner characteristics can be found in that devised by Baldwin and Ford (1988) for transfer of training, which considers three elements fundamental: (i) *training inputs*, in the form of trainee characteristics, training design and work environment; (ii) *training outputs*, in the form of learning and retention; and (iii) *conditions of transfer*. By extension, Holton, Bates, and Ruona (2000), in elucidating the system of influences affecting transfer, converged on three factors derived Baldwin and Ford's model: *trainee (or learner) characteristics,* "including ability, personality and motivation" (p. 334-335); *training design,* "including a strong transfer design and appropriate content", and *work environment,* "including support and opportunity to use" the transferable knowledge.

Thus, in education, while designs such as that of Perkin and Salomon and certain others attend to instructional design and conditions for transfer, the learners' characteristics are sometimes neglected. The present study, therefore, attempts to investigate more fully the role of the learner in transfer of learning, focusing especially on the role of culture and that of the learner's beliefs about knowledge and learning.

Although the pilot study mentioned in this section, because of its narrow scope and small sample size, suffered from a number of limitations, it did alert this researcher to the possibility that, *despite* the absence of many of the conditions that Salomon and Perkins deem necessary to such transfer, many students perceived that they were transferring learning from the EAP course to the disciplines. This perception suggested that factors other than structure or pedagogy might significantly contribute to the transfer of learning.

Limitations to hugging and bridging: *Further support*. In the study (reported above) by Thomas et al. (1992) on late adolescent and adult learners engaged in a three-month parent education course, the strategies suggested by Salomon and Perkins found some support. The researchers developed a general framework based on cognitive principles and specifically employed high-road–low-road instructional strategies. The study, however, revealed a limitation in the framework: while the researchers found support for short-term transfer gains resulting from hugging and bridging, it was impossible to assess the longevity of these gains, leaving unanswered the question as to whether these strategies were sufficient for effective transfer of learning.

Germane to this discussion, an observation by Thomas et al. suggests what these other transfer-enabling factors might be. Thomas et al. admonish educators actively to stimulate, encourage and support learners' *independent* efforts to transfer knowledge during learning. The authors argue that high-road transfer "*depends* [emphasis added] on a *stance of self-directedness* [which] has to do with learners monitoring themselves and viewing themselves as being in charge rather than expecting others, such as the teacher, to direct them" (p. 13).

This assertion by Thomas et al. was an express acknowledgement of the role of learner agency, which is inadequately emphasised in other traditional perspectives of transfer (Green, 2008). Its mention of the students' *views* as to their agency is also indicative of the importance of learners' beliefs about learning to the transfer of learning. Transfer *depends*, moreover, on the learners' stance towards learning—a requirement not adequately explored by Perkins and Salomon, who focus almost solely on the strategies employed by the instructor.

The learner's beliefs about "how learning works" are critical because a learner who relies on the instructor to provide cues for transfer at any given opportunity will most probably fail to do so when autonomy and independence are required (for more complete discussion of this, see Dweck & Elliott, 1983).

In addition to recognising the individual learner's role, it is important to heed sociocultural voices. Pea (1987), for example, drawing extensively on the literacy studies of Scribner and Cole (1981), advocated the need for a "cultural practices framework" (p. 47) that recognised the influence of the learning context and the sociocultural environment on the transfer of learning.

Other frameworks for addressing transfer of learning. The hugging and bridging framework has been an illustrative focus in this section; similar criticism may apply to any framework for achieving transfer of learning that focuses only on instructional strategies while neglecting to attend adequately to the psychological characteristics of the learner and his or her disposition towards learning; attitude and motivation; and beliefs about learning—and to the sociocultural elements identified earlier in Section 2.2.2.

Gagne, Briggs and Wager (1992), for example, promoted a theory of instruction that, in promoting knowledge transfer, formulated nine "events of instruction" as part of a taxonomy of learning outcomes. Central to the taxonomy are what Gagne et al. referred to as *conditions of learning*, which are further subdivided into *external* and *internal*. In an apparent reconciliation of behaviourist and cognitive approaches, the external conditions are concerned with environmental stimuli (the learning context, the materials and other related ecological concerns) and the internal to the individual's learning capabilities. The "events of instruction" are themselves grounded in cognitive information processing learning theory. In practice, first the instructor determines the learning objectives. These are then articulated (and listed) in terms of domains of learning—verbal information, intellectual skills, cognitive strategies, attitudes, and motor skills—using standard performance verbs. The conditions of learning for each of these objectives are then determined by the instructor, and a lesson that encapsulates the events of instruction is compiled around these. While the incorporation of "internal conditions" into the theory does, in part, accommodate what learners bring to the learning process, the focus is still on the instructor as the director of learning. Further possible criticisms of the theory of Gagne et al. are that it is too rigid (for example, the objectives are limited to certain "standard" verbs) and that it perceives transmission of a unified body of learning (see, for example, Carroll, 2002, for constructivist-orientated criticism of this kind of approach). Nevertheless, the theory has had some influence: it is common to see course curricula and subject syllabi objectified in the manner proposed by Gagne et al. (1992), and often research as to transfer of learning is based, at least in part, on examining the transferability of these listed objectives to other target areas (e.g., Burke, Jones, & Doherty, 2005).

As discussed earlier in this section, one of the shortcomings of the earlier cognitive-based frameworks for transfer of learning, such as the hugging-bridging strategies proposed by Salomon and Perkins (1989), is that they were overly-reliant on the instructor and the classroom context, as may be the case with the instructional theory proposed by Gagne et al. (1992). A reliance on such may mean that transfer is short-lived if a student is not inclined, for example, towards a certain autonomy of learning or towards a belief that the source of learning is constructed rather than transmitted through an instructor as the ultimate arbiter of knowledge. Halpern and Hakel (2003) attempt to address potential problems in this regard in their framework, aiming thus for long-term retention and transfer. They revile the "ephemeral 'magic' of quick fixes" (p. 38), advocating instead what they refer to as "empirically validated principles" to enhance long-term retention and transfer of learning.

These principles include ones that have been elaborated upon previously, and are often drawn from cognitive and metacognitive precepts, such as practising at retrieval, varying conditions of learning so that it is not context-bound, "re-presenting" learning in a different form, and focusing on genuine understanding, rather than assessment. In contrast to Salomon and Perkins (1989) and Gagne et al. (1992), what is noteworthy in the principles elaborated by Halpern et al. is an increased focus on what the learner may bring to the process of learning: that "what and how much is learned in any situation depends heavily on prior knowledge and experience; and that *"learning is influenced by both our students' and our own epistemologies"* (p. 39; emphasis added). Halpern et al., furthermore, align *personal* epistemology with academic motivation. They also use the term in the inclusive sense by referring to students' beliefs "about the nature of learning." Their short review of the principles, however, does not elaborate on the precise nature of the relationship between students' beliefs about the nature of learning and the transfer of learning.

A comprehensive review of frameworks for effecting transfer of learning is presented by Haskell (2001). Haskell, in his synthesis of research into transfer of learning elucidates seven major models of transfer, of which the first four are, according to him, primary models. These models, which have been described in more detail in a previous section, include:

- *The formal discipline model of transfer*, whereby learners are expected to generalise certain principles from their studies of classic disciplines, such as Latin—the "faculty psychology" approach, which assumed that automatically transfer would proceed from the classical disciplines because of similarities to inherent cognitive and environmental structures;
- The *identical elements model*, as promoted by Thorndike (1901);
- The *general principle model,* with its focus on the abstraction and transfer of general principles, rather than of identical elements;
- The *stimulus generalisation model,* which still has some currency (particularly in the use of simulations) and proceeds, from a behaviourist perspective, to posit that transfer may be effected through the "evocation of a nonreinforced response to a stimulus that is very *similar* to an original conditioned stimulus" (Haskell, 2001, p. 81; emphasis in original);
- The *cognitive information processing model,* which developed from educational studies and later was adopted by mainstream cognitive psychology, and developed, in particular, enquiry into the actual mechanisms of transfer and frequently invokes the construct of schemata in organising and processing knowledge for transfer;

- The *metacognition model,* which elaborates on the cognitive information-processing model in particular regard to self-monitoring strategies; and
- The *instructional model,* which focuses on the application to instructional frameworks of many of the principles developed in cognitive and metacognitive enquiry.

Haskell argues that these sometimes-competing models need to be incorporated into a general model of transfer. Furthermore, he notes, based on earlier concepts developed by Pea (1987), an element that is omitted from the previous models: the role of context, particularly sociocultural context, in accounting for transfer. As Haskell (2001) observes,

> if we adopt the view that learning is situated, contextually and culturally, that transfer is social in a fundamental way, then we understand also that learning occurs in the context of people engaging in social activities...Once we see that individuals [sic] behaviours, their thought processes, and their mental models are profoundly shaped by social situations, it follows logically that transfer of learning must be understood as a sociocultural process (p. 137).

Since Haskell's comprehensive review of the models and frameworks of learning, the sociocultural element has received more attention (as illustrated previously), and it is towards this endeavour to synthesise the cognitive and metacognitive frameworks with the sociocultural that this study seeks to contribute. Interestingly, Haskell observes that much of the literature related to transfer of *training* in the workplace emphasises organisational culture while literature with regard to transfer of *learning* in education stresses the cognitive aspects. In accordance, a fundamental aim of this present study is to synthesise these two approaches into a general model for transfer. In particular, the proposed model frames students' individual beliefs about knowledge, knowing and learning as a mediating factor between the sociocultural context and the cognitive and metacognitive one as manifested in learning outcomes such as transfer.

2.3. Learners' Beliefs about Knowledge, Knowing, and Learning

If one accepts that the learner's individual characteristics are an important strategic element in achieving transfer of learning, then one would be remiss in not considering the personal belief system of the learner as it related to the nature of knowing, knowledge and learning. Although aspects such as motivation and attitude have had a steady focus in the educational psychology (see, for example, Dweck and Diener, 1983), an emphasis on individuals' belief systems as related to learning contexts, with a specific focus on personal epistemology, is relatively recent. Little or no literature addresses directly the relationship between these individual beliefs and the transfer of learning. However, if effective transfer of learning requires a stance of self-directedness, as has already been argued, such a stance would depend on the learner's view of knowledge as being independently or cooperatively derived without reliance on a higher authority.

In the context of this study, moreover, a focus on personal beliefs allows a reconciliation, in the Vygotskian sense, between the inner and outer workings of the individual learner, in other words between the sociocultural and the psychological (and cognitive). The model that allows this will be elaborated upon in a later section.

2.3.1. Definitions

The term *belief* has been defined in a number of ways. For example, Richardson (1996) describes it as "a proposition that is accepted as true by the person holding the belief" (p. 104), while Pajares (1992) asserts that it is an "individual's judgement of the truth or falsity of a proposition" (p. 316). Most definitions encapsulate, as those above do, the idea of a belief being a conceptualisation of truth. Moreover, a belief is often held to be part of a complex, interrelated, and sometimes, hierarchical system (McAlpine, Eriks-Brophy, & Crago, 1996). Accordingly, Fives & Buehl (2012), writing in the context of teachers' beliefs, characterise these belief systems as necessarily "messy," a description that can be used to classify social research in general, in the way that it often defies "neat" theoretical classification. Beliefs about knowledge, in particular, are described as complex, interactive and multidimensional (Buehl & Alexander, 2006).

The "messiness" of social research, in general, and belief systems, in particular, however, has not precluded the quest for conceptual clarity. As a case in point, much of the conceptual and empirical development concerning learners' beliefs has occurred under the banner of *personal epistemology*. Unfortunately, definitions of personal epistemology are as fraught as those of transfer of learning. Recent debate has centred around whether personal epistemology should include views on both the nature of knowledge and knowing *and* those on the nature of learning. Hofer and Pintrich (1997) and Sandoval (2005), for example, have argued for the narrower perspective, while Elby (2009) has countered that it is not productive to converge on a single definition until further exploration has been made in the field. For these reasons, this study, in considering the term *personal epistemology*, recognises that the trend in the literature, while not unanimous, is to take a narrower view (this development is illustrated below), and to exclude beliefs about learning from a definition of personal epistemology. Pending clarity resulting from more investigation of the kind suggested by Elby, the term "learners' beliefs about knowledge, knowing, and learning," sometimes abbreviated to "learners' beliefs about knowledge and learning," or merely "learners' beliefs" to connote the full term, will be preferred in this report to the term "personal epistemology."

2.3.2. Conceptual Development

Epistemic and ontological enquiry has been well-trodden ground for millennia, following the philosophical predilections of each era and each geographic region. In the West, this enquiry begins with classical views, mainly evinced by Plato (1993), that what constitutes true knowledge is its justification, truth and belief, and by Aristotle, who extended to this the importance of rational and evidentiary enquiry (Taylor, 1990). Post-renaissance views expanded upon concerns of rationalism and empiricism as both sources and constituents of knowledge; while the former (as represented by Descartes) presupposes the internal mental element of knowledge, the latter (as propounded by Locke) is more concerned with an external, objective reality (Packer & Addison, 1989). Both, however, in terms of assumptions about knowledge, perceive a mind-world duality. Kant argued that, beyond rationalism and empiricism, there were two other discrete sources of knowledge: intuition and understanding (Muis, Bendixen, & Haerle, 2006).

Following on the ideas of Kant as to the sources of knowledge, the structuralists—pre-eminently Lévis-Strauss—attempted to explain sources of knowledge by way of a social rationality that could be observed through a detailed explication of social structures. It is by means of these social structures that knowledge is communicated: the objective reality is, therefore, a perceivable social reality (Audi, 1999). In this conceptualisation, Lévis-Strauss attempted to reconcile empiricism—data gained by means of an individual's senses—and rationalism—knowledge derived by applying inference and deduction processes to the empirical data so derived. The individual's role as an interpreter thus became crucial.

While Marxist dialectic materialism is a post-structuralist position, it can be argued that the previous structuralist view is also compatible with dialectics. This is true if the collective, societal reality is seen as an opposite but interconnected reality to that of the individual; and if knowledge, while being shaped by social constructs, such as culture, is both manifested in and interpreted by individuals, with that interpretation conversely shaping the social constructs. This is of particular relevance to the interconnectivity between these spheres in the cultural matrix of social psychology by Fiske, Kitayama, Markus and Nisbett (1998). The cultural matrix is adopted as a framework for this present study; it is employed as a model that explains learning transfer as an individual manifestation of beliefs about knowledge and learning that are formed by culture, and transferred via the values reflected in social structures and institutions. Structuralism is also reflected in the work of Piaget (as perceived by Packer & Addison, 1989) and of Vygotsky (1978), the latter of whose views also inform the framework of this study, in particular in the explanation of how the *inter*personal (in this instance, social structures and values) becomes the *intra*personal (individually-held beliefs).

An overview of the philosophical predilections towards knowledge and knowing would, of course, not be comprehensive without considering post-modernist and post-structuralist contributions. As Muis et al. (2006) have pointed out, the postmodernist view is diverse, but convergences in a number of propositions:

> First, postmodernist positions recognise the plasticity and constant change of reality and knowledge, stress the importance of concrete experience over fixed abstract principles, and believe that no single a priori thought system should dominate belief or investigation. Postmodernists argue that knowledge is subjectively determined by multiple factors, and things-in-themselves are neither comprehensible nor positable. Further, they stress that all knowledge and assumptions must be continually subjected to direct testing. Those in search of advancing knowledge must be tolerant of

ambiguity and pluralism, and recognise that knowledge is relative and fallible rather than absolute and certain (p. 9).

Of course, these principles concerning the sources and certainty of knowledge are of themselves epistemic constructs that bear further enquiry. The acknowledgement that no thought system should dominate belief or investigation is one that is accommodated by this study. What is recognised, in accordance with this, is that a universalistic stance that fails to investigate the sources of beliefs in social constructs (as in earlier enquiries as to personal epistemology) is untenable. In fact, these very constructs account for, or at least interact with, diverse individual beliefs that, in terms of the cultural matrix, are manifested in actions such as learning transfer.

To complete the overview of the development of thought as to the nature, sources, and limits of human knowledge, one must also acknowledge the views of the post-structuralists. These perspectives (e.g., those of Derrida and Foucault), as opposed to those of the structuralists, are much more focused on social dissonance, rather than on the cohesion of social structures. Post-structuralists question the binary positions that are inherent to either structuralism ("Post-structuralism," 1998) or, for that matter, to dialecticism. These ideas notwithstanding, because this study is concerned with sociocultural institutions, and thus assumes that these institutions represent consonant human endeavours, and because the study presents a model for the interrelationship of apparently opposite elements (*the individual* vs. *the collective*), it is more closely informed by both structuralism and dialecticism.

Despite the divergent positions adopted by these (in some cases, rather loosely defined) schools of thought, a common thread is that all have concerned themselves with three central areas of enquiry: the limits, the sources, and the nature of human knowledge (Arner, 1972). Regardless of whether personal epistemology is defined narrowly or broadly (as further elaborated upon in the next section), the enquiry in this present study is closely concerned with the second and the third of these. As will be seen, Schommer-Aikins's constructs (Schommer, 1990, 1994) address either the nature of knowledge (e.g. *certain* vs. *uncertain*), the sources of knowledge (e.g., whether transmitted via "omniscient authority"), or a combination (whether or not knowledge and knowing is innate to individuals). Schommer-Aikins was explicit in this inclusive conceptualisation; she "postulated five beliefs about the nature of knowing *and learning* (Schommer, 1994, p. 300; emphasis added).

While the epistemological and ontological concerns outlined above have long pre-occupied philosophical thought in general, it is only comparably recently that, in educational psychology, learners' belief systems have been theorised and studied in a comparably structured way. In this field, studies as to learner's attitudes to learning, learner motivation, and the interrelationship between these constructs and learning have long been common (e.g. Bandura, 1977; Dweck, 1975); however, it is only much more recently, particularly since the 1990s, that a more concentrated and structured enquiry into learner's beliefs about knowledge and learning has arisen. Perry (1970), in his research into Harvard undergraduate students' intellectual and ethical development, is considered to be the progenitor of much of this research and theory-building, which was revived and given much of its definition during—and since—the 1990s by scholars such as Hofer and colleagues (e.g., Hofer & Pintrich, 1997) and Schommer-Aikins (Schommer, 1990, 1994). The sections below outline, at least illustratively, and in relation to this particular study, much of the conceptualisation and empirical enquiry that have been conducted by these and other scholars in the last three decades.

What potentially problematises closer investigation between learner belief systems and any aspect of learning, such as transfer of learning, is the debates that have subsisted in the conceptualisation of these belief systems. The first of these debates concerns the inclusivity of types of beliefs in the term *personal epistemology*, while the second concerns the *domain-generality* or *-specificity* of these belief systems, whether or not they may be labelled *personal epistemology*.

Defining *personal epistemology*. Most of the studies concerning learners' beliefs as they relate to learning are situated, at least nominally, within the domain of personal epistemology. Because of problems in the conceptualisation of personal epistemology and the elements, such as cognition, that it subsumes, Schunk (2008, in Hofer & Sinatra, 2009) advises that researchers "provide clear definitions, situate the definitions theoretically, use methods consistent with the definitions, and then link these processes with educational outcomes" (p. 115). In accordance with this suggestion, it is important to establish an operational definition of individual epistemic beliefs and of personal epistemology, and to situate these in relation to learners' beliefs about knowledge and learning.

Definitions of personal epistemology and the epistemic beliefs that are encompassed by the term tend to converge on beliefs about knowledge and knowing. Hofer and Pintrich (1997), at the time when writing about personal epistemology and learning outcomes was becoming prolific, posited that epistemic beliefs are concerned with the nature, source, structure, and justification of knowledge while a recent definition by Bendixen and Feucht (2013) asserts that personal epistemology is "the study of beliefs *associated with* knowledge and knowing" (front material; emphasis added).

The question that arises is as to whether epistemic beliefs, and hence, personal epistemology, should include, in addition to beliefs about knowing and knowledge, beliefs about learning. This is a pertinent question in this research context, since beliefs about learning are clearly closely associated with beliefs about knowledge and knowing, particularly in an educational setting.

Intuition provides that beliefs about knowledge and beliefs about learning be closely related, particularly when one considers, as Hofer and Pintrich (1997) have asserted, that epistemic beliefs are concerned with the sources of knowledge. Surely, from such an inclusive view, *learning* is inextricable from these sources, whether the source of knowledge is considered to be by transmission or by construction. Hofer and Pintrich recognise this argument, but they also asserted that beliefs about learning (as with beliefs about teaching) are not concerned with the nature and justification of knowledge. By extension, and by philosophical tradition, which requires that epistemic enquiry include these latter concerns, they argue for a narrower definition that excludes beliefs about learning. Sandoval (2005) concurred with Hofer and Pintrich (2005) in arguing for a narrow definition, pointing out that "conflation" of the definition by including beliefs about learning has been detrimental to psychological research, and that a narrower definition would assist in clarifying theoretical development and research.

However, dissenting voices have argued that beliefs about knowing and knowledge should subsume beliefs about learning, or that beliefs about learning need not be separated, of conceptual or empirical imperative, from epistemic beliefs. Schommer-Aikins (Schommer, 1990, 1994) has taken such an inclusive view in the development of her belief constructs, defining personal epistemology, in the educational context as "what students believe about the nature of knowledge *and learning*" (1990, p. 498; emphasis added). In her synthesis of the literature concerning epistemological beliefs (1994), she recognised that the term "personal epistemology" assumed many different "shades of meaning from study to study" (p. 294) and that, in cognitive research, conceptions of personal epistemology diverge from traditional philosophical enquiry. She summarised key studies in the area, concluding that key concerns of personal epistemology, from a cognitive research perspective, include "individual's beliefs in the source, certainty, and organisation of knowledge, as well as the speed, and control of knowledge acquisition" (p. 302). She added, in interesting contradistinction to Hofer and Pintrich (1997), that "while philosophers may find these conceptualisations of knowledge too simplistic or too applied... for educational psychologists, the applied aspects are as important as the theoretical."

Elby's (2009) is another voice that argued against a definition of personal epistemology that, of necessity, excludes beliefs about learning. He countered the arguments by Hofer and Pintrich (1997) and Sandoval (2005) that proffered that an inclusive definition was undesirable for three major reasons: that such an inclusive definition suffered from conflation; that it departed from the philosophical tradition of enquiry into epistemic beliefs, and that an overly-broad definition of personal epistemology was in fact an impediment to clarity in research and theory building. In addressing the conflation argument, Elby noted that Sandoval (2005) based his objection to an inclusive definition on the premise that many purported studies into students' epistemic beliefs included students' *expectations* of learning. While Elby (2009) conceded this point, he asserted that this was not a valid reason for excluding beliefs about learning from a definition of personal epistemology, as, in many cases expectations can be extricated from epistemology, notwithstanding the failure of some psychological researchers to do so.

Concerning Hofer and Pintrich's (1997) argument that a definition of personal epistemology should be narrow in order to align it with the philosophical tradition, Elby countered this by averring that "naïve psychological constructs do not necessarily align with disciplinary constructs defined by experts" (p. 140). Specifically, he elaborated that "some elements of students' personal epistemologies cut across the categories *views about knowledge and knowing* and *views about learning,*" concluding that, on this basis, a narrow, disciplinary-imposed definition could, in fact, hamper enquiry into "the substance and cognitive structure of students' epistemologies."

In addressing the argument for conceptual clarity, Elby (2009) concludes that the field of personal epistemology should be defined by empirical and conceptual development, rather than demarcated ab initio. A consensual view of personal epistemology that includes beliefs about learning, in this sense, could provide equal clarity to one that is more narrowly defined, provided this facilitates communication in the field by virtue of being indeed, consensual and shared.

While this researcher concurs with Elby that a narrow disciplinary definition would limit enquiry into the nature of students' beliefs as they relate as a cognitive complex to learning, this is with equal recognition, again in accordance with Elby's concluding recommendation, that developing consensus in the field tends towards a definition of personal epistemology that does exclude beliefs about learning. In concurrence with Hofer and Pintrich (1997), many later authors (e.g., Greene, Azevedo, & Torney-Purta, 2008; Stahl & Bromme, 2007) have recognised that learning beliefs are, of course, related to epistemic beliefs; however, they argue that this does not imply that the latter include the former. In terms of the research that has been conducted in the field, the construct "epistemic beliefs" should accordingly be conceptualised in a more accurate way—that, in other words, beliefs about the nature of knowledge and knowing should be considered separately from learning beliefs, both theoretically and empirically.

These arguments have some implications for the instrument used to investigate students beliefs in this study, the Epistemic Beliefs Inventory (EBI; Schraw, Bendixen & Dunkle, 2002). It may be claimed that, in the decades since Schommer-Aikins's (Schommer, 1990) conceptualisation of epistemic constructs, and since the development of the EBI, the concept of what constitutes epistemic beliefs, which the instrument purports to measure, has changed. In particular, following Hofer and Pintrich's (1997) well-known critique, this researcher acknowledges that there has been some agreement (e.g., Greene, Azevedo, & Torney-Purta, 2008; Stahl & Bromme) that not all of Schommer-Aikins's (Schommer,

1990, 1994) hypothesised constructs and, therefore, not all the dimensions emerging from the EBI, are epistemic in a genuine sense.

Admittedly, thus, the EBI incorporates both epistemic beliefs and learning beliefs. Two of the originally-hypothesised dimensions do not address directly the nature of knowledge and the knowing process. Specifically, it can be argued that beliefs about the *speed* of learning and beliefs about the *ability* to learn should not be included among "pure" epistemic beliefs concerning the source and nature of knowledge (this is discussed in a later section).

Nevertheless, while this researcher recognises the growing consensus towards a definition of personal epistemology that excludes beliefs about learning, the purpose of this study is not to indulge in minute conceptual scrutiny or seek definitive clarity on personal epistemology itself. Rather it concurs with a recent assertion by Östman & Wickman (2014) that researchers take a pragmatic view of learners' epistemic beliefs that is social and transactional, one, moreover, that is thus situated in educational practice (p. 375) and includes beliefs about learning. In addition, this present study has broader aims than an over-specification of learners' beliefs would facilitate: it recognises that beliefs are indeed "messy" (Fives & Buehl, 2012), notwithstanding the quest for conceptual clarity, and are an intricate and interrelated complex (e.g., Buehl & Alexander, 2006) when considered in connection with learning outcomes such as transfer. The researcher heeds Elby's (2009) admonition that "naïve psychological constructs do not necessarily align with disciplinary constructs defined by experts," by seeking a working model to account for transfer of learning as both a cultural and cognitive phenomenon. What is more useful here is a general approach that sees a learner's beliefs as they are related to learning—whether with regard to the nature, source or process—as part of an intermediary process between sociocultural context and its manifestations in terms of learning transfer. Thus, in view of the conflicting opinions outlined above, and in view of this broader goal, this study has taken an accommodative approach; it refers, in concurrence with Schommer-Aikins's apparent acknowledgement of the objections to including beliefs about learning in epistemic beliefs in later work (e.g., Duell & Schommer-Aikins, 2001), to learner's *beliefs about knowledge and learning*.

For the reasons outlined above, it was not considered problematic, in terms of these broader goals, that the EBI, although labelled "epistemic," might contain constructs related to both beliefs about learning and beliefs about knowing and knowledge. Rather, relevant *learning-related belief structures as a complex* are seen as an internalisation (in Vygotsky's sense) of the external, as represented in the cultural psychological matrix adopted in this study. In addition, both are included in further acknowledgement to Elby (2009) that a priori definition of personal epistemology should be reserved pending empirical development. While Elby refers to the field as a whole, this is adopted in a microcosmic sense to this study: classification was suspended in anticipation of the empirical findings of this particular study, and specifically of the outcome of the dimension reduction of the EBI.

Macrocosmically, the possibility existed that the process of validating the constructs of the EBI, while not the major focus of this study, might contribute in a small but significant way to understanding a distinction, if one existed, between beliefs about learning and beliefs about knowledge and knowing. Although it was not the express purpose of this research to either support or refute a particular definition of personal epistemology, the analysis allowed, based on the emerging factors, for a possible extrication of dimensions relating to *beliefs about learning* from those concerning *beliefs about knowing and knowledge*. Its findings may thus contribute to the conceptual clarity sought by scholars of personal epistemology, such as Hofer and Pintrich (1997) and Sandoval (2005).

As reported in Chapters 4 and 5, the conceptual development discussed above in relation to students' beliefs did, indeed, emerge from the principal components and confirmatory factor analyses of the EBI. The components that the analysis yielded suggested that beliefs about knowledge were, in fact, discrete from those about ability. This contributed, together with the theoretical development already outlined, to a decision to re-label, throughout this study, what had initially been termed as "personal epistemology" as "beliefs about knowledge and learning."

Domain-specific or domain-general. Other than the question as to whether beliefs about learning should be included in a definition of personal epistemology, the field is framed by a second debate: whether an individual's epistemic beliefs relate to learning in general, or whether different epistemic beliefs apply to different subject areas. In other words, the consideration is whether personal epistemology is, in the first instance, *domain-general*, or in the second, *domain-specific*. Domain knowledge is knowledge held by individuals about a particular field of studies (Alexander & Judy, 1988), which can further be classified into different types of knowledge: conditional, declarative, or procedural, according to Paris, Lipson, and Wixson (1983).

Sternberg (1989) asserts that it is an oversimplification to declare any phenomenon related to learning and cognition as either exclusively domain-specific or domain-general. Many studies support this assertion, indicating that certain types of knowledge may have aspects of both, that there are inevitable correlations between apparently discrete epistemological dimensions, and that what emerges from a particular study—domain-specificity or domain-generality—depends, often, on the nature of the study and the instrument used (Buehl & Alexander, 2002; Muis, Bendixen & Haerle, 2006). Buehl and Alexander (2002), in addressing the question as to whether schooled knowledge is domain-specific or domain-general, observed that that because knowledge itself is multifaceted, it follows that knowledge-related beliefs are similarly multifaceted. They further reasoned that "if individuals can retain varied and sometimes opposing forms of knowledge in memory, then it is conceivable that the beliefs they hold about such knowledge can be similarly varied and even oppositional" (p. 416). Hence, students may simultaneously hold domain-general and domain-specific beliefs, and these beliefs themselves may be dependent on specific variables such as gender, for instance, on the relative formality of the learning context, or on how well-structured a certain domain is in relation to another. This means that a particular learner may hold more domain-general beliefs in a certain setting in a certain discipline while holding more domain-specific beliefs in another.

The question as to the relative structure of a domain is of particular relevance here; the present research, conducted in an academic setting, and explicitly investigating the transfer of academic literacy skills as they related to knowledge and learning, is concerned particularly with *academic* domains. According to Muis et al. (2006), who traced much of the development of specificity-generality debate through their review of research in into epistemic beliefs, academic domains may be classified by a number of structural distinctions, as derived from Biglan (1973). These include:

- Paradigm: whether the domain is "hard," i.e. relatively rigid in its approaches, or "soft";
- Practical applications of problems: whether a domain is considered "pure," focusing on theoretical development (e.g., Mathematics, or "applied," focusing on practical application (e.g., Food Sciences);
- Concern with life systems: whether the domain considers life (e.g., Biology) or non-life systems (e.g. Physics).

While Muis et al. pointed out that these classifications are not absolute, they nevertheless stressed that they, particularly the first two, may be crucial in considering the domain-specificity or domain-generality question.

Aligning themselves with Royce's (1978) hypothesis that epistemic knowledge becomes more specialised as learners progress through their education (in correspondence with greater levels of specialisation in knowledge itself), Muis et al. further recounted that much of the early research as to epistemic beliefs in *experts* tended to support domain-specificity (e.g., Donald, 1990; Royce & Mos, 1980). In accordance, the beliefs of experts—often university professors in the domains under comparison—with regard to the certainty of knowledge seemed to depend on the academic domain under examination: Physics, for example, seemed to be subject to more epistemic certainty than did Psychology. What this indicated was the significance of the classification system outlined above: in particular, domains such as Physics, relative to the Social Sciences, could be considered well-structured, in possession of a "hard" paradigm, and "pure," while, because the opposite is true in Psychology; experts in this latter field would perceive knowledge to be less certain. So, as Muis et al. concluded,

> individuals develop more specialised forms of knowledge as they progress through higher levels of education. Thus, one would expect that, because specialised forms of knowledge are dependent on particular epistemologies, individuals' beliefs become more consistent with the epistemic patterns of their domains of study (p. 14).

What, then, of novices who have not had the exposure of experts to academic domains? One would assume that the converse would be valid: that, because of this lack of exposure, and because, perhaps, of a more general educational background through their secondary education, undergraduate students, particularly in the first year of study, would have more in common than experts in terms of their epistemic beliefs. When it comes to comparing students' epistemic beliefs across domains, empirical investigation is divided as to support for this reverse hypothesis. Again, Muis et al. provided a critical review of studies that support either domain-generality or domain-specificity. They classified studies by whether they employed a between-subjects design—whereby different sets of participants are surveyed with regard to their epistemology across more than one major or domain, for the sake of comparison—or a within-subjects design—whereby the same set of participants is surveyed as to their beliefs regarding different majors or domains.

All eight of the between-subjects designs that Muis et al. (2006) reviewed used a questionnaire designed to measure general beliefs. They included studies by Jehng, Johnson, and Anderson (1993); Paulsen and Wells (1998); and Schommer-Aikins (Schommer, 1993); all of whom, as in this present study, used an instrument either identical to or derived from Schommer-Aikins's (Schommer, 1990) epistemological questionnaire, and included, as a result, dimensions considered to be related to beliefs both about knowing and knowledge. All of the studies found some support for domain-specificity, but only so in certain dimensions, providing for the assumption of commonality or generality in the others.

In examining the within-subjects designs—those that investigated learners' beliefs as contextualised with two or more domains—Muis et al. (2006) considered 11 studies, eight of which involved as participants university students (e.g., Buehl, Alexander, & Murphy, 2002; Estes, Chandler, Horvath, & Backus, 2003; Hofer, 2000; Mori, 1999; Schommer & Walker, 1995), and all of which examined three or more belief dimensions. For these within-subjects designs, Muis et al. reported mixed results: two of the 11 studies found predominant support for domain generality, while the remaining nine found evidence in favour of domain specificity. Moreover, of the nine that found a preponderance of support for domain specificity, six also found support for domain generality. Similarly to the between-subjects studies, in none of the studies did domain-specific beliefs extend to all dimensions.

Not only did domain-specific beliefs not extend to all dimensions, but Muis et al. (2006) also observed that different analytic methods produced different results: those that used correlation and regression methods tended to find support for domain- generality, while those that compared the means of beliefs across domains, domain-specificity. Furthermore, different conceptual frameworks could be considered to produce different results. In terms of these observations, Muis et al.

proposed that data collection, methodological, and conceptual issues have limited the ability of researchers to deliver conclusive evidence as to whether epistemic beliefs are domain specific or domain general. However, from their investigations, they developed a conceptualisation of the relationship between domain-specific and general beliefs.

First, they defined general epistemic beliefs as "as beliefs about knowledge and knowing that develop in non-academic contexts such as the home environment, in interactions with peers, in work-related environments, and in any other non-academic environments" (p. 33). They distinguished between these general epistemic beliefs and academic epistemic beliefs, which "*begin to develop* once individuals enter an educational system" (p. 34; emphasis added), remarking that these beliefs reflect, at first, general epistemic beliefs, but that they become more distinct, to the extent of domain specificity, during the course of exposure to higher education, particularly in a particular domain.

These belief systems, thus, may exist in parallel; this co-existence, at times, may manifest itself in apparently contradictory beliefs that may at once be both domain-general and domain-specific (De Corte & Op 't Eynde, 2003). This perspective is consistent with that of Hofer (2000), who held that while students may retain general epistemic beliefs, they make distinctions as to various dimensions of that knowledge, particularly when certain contextual schemata are instantiated, whether at the level of academic domain, or of the classroom context (Hammer & Elby, 2002; Louca, Elby, Hammer, & Kagey, 2004).

The notion of domain-specific beliefs developing over time and from a stock of more general beliefs was shared by Schommer-Aikins (2002). In addition, Buehl and Alexander (2006) recognised what they referred to as the dual nature of beliefs, positing that general beliefs apply particularly in situations where students access previous learning, and that more domain-specific beliefs are actively and increasingly evoked in certain contexts, but may still exist co-exist with the more general beliefs. They argue, moreover, that "the type of beliefs that are most salient and explicitly available for consideration will vary depending on the context" (p. 39). The classroom or the culture may provide this context.

The idea that learners draw from a stock of general beliefs as they develop more domain-specific beliefs was shared by Limón (2006), who described this view of domain-general—domain-specific duality as the "developmental" approach. She proposed that domain-general beliefs alone could be referred to as "pure" epistemic beliefs and, hence, only these should be termed *personal epistemology*.

Methodologically, Limón claims, it is only general beliefs that instruments such as Schommer-Aikins's Epistemological Questionnaire (and, by extension, instruments derived from it, such as the EBI) are designed to capture. These instruments are not designed to measure domain-specific beliefs, even if they sometimes do detect these incidentally, because they are not sufficiently sensitive. In terms of the current study, this view is not problematic: the current study, by means of the EBI, aims to capture students' general beliefs about knowledge and learning.

In relation to the concepts of general epistemic beliefs and academic epistemic beliefs, the developmental framework devised by Muis et al. (2006) has a strong relationship to the conceptual framework—the cultural matrix of Fiske et al. (1994)—adopted in this study, particularly with regard to the sociocultural influences on beliefs. It assists in situating the current research with regard to its orientation towards domain-generality or -specificity. The majority of participants in this study are second-year undergraduate students who have newly commenced their majors while still in the process of completing their general education requirements. Therefore, it can be argued, in accordance with the theoretical views expressed above, that their academic beliefs about knowing and learning are still largely general in nature. Furthermore, the study does not aim to instantiate any domain-specific schemata; rather, it is conducted in a general education setting and does not require the participants to consider the questionnaire items in relation to any specific disciplinary context.

While one may argue that conducting the survey within an academic literacy class does indeed evoke a particular context, this context could be classified as ill-structured and, in Biglan's (1973) terms, as "soft," "applied," and non-life-sciences related: such contexts seldom support a domain-specific invocation on the part of students (Schommer-Aikins & Duell, 2013). That data are derived from second-year, non-expert students, that no well-structured, hard contextual domain is instantiated by the questions, that the research concerns, ultimately, the transfer of general-education knowledge to the disciplines is justification for the focus of this study on domain-general beliefs about knowledge and learning.

2.3.3. Beliefs and Learning

As explicated above, despite a long tradition of philosophical enquiry into epistemology, it is only relatively recently that scholastic enquiry has focused itself more particularly on epistemic and associated beliefs as they relate to learning in the educational sphere (Muis, Bendixen, & Haerle, 2006). This development, which is the result of the merging of philosophical and psychological enquiry, became especially prolific in the 1990s (e.g., Schommer, 1990, 1994; Hofer & Pintrich, 1997). Hofer and Pintrich (1997, 2002), for example, traced the implications of epistemic beliefs for cognitive processing, comprehension and strategy use. Other empirical studies have supported, in broad terms, a relationship between a learner's epistemic beliefs and aspects directly related to learning (Muis, Bendixen, & Haerle, 2006), whether, for example, more specifically to achievement (Schommer, 2004), to cognition and metacognition (Schommer et al., 1992; Muis, 2004), or to motivation (Muis, 2004).

Much of the theoretical conceptualisation and empirical investigation that has already been mentioned in this section has established the existence of clear associations between these beliefs, on the one hand, and motivational and cognitive processes, on the other (Hofer & Pintrich, 1997; Muis, Bendixen, & Haerle, 2006). In particular, much of the research that has focused on students and teachers has revealed, more-or-less uncontroversially, a relationship between personal epistemology and learning, motivation, and achievement (Muis, 2004). Muis, Bendixen, & Haerle (2006) have outlined how most of these studies have focused on learning-related processes, such as those involved in learners' problem-solving (Schommer, 1990), their metacognitive processes in comprehending material (Schommer, Crouse, & Rhodes, 1992), and in academic achievement. Other, more recent studies have investigated, to present an illustrative chronology: learners' approaches to and avoidance of arguments (Nussbaum & Bendixen, 2003); learners' self-regulation (Hofer & Sinatra, 2010), including how it relates to second language reading (Ayatollahi, Rasekh, & Tavakoli, 2012) and critical thinking (Chan, Ho, & Ku, 2011). These studies have been conducted on diverse groups of learners (usually secondary school or undergraduate) in a number of different societal and institutional contexts.

Beliefs and transfer of learning. While many of the elements and processes of learning discussed above are related to transfer of learning, particularly in terms of the metacognition and problem-solving processes involved, none has focused specifically on transfer. Green (2013) has hypothesised such a relationship, but the direct association, as far as this review has been able to determine, has not yet been empirically established (as this study aims to do). It seems reasonable to suppose, nevertheless, that if a preponderance of research has supported the existence of relationships between learners' beliefs and other learning-related processes—those that are central to learning transfer—then one may, by reasonable extension, suppose that such a relationship exists between learners' beliefs about knowing, knowledge, and learning and transfer of learning.

Moreover, a relationship between learners' beliefs and transfer of learning becomes increasingly plausible if one considers the convergence of metacognitive mechanisms in both. A preponderance of the theorising concerning learning transfer, as discussed in a previous section, has been metacognitive in nature. Perkins and Salomon (1989), for example, posited that high road transfer, the kind that tends to fail if not explicitly addressed, is dependent on mindfulness and conscious abstraction of principles from the learning contexts.

The relationship between metacognition and transfer of learning has already been established in this discussion. As is the case for transfer of learning, theorists have made explicit references to epistemic beliefs being metacognitive in nature. Metacognition implies a consciousness of one's thinking processes; according to Hofer and Sinatra (2010), beliefs about knowledge and learning could only be considered where learners were aware of such beliefs or where they were actively applying these beliefs to learning tasks. To elaborate, learners are "aware of their beliefs about the nature, source, structure, and justification of knowledge, and/or be using their beliefs about the nature, source, structure, and justification of knowledge to regulate their cognition" (p. 115). In this respect, Barzilai and Zohar (2014) offered a theoretical perspective that argues explicitly for personal epistemology as metacognitive in nature: these areas intersect, according to these authors, in many of their complex facets, such as metacognitive skills, metacognitive knowledge about social context, tasks and relationships, and metacognitive experiences (p. 13).

Beliefs about knowledge and learning would be accessed by the learner in the ways described by Hofer and Sinatra, particularly in anticipating, self-regulating and strategising in completing tasks. In the first of these, for example, Bromme, Piesch and Stahl (in Hofer & Sinatra, 2010) have remarked that learners' beliefs systems help them prepare for a specific learning task through anticipation—or through an instantiation of schemata. In other words, what learners have encountered previously influences their beliefs about the nature of the task and thus equips them to negotiate a new task that they perceive to be similar in operation. The second of these, self-regulation, another important metacognitive function, has been linked by Bråten, Strømsø, and Samuelstuen (2008) and Muis and Franco (2009) to learners' epistemic beliefs, this self-regulation being moderated by the last of these, the strategy choices that learners make. The choices that learners make in adopting what they refer to as "epistemic strategies" are based, according to Richter and Schmid (2010), on learners validating their knowledge bases and validating this knowledge against new learning tasks.

Considering these metacognitive functions as a whole, a strong implicit link to transfer of learning emerges here: learners access previously gained knowledge, aggregated in a systemic form, and assess its utility in completing new learning tasks. In this regard, Hofer & Sinatra (2010), in assessing the metacognitive role of epistemic beliefs, observe that research has strongly indicated that metacognitive beliefs are teachable, which not only accords with the bridging approach advocated by Perkins & Salomon (1988) in engaging transfer of learning, but also evokes the speculation that epistemic metacognition might be equally teachable.

These views as to the nature and role of beliefs notwithstanding, it has been difficult to locate in the field of educational psychology, until fairly recently, an express focus on learners' personal beliefs in relation to learning itself. While much of the literature surrounding learning and cognition has taken into account related learner characteristics such as attitude, motivation and self-esteem (e.g., Anderson, 1982; Brophy, 1997; Dweck & Elliott, 1983; and, in language learning, Krashen, 1981; Dörnyei, 1994), there was not until recently, explicit mention of the terms "personal epistemology," or its concomitant beliefs, other than the concern for learner agency that is expressed, illustratively, by Thomas et al. (1992) of a need to extend the framework of Salomon and Perkins. Nevertheless, factors subsumed by what may be termed a "positive" epistemology—one conducive towards learning in general and transfer in particular—have been, in fact, invoked by many of the earlier frameworks and studies already discussed here. In particular, despite debate in the literature surrounding mechanisms of transfer (e.g., Gick & Holyoak, 1983; Kaminski, Sloutsky, & Heckler, 2008) and about what exactly is transferred (e.g., Detterman, 1993; Cox, 1997), there is general agreement as to the necessity of positive values and beliefs in the learner (Pea, 1988; Perkins & Salomon, 1988).

It has already been seen how many teaching-for-transfer frameworks stress a three-pronged approach that address structure (including learning environment and contextual), task (including instructional approaches to the task) and the learner. In yet another non-explicit reference to epistemological concerns, Macaulay and Cree (1999) claim a focus on the last of these elements, the learner, as they explore the cognitive features of transfer, specifically in relation to active learning. Macaulay and Cree note that "the centrality of the learner (as opposed to the learning task) has, for some time been a basic tenet of non-formal adult education" (p 186), and observe the extent to which such affective features as lack of self-confidence and anxiety impede the learning process. They emphasise, further, that "the experience of the learner is not merely seen as something to take account of—it is crucial to the learning process" (p. 186). Furthermore, they advocate the need for a pedagogy that recognises and integrates the learning experience of students and which, in addition to taking into account affective elements, "allows time for reflection, encourages a 'deep' as opposed to a 'surface' approach to learning, and promotes self-direction" (p. 192). Experience, thus, shapes the beliefs of the learner about the nature of knowledge and about the process of "coming to know."

These authors' observations regarding the effects of previous learning, drawing on those of Entwistle (1987), pertain particularly to undergraduate students and, thus, to learners in EAP programmes:

> Students often enter Higher Education with a conception of learning as a process of memorisation (a procedure that may have proved effective in attaining the qualification to gain entrance to a course) rather than as developing insight. This often leads to the use of "surface" learning strategies involving rote learning and a lack of reflectiveness, rather than "deep processing" which involves an intention to understand complex ideas and make connections between new concepts and previous knowledge (p. 189).

Observations such as that by Macaulay and Cree are particularly relevant to an investigation of the learning beliefs of first-year students in a Thai university. The researcher's personal experience can attest that Thailand's education system, although now recognising an urgent need to reform, has been for generations characterised by the "rote-learning and lack of reflectiveness" that Macaulay and Cree mention. Mahidol University International College, the institutional focus of this research, receives students from government schools that are still heavily influenced by the traditional system, as well as students from the more progressive international schools. It seems fair to argue that these different environments influence learners' beliefs and values about learning and, in so doing, have an impact on the transfer question itself (this being the central assertion being developed in this discussion).

Many authors have thus addressed issues of knowledge and learning that may justifiably be subsumed by learners' beliefs about knowledge and learning. Recently, moreover, an increasing focus has been noted by some on "how a student's *beliefs about knowledge and knowing* are a part of the process of learning and how these beliefs affect or mediate the knowledge-acquisition and knowledge construction process" (Hofer, 2001, p. 354).

Studies and frameworks that explore learners' epistemology expressly in instructional contexts have emerged: Halpern (2003), for example, in elucidating principles of teaching for transfer, stresses the need for teachers to at least understand their students' epistemology, while, even more recently, Boden et al., (2008) have investigated university-level instructors' use of specific interventions or methods to foster learners' epistemology and self-reliance.

Beliefs, metacognition and literacy. As this study considers transfer of academic literacy learning to the disciplines, it also germane to examine how epistemic and attendant beliefs relate to literacy itself. One of the most seminal works in this regard is that of Scribner and Cole (1981), who conducted a five-year study on the Vai people, a small ethnic group in Liberia. The study sought to better understand the relationship between social situations and learning, particularly in the form of literacy.

Because the Vai had established their own writing system that they used to conduct affairs amongst themselves, Scribner and Cole were able to consider schooling as an independent variable discrete from other social influences. They found that "formal schooling with instruction in English increased ability to provide a verbal explanation of the principles involved in performing the various tasks" (p. 130), an ability that was lower in participants who had learnt only the Vai script, and that, by implication, literacy involved more than mere knowledge of a script but included also the application of this knowledge to specific social contexts. A further implication is that particular social contexts, such as that of the school or the community, may be conversely associated with literacy and literacy tasks. One may argue, for example, that the schooling context engenders the type of mindful abstraction that high-road transfer involves (Salomon & Perkins, 1989).

In a context that closely reflects that of this present study, Carroll (2002), in her longitudinal study of first-year college writing at Pepperdine University in the US, charts the development of the related "literacy complex" of a cohort of students. She notes that one of the major challenges that new undergraduates encounter is that of transforming their initial belief in a single correct answer to a view that incorporates a careful, reasoned consideration of a variety of sometimes-conflicting viewpoints in order to construct an essay. In the terms developed in this present study (see the subsection below, "Belief constructs and learning"), this entails a shift in the student's personal beliefs about knowledge from the *less-availing* (of learning) belief of knowledge as reified and simple to a *more-availing* one that is cognisant of complexity and contextual relativity (for a further explanation of the use of the terms *availing* and *non-availing* in this study, see Section 2.3.4.). Ultimately, success in academic literacy tasks, such as researching and writing an essay, is predicated on a shift in the learner's beliefs.

Moreover, Carroll frequently mentions the relationship between the development of literacy knowledge and metacognition—in the form of reflection, for example—in her study. A reflective learner, in terms of the belief constructs developed in this study, would also be in possession of an availing belief that knowledge can be constructed by all participants in the learning process (including the individual learner, through such reflection), rather than being passed down by an authoritative source. Such beliefs would accord with more constructivist approaches to education:

> Current theorists in composition, especially those who draw on postmodernist views of knowledge and discourse as socially constructed, challenge the notion of a stable, unified "writing ability" (Carroll, p. 2)

It would make sense that a learner who adopted beliefs that corresponded to these postmodernist approaches would be successful in such an environment.

Defining beliefs conducive to transfer of learning. The question remains as to the kind of beliefs that would be conducive to the sought-after transfer of learning. In the context of a belief system that perceives the importance of learner self-directedness to the high road-low road/hugging-bridging framework, it is once again worth heeding the remarks of Thomas et al. (1992):

> [T]he nature of high road transfer as personal intent-driven raises the question of what kind of teaching and learning will help learners develop their desire and capacities to initiate and engage in these processes on their own. At its core, high road transfer entails the assumption of responsibility for self-initiated generation of new meanings and connections. A critical thing that must happen in teaching and learning for high road transfer is that this *responsibility must be passed from the teacher to the learner*" (p. 21; emphasis added).

The learner must not only assume responsibility for learning, but there is general agreement in the literature (e.g. Perkins & Salomon, 1988; Pea, 1988; Ngeow, 1998) that such a learner must also be in possession of certain values and beliefs that include "risk-taking attitudes, mindfulness or attentiveness, and a sense of responsibility for learning" (Ngeow, par.5).

An earlier focus by Dweck and Elliott (1983) on achievement motivation makes a useful contribution to this discussion by providing links between mechanisms of cognition (in the form of goals), the learners' beliefs, and learning. This conceptualisation is especially useful in giving substance to the beliefs that would be conducive to transfer of learning.

The authors address elements that are central not only to an individual's need for achievement, but also to his or her theories of knowledge and knowing. Theory, of course, may be described as a set of beliefs. Of particular interest here is these authors' reference to the attributional and learned helplessness approaches, both of which are "based on the assumption that individuals' *beliefs* [emphasis added] about the outcomes they experience guide their subsequent behaviour in that and analogous situations" (p. 651). Thus, for example, if learners are successful in achieving class objectives because of rote learning and memorisation (which is so often the case in Thailand's state schools), rather than through the conceptualisation and abstraction demanded by high road transfer, they are likely to continue applying the methods that led to such success. Similarly, if a culture is characterised by a high power distance, as in Thailand (Hofstede, 2001), that fosters the perception in the learners that it is the instructor who is the ultimate authority in the classroom, and hence the repository of all knowledge, then the learner is likely to continue in an attitude of dependence on the instructor.

Dweck and Elliott argue that what orientates young learners towards divergent achievement goals—on the one hand, actively questing for learning and, on the other, seeking approval for competence—is their personal "theories, hypotheses and sets that orient them towards particular goals" (p. 654), all of which may be subsumed under a general definition of epistemology. Diener and Dweck (1978) define these dispositions to learning as "mastery-oriented" striving as opposed to learned "helplessness," both of which, as seen earlier, are directly influenced by a learner's beliefs about knowledge and learning.

Clearly, a learner who will take responsibility for learning, and seek opportunities for transfer of such learning, will be in possession of a belief system that is mastery-oriented. Task-based instructional strategies, such as those of Salomon and Perkins (1988), although useful, are highly unlikely to foster such a learner, as they are instructor- rather than learner-orientated. There is a need to augment such pedagogical strategies in a way that also develops, in the learners, a system of beliefs that will ultimately be independent of instructional interventions in seeking transfer of learning. The question remains as to how to develop such a belief set in learners. The answer may lie in sociocultural factors.

Belief constructs and learning. Employing the term *personal epistemology* in its most inclusive sense (i.e., as subsuming *both* learners' beliefs about knowledge and knowing *and* their beliefs about learning, Schommer-Aikins (Schommer, 1990, 1994) theorised a number of underlying constructs to these epistemic beliefs. Although epistemic beliefs had previously been examined in a more general sense (Bendixen, Schraw, & Dunkle, 1998), Schommer-Aikin was the first to recognise the shortcomings of previous work that had perceived personal epistemology as one-dimensional and as progressing through fixed stages of development. In her words, "beliefs about the nature of knowledge are far too complex to be captured in a single dimension" (p. 498); her theorising, therefore, examined the individual contributions of multidimensional beliefs to adult cognition in detail, and thus influenced a large amount of conceptual and empirical development in considering these types of beliefs.

Schommer-Aikin derived her notions as to the multidimensionality of beliefs from previous research, particularly that of Perry (1970), which focused on structure, certainty and source, and that of Dweck and colleagues (e.g., Dweck and Legget, 1988), which contemplated the nature of intelligence (the latter ideas are discussed, in relation to transfer of learning and belief systems, in the previous subsection, "Defining beliefs conducive to transfer of learning"). She thus hypothesised five epistemic dimensions that correspond to beliefs pertaining to the following (p.499):

- *Simple knowledge:* "Knowledge is simple rather than complex"
- *Omniscient authority:* "Knowledge is handed down by authority rather than derived from reason"
- *Certain knowledge*: "Knowledge is certain rather than tentative"
- *Innate ability:* "The ability to learn is innate rather than acquired"
- *Quick learning*: "Learning is quick or not at all"

In the context of broader and comparative views of culture and social psychology, as elucidated below, Schommer-Aikins's labelling of learners' personal epistemology as either *naïve* or *sophisticated* may be subject to criticism. For one, the labelling assumes a universalistic position: that certain constructs are superior to others, and by extension, more desirable in any given learning context. This seems to take little consideration of an alternative position that holds that belief systems are more relativistic in nature, and that what is desirable, or valued, in one particular culture is equally desirable and valued in another (see, for example, Fiske et al., 1998; Green, 2013; Hofer, 2008).

To label what is valued in one culture, such as interdependence and harmony, as "naïve," and that in another culture, such as independence and autonomy, as "sophisticated" could be perceived of as an instance of what post-colonialist writer Spivak (1988) terms "epistemic violence"—a tendency to assume that Western beliefs and culture are superior to those of other cultures, thus resulting in a marginalisation of these other cultures (see Green, 2013). Furthermore, at least one study, that of Bråten, Strømsø, and Samuelstuen (2008) has called into question whether a more "sophisticated" personal epistemology is indeed "better," particularly when one considers source beliefs. The study found that students who held a "sophisticated" knowledge construction view of a particular subject faired more poorly in achievement tests than did students with a more "naïve" knowledge transmission view.

In addressing the first concern, that related to the cultural dimension of beliefs, Schommer-Aikins's nomenclature is defensible in that personal epistemology and its underlying constructs can indeed be conceived of as hierarchical in one sense: within and individual or a cohort, they represent a cognitive or epistemic progression of development. The initial nomenclature was based on theorising by Perry (1968, in Schommer, 1990) that proposed that

> students go through stages of development of epistemological beliefs. In the early stages, students see knowledge as either right or wrong and believe that authority figures know the answers. When students reach the late stages of development, they realise that there are multiple possibilities for knowledge and there are times when one must make a strong, yet tentative commitment to some ideas (p.498).

Perry, in drawing these conclusions, had conducted annual interviews within cohorts of undergraduate students. These interviews sought to gauge students' intellectual development through progressive exposure to the Harvard institutional culture, which was more relativistic and constructivist than were the secondary school backgrounds of the students. Perry's research led him to a nine-stage developmental model, from which Schommer-Aikins drew her conceptualisation of continua ranging from basic, or *naïve* beliefs, to more advanced, or *sophisticated*, ones.

However, a more critical stance would question the universal desirability of the "moral and intellectual relativism" (Perry, 1970) that was prevalent at Harvard, which was, and still is, considered by many to epitomise a certain American cultural niche. Did the ideals of an elite American institution and a very select student body represent the educational aspirations and values of all humanity? Perry developed his conceptualisation at a time at which much of the relevant seminal research was conducted in these similar American institutions. Compared to contemporary concerns over representing cultural diversity, the *Zeitgeist* evinced only nascent awareness of cultural sensitivities and little consideration was given to the possibility that these development stages might reflect ideals in one sociocultural context and not another.

2.3.4. Beliefs and Cross-Cultural Studies

Even more recent to the field of learners' belief systems (epistemic or otherwise) are studies examining the relationship between sociocultural factors and personal epistemology. These studies tend to take increased stock of cultural diversity and how different cultural contexts may influence individual's beliefs about knowledge and learning.

It should be noted here that the pioneering studies in personal epistemology were conducted, as has already been discussed, with single cohorts of students, as was the case in Perry's (1970) study of the intellectual development of Harvard undergraduate students. Students were perceived to be unsophisticated at the beginning of their studies, and, as they progressed within their academic paths, they were observed to become increasingly sophisticated. The models so derived were developmental and hierarchical in nature; the conceptualisations and the concomitant labels reflect this development, hence the use by Schommer-Aikins (Schommer, 1990, 1994), in her synthesis of personal epistemology, of the terms *naïve* and *sophisticated*.

However, much of the more recent enquiry into personal epistemology does not engage in the kind of longitudinal single-cohort studies that initiated the field. Instead, there has been increased interest (as in this present study) in culturally-situated (and cross-culturally comparative) investigation as to learners' personal epistemology, whether in national cultures (e.g., Bråten, Gil, Strømsø, & Vidal-Abarca, 2009; Chan, Ho, & Ku, 2011; Fujiwara & Phillips, 2006), or institutional ones (e.g., Muis & Sinatra, 2008).

Hofer (2008) has developed an explication of culture and personal epistemology that is critical of universalistic assumptions as to personal epistemology, pointing out that the pioneering studies as to the beliefs of students was conducted on "white males at an elite institution in the 1950s and 60s" (p. 3). She refers to Perry's (1970) study, which was conducted at Harvard. Hofer further remarks that "measurement of epistemic beliefs has typically been formulated and validated in the USA and then applied in other cultures by translating existing instruments and presuming similar factor structures."

In other words, assumptions as to belief structures formulated at elite institutions in the US may not be valid for specific populations in, for example, Turkey, China or Thailand. From this more contemporary perspective, Muis (2004) has proposed alternative labels that address both what may be conceived of as cultural insensitivity and the actual contribution of the beliefs to learning. In the context of learning, rather than adopt the labels *naïve* or *sophisticated*, she proposes the use of the terms *availing* or *non-availing* of learning. This latter nomenclature is preferable in this present study; when one considers the socioculturally situated relationship between students' beliefs and transfer of learning, one may focus on whether such beliefs are availing of such transfer. It should also be noted that even transfer itself may be culturally situated; one may question the extent, for example, that transfer is a preeminent goal in *all* schooling models (see Green, 2013).

An increasing number of studies have situated beliefs about knowledge and knowing socioculturally: these beliefs are actively constructed by learners engaging in a social environment, the duration of the engagement influencing the development of beliefs (e.g., Belenky, Clinchy, Goldberger, & Tarule, 1986; Bendixen & Rule (2004); Hofer & Pintrich, 1997; Muis, Bendixen, & Haerle, 2006).

Particularly in beliefs concerning academic knowledge and learning, the educational context is arguably the primary sociocultural influence. In developing their explanatory framework of domain specificity and domain generality, Muis et al. (2006) account for this while also considering wider cultural influences in an overall view that accords with the cultural matrix (Fiske et al., 1998) adopted for this present study:

> It is the dynamic interaction of cognitive and brain capacities with environmental demands that characterises advancement in epistemic beliefs... Accordingly, to improve our understanding of individuals' beliefs, we suggest that researchers consider three different but related contexts: the larger societal and cultural context, the academic context, and the instructional context. Each of these perspectives allows a finer grained examination of how individuals' beliefs may develop within each context (p. 32).

A number of studies support a view of epistemic belief development as a process of enculturation, foremost of these being research by Jehng, Johnson, & Anderson (1993) that compared the epistemic beliefs of undergraduate and graduate students. These studies concluded that, through this process of enculturation, students' beliefs evolve with increased exposure to increasingly advanced levels of education, and in accordance with the domain that provides the academic context. Successive studies support these assumptions, both in terms of broader social context and narrower academic institutional culture. Bråten, Gil, Strømsø and Vidal-Abarca (2009), for example, compared students' personal epistemology across a Norwegian and Spanish context, finding "cultural embeddedness" in topic-specific beliefs. In terms of the instrument used for measuring beliefs about knowledge and learning used in the present study, the EBI, comparisons of similar studies using the same instrument (e.g., Cam, Topfu, Sulun, Guven, and Arabacioglu, 2012; Chan et al., 2011) also suggest that culture has an impact.

While, with notable exceptions (e.g., Nussbaum & Bendixen, 2003), studies using the EBI conducted in the US (e.g., Schraw, Bendixen & Dunkle, 2002) have tended to support belief structures identical or similar to the five dimensions as originally hypothesised by Schommer-Aikins (Schommer, 1990), similar analysis of the instrument in many non-Western contexts has failed to do so. This analysis often converges on only three conceptually defensible and statistically feasible dimensions: For example, Cam et al. (2012), in their validation of a Turkish translation of the instrument with Turkish students, identified these as *quick learning, innate ability,* and *certain knowledge*; and Chan, Ho, and Ku (2011), in investigating the epistemic beliefs and critical thinking of Chinese students, identified *innate ability, certain knowledge* and *simple knowledge* as factors. These findings, however tentatively, suggest that there may be cultural differences in the dimensionality of beliefs about knowing and learning; what could confirm this are replications conducted in similar contexts that reproduce higher dimensional correlations for arguably similar cultural contexts and, conversely, lower correlations for those that are markedly dissimilar, such as the American and Chinese cultural context.

However, as discussed above, in an enculturation framework the educational institution has a relationship closer than that of broader national culture to epistemic and related beliefs. In this regard, Muis and Sinatra (2008) found differences in the epistemic beliefs of students from culturally similar countries, but from culturally divergent academic institutions. They suggested that these findings were at least partially the result of instructional practices, such as the tutorial system in one of the institutions. The findings of these and other related studies (e.g., Ventura et al., 2008) support the application of the cultural matrix employed in this study as a framework for studying the interrelationship between culture in the broader, national or ethnic sense; its enactment and embodiment through institutions such as schools; individuals' beliefs about knowledge and learning; and, ultimately, its manifestation through transfer of learning. (Culture, its definitions, and its forms are elaborated upon in the following section).

In its investigation of the relationship between culture and learners' beliefs about knowledge and learning, this study, moreover, responds to another observation and exhortation by Hofer (2008). She observes, firstly, that there are, according to Heine & Norenzayan (2006, in Hofer, 2008) two stages of scientific enquiry as to cultural research in psychology. The first stage is "seeking cultural differences and establishing the boundaries of a phenomenon" (p. 15). It can be argued that many of the studies as to personal epistemology in various broader or narrower cultural contexts, as exemplified in this section, have satisfied, or are in the processing of satisfying the requirements of this stage. The present study, too, attempts to investigate further the nature of cultural differences as to epistemic and related beliefs.

The second stage that Hofer invokes is "the pursuit of underlying mechanisms" (p. 15) of the cultural differences that have thus been identified. She reflects that much research is needed in this sphere, particularly in terms of investigating highly divergent cultures for which variations in the nature of learning makes for differences in beliefs about knowledge and learning. In drawing from a highly diverse student population, some members of which are influenced by either Western or Asian philosophies and their respective habits of thought, as encapsulated by concomitant institutions and methods, this study is well placed to contribute in this last regard.

2.4. Culture

Because of the cultural diversity of the research context, and because of its centrality as an element of the research framework adopted in this study, a focus in this project was on the construct of culture itself and its relationship to both learners' beliefs and to transfer of learning.

2.4.1. Definitions of Culture

Culture has been defined in a number of ways. It is not employed here in the sense of social refinement and the arts (as in "high culture"), but rather in the sense of the collective consciousness of a social group with common points of reference. It relates to values shared by members of broader society, or of a particular institution. Borofsky, in his introductory remarks in Borofsky, Barth, Schweder, Rodseth and Stolzenberg (2001) notes the plethora of definitions, some converging, others not. *Culture* is not a set term; it is therefore difficult to locate concurring definitions. Borofsky proposes that "rather than seeking the concepts's [sic] underlying essence or reality, we should view it as a conceptual tool that can be applied in different ways for different ends with different effectiveness." p. 433). This flexible, pragmatic approach is adopted in the current study: elements of culture are identified along with relevant issues as they apply to the conceptual framework—specifically in relation to learning and beliefs about knowledge and learning.

In recognising that culture may be defined and contextualised in diverse ways, it is important to note the existence of a number of paradigms, each of which defines culture in its own way (Hofstede, 2003). Of direct relevance to the framework of this study, these include the anthropological paradigm, which tends to draw its definition from Tylor (1871), who, in developing a theory of the evolution of religion, proposed that culture was "that complex whole which includes knowledge, belief, art, law, morals, custom, and any other capabilities and habits acquired by man as a member of society" (p. 1).

The American anthropological tradition diverges somewhat from the broad collective expressed by Tylor in that it focuses on the symbolic interpretation and dissemination of human experience. This is reflected in Kroeber and Kluckhohn's (1952) classical definition: "culture consists in patterned ways of thinking, feeling and reacting, acquired and transmitted mainly by symbols; the essential core of culture consists of traditional ideas and especially their attached values" (p. 223). The concept of the symbol in this definition of culture is perhaps most pertinently rendered by Zimmer (1969):

> Concepts and words are symbols, just as visions, rituals, and images are; so too are the manners and customs of daily life. Through all of these, a transcendent reality is mirrored. They are so many metaphors reflecting and implying something that, though thus variously expressed, is ineffable, though thus rendered multiform, remains inscrutable. Symbols hold the mind to truth but are not themselves the truth, hence it is delusory to borrow them. Each civilisation, every age, must bring forth its own (pp. 1-2).

The emphasis on symbols as prerequisites for the separate identity of a civilisation or an age, and as metaphors reflecting a perceived reality, is adopted microcosmically by proponents of business management in their consideration of organisation culture. Harragan (1977), for example, remarks on how "the modern cultural building reeks with symbolism" (p. 211), which may subsist in the architecture, the spaces, and even the carpets of a corporation.

The centrality of the symbol is also evident in the views of the sociologists, but with the focus on society as a whole. Culture is defined in this sense as pertaining to how a society thinks and acts, and is held to manifest itself in both material and non-material ways (Macionis & Gerber, 2010).

In terms of the material manifestations of culture, approaches that are subsumed by cultural studies emerge, such as that of Marx's dialectic materialism: control of material goods, by regulating the means of production, might lead to collective cultural change, which could then be manifested in individual action. (The converse is, of course, also possible in terms of the overall dialectic). The field of cultural studies is not limited to material manifestations of culture, however, and concerns itself, broadly, with the relationship between cultural practices, as evidenced in the meanings and practices of daily existence and their relationship to power, or hegemony (Sardar, 1994). It is also concerned with epistemology: Barth (1995) observes that culture is directly concerned with knowledge and ways of knowing.

There are, of course, many other interpretations of culture. This study, however, is informed by a synthesis of the controlling concepts mentioned here. In its treatment of both organisational and societal culture, the study is concerned, in the broader sense, with the knowledge, beliefs, customs, and habits that Tylor recognises as key cultural attributes and with the templates of thinking and feeling and reacting that Kroeber and Kluckhohn elucidate. Specifically, knowledge and beliefs are a direct concern of this study in its consideration of learning and learners' beliefs, while the customs and habits of the educational institution are also scrutinised in relation to these beliefs. Customs and habits are frequently transmitted to individuals within an organisation, such as a school, through everyday activities and the many symbols, including rituals, that give meaning to these activities. These elements all find expression in the cultural matrix of social psychology (Fiske et al.,

1998) adopted as the framework of this study (elucidated in Section 2.5.2.), which in itself acts as a dialectic between, ultimately, societal culture and individual action and, more immediately, between sociocultural forces and individual psychology.

In this overall development, this study is concerned with culture at two levels: indirectly, with societal culture and, more directly, with organisational culture (as manifested in the secondary school context).

2.4.2. Societal Culture

Disclaimer. Most of the definitions given above were developed in relation to considerations of culture at a societal level, whether that is ethnically or nationally defined. It is important at this stage to acknowledge that in deriving classifications based on shared symbols, practices and beliefs, any scholar of culture is bound by generalisations that may not be applicable to each individual member of a group that is so defined. It is a difficult task to avoid accusations of stereotyping in performing this task. This researcher is acutely aware of this problem but makes every effort to avoid unthinking and prejudicial classifications of social groups. Where possible, only typologies that are empirically substantiated are employed, with full recognition that the constructs so identified are dynamic and may not reflect the full reality. This study is based on a model that, by being guided by Occam's razor, is of necessity general in nature in seeking a parsimonious explanation. It does not, nevertheless, seek to negate the individual and individual agency; it is worth remaining cognisant of the overall framework, by which it is held that societal and organisation norms and practices do indeed shape the individual, but that the individual also has the potential to shape, conversely, society through his or her actions and beliefs.

In brief, the researcher acknowledges that the classifications that follow are very broad, but wishes to emphasise that these reflect tendencies only, and do not purport to portray accurately even significantly divergent minorities within these broad classifications.

Classifications of societal culture. The more traditional focus of societal culture, as distinct from organisational culture, may encompass various, frequently-overlapping group units, such as ethnic groups, nationalities, or even "blocs" or groups of nationalities, such as in the pervasive East-West binary. These units may be distinguished on a geographic basis, but with the increasing diaspora of peoples in the past few decades, this may not be the most resilient distinction to make.

In most cases, it is necessary to examine historical and philosophical elements, in addition to current social science-based means of investigating culture, such as ethnographies. While there have been a plethora of efforts to classify culture by these means, this review will briefly visit a distinction between cultures by Hall (1976) before drawing on the efforts of two scholars, Richard E. Nisbett and Geert Hofstede, the former because his work is a compendium of thinking regarding the East-West divide and, simultaneously develops a model that is closely related to the framework adopted by the current study; the latter because of the volume of empirical evidence he has brought to bear on the classification of cultures, and because he has been so highly influential in defining and classifying both societal and organisational culture.

High-context vs. low-context cultures. These terms, developed by anthropologist Hall (1976) as a means of comparing messages in routine communication in different cultures, are useful in a discussion of transfer of learning. The relation of learners to context itself in terms of context-bound or context-free processing is closely associated conceptually to the extent to which *high-road* learning, in particular, will occur (Perkins & Salomon, 1988). The abstraction of principles from one context to another is an essential quality of *high-road* transfer; it follows that individuals who are accustomed to low-context situations will be better adapted to this.

Hall did not apply *high-context* or *low-context* labels to cultures in the absolute sense; rather, these terms described speaking styles from which the observer could draw certain group inferences. Hence, although Hall acknowledged individual differences in style (which might also vary according to situation), certain societies that emphasised interpersonal relationships, and that were more contemplative and collective in nature, and that valued more indirect communication were considered to be *high-context*, while other societies that were task-orientated, individualistic, and logical, favouring direct communication, *lower-context*. Most countries in North American and European were considered to be *lower-context*, while many in Africa, the Middle East, and Asia, were *higher-context*. Thailand was an explicit example of the latter group. This was not to imply that countries or cultures could not change in their orientation; as social anthropologists Nishimura, Nevgi, and Tella (2008) observed, changes could be observed in the overall positioning of countries such as Finland, India, and Japan in the decades following the inception of Hall's classification. For example, while Japan was originally cited as an high-context exemplar, the country, as a result of modernisation and the inevitable Western cultural influences, has become lower-context. Similar cultural influence are extant in Thailand with possibly analogous results.

The *high-context—low-context* distinction is conceptually related to Nisbett's focus on *field-dependency* (discussed below) as a means of distinguishing the "habits of thought" of Asian and Western cultures.
Eastern, or Asian culture vs. Western culture. Nisbett, who is represented frequently in this study with reference to the relationship between culture and individual thought and in relation to the development of a cultural matrix of social psychology, developed much of his thinking with regard to differences between Eastern and Western cultures in his book *The Geography of Thought: How Asians and Westerners Think Differently... and Why* (2003). He began with an operational definition of "Eastern cultures" as those pertaining to China and those countries in East Asia that are highly influenced by its culture, such as the Koreas and Japan. "Western culture," on the other hand, characterises those countries that are mostly inhabited by people of European culture. Although he recognised that each of these terms may in turn encompass myriad distinct cultures and subcultures, he justified the classification by maintaining that these are as socially and politically similar in the case of Eastern cultures as they are distinct from Western cultures and subcultures.

Nisbett's classifications are based on a number of distinguishing features between the cultures. He focused particularly on the origins of the divide in classical thought, particularly in the distinction between "the syllogism and the Tao." Westerners draw from a classical tradition, based mostly on that of the Greeks, that is accompanied by an emphasis on individual identity and personal agency, coupled with a strong "sense of curiosity about the world" (p. 4) that fuelled explanatory models based on speculation and classification of underlying principles. Moreover, the

Greeks would focus on individual elements, rather than their contextual background, considering these elements "particulate and separate" (p.10). A further tendency of Greek antiquity was the idea of the cosmos as static, rather than dynamic.

In contrast to these classical Greek underpinnings of Western thought, the Chinese counterpart to individualism was harmony: "For the early Confucians, there can be no me in isolation, to be considered in isolation" (Rosemont, in Nisbett, p. 5). The blended philosophies of Taoism, Confucianism and Taoism resulted in a greater focus on the collective, on a "harmonious social network," on minimising discord, and on a collective agency (rather than, one would assume from a Western perspective, a sense of individual helplessness). In addition, in contrast to the constant desire of the Greeks to explain natural phenomena in terms of underlying principles and rational models and to constantly revise and refine these principles and models, the Chinese tendency was, according to Nisbett, to lose interest in the links between cosmic events and worldly phenomena once these were understood. As distinct from the Greek notion of cosmic stasis, often expressed as binaries, the Chinese perceived the world as a comprised of sometimes apparently opposing elements that complemented and balanced each other as a dynamic whole, as in the famous *yin-yang*.

Hofstede's dimensions. Hofstede (2002) developed the West-East distinction further by adding not only groups to the classification of culture, but also dimensions of divergence. Hofstede's initial study, conducted in the 1960s and 70s and published in 1980, is notable because it is regarded as the first to draw cultural dimensions from empirical data collection. In many respects, it also bridges any apparent gap between societal and organisational culture: Hofstede, from a management stance, initially collected his data from a global survey of IBM employees, using this data to classify national culture along the dimensions extracted through factor analysis. These dimensions were then confirmed over a number of decades by studies in different organisational contexts.

In sum, Hofstede, informed by Kroeber's classical definition (see Section 2.4.1.), particularly with regard to the importance of values, defines culture as the "collective programming of the mind that distinguishes the members of one group or category of people from another" (p. 9), elaborating that *mind* refers to "thinking, feeling, and acting, with consequences for beliefs, attitudes, and skills." While Hofstede recognised that more recent cross-cultural enquiry in cultural anthropology had focused on the complexity of society, as his unit of societal culture Hofstede focused on *national culture,* because, he averred, national character had been a stable subject of enquiry with much historical precedent, and it remained a concern within social psychology. He added that information about a population may be considered scientifically valid—as opposed to stereotypically defined—by meeting a number of criteria:

1. It is descriptive, rather than evaluative;
2. It is verifiable from more than one source;
3. It is applicable to a statistical majority;
4. It discriminates on population from another by indicating those characteristics for which this population differs from others (p. 14).

Hofstede maintained that his focus on national culture was justified by an adherence to these criteria, and he went to substantial effort in observing these criteria throughout his discourse.

From his focus on characteristics that distinguish certain cultures from others, Hofstede originally drew from his questionnaire data the following dimensions: *power distance*; *uncertainty avoidance*; *individualism and collectivism*; and *masculinity and femininity.* As these speak to the cultural considerations adopted in this study, they will now be defined in relation to a specific national culture, that of Thailand, as both illustration and overall situational context.

Power distance. According to Hofstede, this dimension is concerned with how different societies come to terms with human inequality in the areas of prestige, wealth, and power. Specifically, it is "a measure of the interpersonal power or influence between [a boss] and [a subordinate] as perceived the less powerful of the two" (p. 83), and is taken from Dutch social psychologist Mulder (1976, 1977, in Hofstede, 2002). Different societies show different power distances in their social hierarchies: a less egalitarian society will be considered to rank more highly than a more egalitarian society in the power-distance index, and would be more accepting of an unequal power distribution in, for example, the family and in institutions such as schools. Thailand ranks relatively highly in power-distance; the Thai cosmology is highly hierarchical in nature (Pagram & Pagram, 2006; Wyatt, 2003) and a Thai subordinate, for instance, would be less likely that an American one to question an authority figure such as a manager, parent or schoolteacher (Hallinger & Kantamara, 2001).

Uncertainty avoidance. Concerned particularly with the domains of technology, law, and religion, the term *uncertainty avoidance* is derived by Hofstede from organisational theorists Cyert and March (1963, in Hofstede, 2002) and reflects a culture's tolerance of ambiguity. Similarly to *power distance*, it is defined as part of a society's cultural heritage. Moreover, it concerns of ways of managing uncertainty as they are "transferred and reinforced through basic institutions such as the family, the state, and the school" (Hofstede, p. 146). People in uncertainty-avoiding cultures "look for structure in their organisations, institutions, and relationships." Thai culture, according to Hofstede's research, displays a slight tendency towards uncertainty avoidance. Certain ambiguities, concerning, for example, gender and sexual roles, are tolerated, but despite a somewhat lackadaisical and erratic approach to law *enforcement*, law *enactment* is sometimes draconian (The Hofstede Centre, 2014), indicating a high aversion to change and to risk. In the US, by way of comparison, uncertainty avoidance is relatively low: new ideas and innovations are generally well supported by society; there is also a tolerance for conflicting opinions and an encouragement of freedom of expression.

Individualism and collectivism. This binary, which is common to both Nisbett's (2003) and Hofstede's (2002) conceptualisation, enjoys considerable attention in cross-cultural literature, and describes "the relationship between the individual and the collectivity that prevails in a given society" (p. 209). As a commonly cited example, Chinese society, and those societies within the traditional sphere of influence of China, place more value on the collective than on the individual, whereas individualism and personal achievement is seen as an American ideal. More collective societies demand greater emotional commitment of their members towards their organisations, and "the level of individualism or collectivism in society will affect the organisation's members ' reasons for complying with organisational requirements" (p. 213).

In terms of this paradigm, as in most East Asian and Southeast Asian societies, Thai culture favours the collective; extended families remain the norm, although modernisation and industrialisation have resulted in some erosion of this. Harmony, compliance and interdependence are encouraged in the family and schools (Hallinger & Kantamara, 2001; Sirikanchana, 1998), and the preoccupations with autonomy, self-efficacy and personal mastery that are seen as schooling imperatives in the West (see, for example, Bandura, 1977; Dweck & Elliott, 1983) seldom emerge in traditional schooling. Compliance with group norms is high, and individual exposure to attention is seen as a potential source of embarrassment in business meetings or the classroom. In this researcher's fourteen years of experience as an educator in Thailand, individual learners rarely assert themselves in the classroom, and learning tends to be cooperative and interdependent.

Masculinity and femininity. Hofstede cited research (his own, in addition to that of others) that demonstrates that men tend to be more task- or ego-driven, as evinced in concerns such as careers and earnings, while women are more inclined to focus on social aspects, for example, relationships, assisting others, and the physical environment (p. 279). A culture that values a task- or ego-orientation will rank highly in Hofstede's Masculinity Index, with the converse being true for one that tends more towards social concerns. Hofstede contended that the male-female duality was elemental to human existence as one of the first that "each society has had to cope with in its individual way" (p. 280); it is therefore at the core of cultural norms. He referred, in this duality, to gender as a social function that has engendered, through male assertiveness and female "nurturance," male political and economic dominance. He further asserts that within households and, by extension, in organisations, different distributions of power may be observed across different societies.

In the workplace, Hofstede's research at IBM indicated that, to men, career advancement, earnings, training, and "up-to-datedness" were more important, and that, to women, a friendly atmosphere, position security, physical conditions, the manager, and cooperation were most important. These concerns could be projected to societies as a whole, facilitating their classification as either masculine or feminine in orientation. Societies in countries such as the UK, USA and Australia tend to be, in addition to individualistic, masculine in orientation because of the high value placed on achievement, competition and success, while in Thailand, higher value is placed on quality of life and on caring for others, with individual prominence spurned, resulting in Thai culture being considered feminine in orientation.

Interestingly, the juxtaposition of the dimensions of individuality and masculinity (as with juxtapositions of Hofstede's other dimensions) make possible comparisons that extend beyond the more simplistic East-West duality; for example, Japan, while sharing with Thailand a collectivistic orientation, is classified as one of the world's most masculine societies—rather than competition between individuals, however, as one would see in the USA, serious competition occurs amongst groups in Japan (The Hofstede Centre, 2014).

Other dimensions. Subsequent to the analysis of the data from the IBM studies and derivative research, discussed in this section, Hofstede added, to the initial four dimensions, two dimensions for the further consideration of cultural differences. These include *long- versus short-term orientation, indulgence,* and *pragmatism.*

The *long- versus short-term orientation* dimension emerged from research conducted in Hong Kong by Bond and others (e.g., Bond, Wan, Leung, & Giacalone, 1985). Here, Hofstede acknowledged the weakness of an instrument (his own in relation to the original IBM studies) that is designed by "Western minds" and applied to Asian contexts. The long- versus short-term orientation (LTO) dimension was suggested to Bond by Chinese scholars, and "appears to be based on ideas reminiscent of the teachings of Confucius" and places in contradistinction "long-term to short-term aspects of Confucian [sic] thinking: persistence and thrift to personal stability and respect for tradition" (p. 351). Broadly, East Asian countries scored more highly in terms of their long-term orientation that did Western countries. The LTO dimension was later subsumed by the pragmatism dimension discussed below.

The dimension of *indulgence (vs. restraint)* was added after collaboration with Minkov (Hofstede, Hofstede, & Minkov, 2010). Indulgent cultures are those that allow their members relatively free expression and gratification of their individual urges, particularly with regard to pleasure gratification, tending to focus thus on individual happiness, whereas more restrained societies strictly control these urges, discouraging such expressions and proscribing them by means of exacting social norms. Many Western societies tend to be high indulgence cultures, while most Asian countries incline more towards low indulgence. Thailand scores a mid, indeterminate position in this dimension (The Hofstede Centre, 2014).

A *pragmatic* (*vs. normative*) dimension has been most recently added to the list of dimensions. It describes the desire of people to explain environmental (including social) phenomena. Pragmatic societies are not inclined to attempt such explication of all such phenomena, and do not seek an ultimate and universal truth to inform such explanations. They tend, instead towards a contextual orientation: it is impossible to rationalise everything; life is complex and cannot be fully comprehended; and truth is dependent on situation, context and time (The Hofstede Centre, 2014). This dimension subsumes the LTO orientation in that pragmatic societies tend towards long-term goals that are achieved by thriftiness and perseverance. Normative societies, on the other hand, focus on rapid results and demonstrate a concern for establishing an absolute truth that applies to all situations. Moreover, this dimension resonates strongly with Nisbett's (2003) views of the folk metaphysics that distinguish Chinese and Western culture, and with the dimensions of *quick learning* and *certain knowledge* that Schommer-Aikins (Schommer, 1990, 1994) hypothesised. Thailand scores lowly on the pragmatism index, indicating a normative orientation.

Criticisms of Hofstede's cultural dimensions. As Ailon (2008) has asserted, one should approach Hofstede's cultural dimensions theory with caution, especially in view of the broad cultural generalisations that it engenders. In a work so influential, critiques are many, but include, illustratively, those of McSweeney (2002) who questions the validity of the survey-based research in measuring cultural differences, challenges the currency of the IBM data, and further notes the difficulties in generalising concepts to whole nations based on in-company research, and Baskerville (2003) who shares McSweeney's reservations as to the suitability of measuring culture by manner of statistical analysis, and who additionally questions the assumption that nation should be equated with culture. Hofstede makes an effort to respond to criticisms such as these (see, for example, Hofstede, 2002, 2003): he counters, for example, that surveys and the statistical information they provide are useful, but makes the accommodations that they should be used in conjunction with other methods. Furthermore, he asserts that, in addressing differences between countries, the comprehensive data from the IBM sample were significantly correlated with information from other studies that examined these differences. In addressing the question as to the currency of the data from the IBM studies, he observes that "the dimensions found are assumed to have centuries-old roots; only data which remained stable across two subsequent surveys were maintained; and that they have since been validated against all kinds of external measurements" (2002, p.2). Nevertheless, these concerns remain valid and this researcher proceeds with some caution in this regard.

The use of the cultural dimensions in this study. Despite the criticisms described above, Hofstede's cultural dimensions theory remains useful as a departure point for discussion; it is not adopted as a *sine qua non* of this particular study. Rather, it is adopted as an empirically sound manner of informing discussions of culture that transcends stereotypes—as Hofstede is at pains to establish in the principles discussed previously—and the more simplistic East-West duality that subsists in much of the earlier discussions of cross-cultural comparisons. It has been shown here, for example, how certain dimensions are useful in not only differentiating between US culture and that of East Asia (as in Nisbett's work), but also in differentiating between, for instance, Thai cultural tendencies and those of Chinese society (in the pragmatic index, while China scores highly, Thailand's score is low). The dimensions serve, therefore, in potential consideration of differences on a regional level, and on a global level, all of which are reflected in the schooling backgrounds of the participants in this particular study.

In addition, while the study does not seek direct relationships between Hofstede's cultural dimensions and the dimensions of learners' beliefs about knowledge and learning as developed by Schommer-Aikins (Schommer, 1990, 1994) and adopted in the EBI, there are some notable overlaps that add to the usefulness of the cultural dimensions as a point of departure for consideration and discussion. This includes, but is not limited to, the concurrence between the *pragmatic-normative* cultural dimension (where normative cultures pursue absolute truth, certainty of knowledge and rapidly-gained knowledge) and the dimensions of *certain knowledge* and *quick knowledge* reflected in the beliefs dimensions.

Thus, while the study recognises the limitations of Hofstede's cultural dimensions, it is also cognisant of the comprehensive nature of the theory and its applicability to cross-cultural examination. That is not to assert, however, that it is employed in this study to the exclusion of other frameworks or cultural considerations. Hofstede himself recognises, for example, that the theory is useful in comparing national cultures, but not of organisations within national cultures; the theory is only useful to the extent, therefore, that the organisation—or, in this case, school—culture converges with national culture. In respect of discussions of divergent organisation cultures, other dimensions may need to be employed.

Accounting for cultural differences. Nisbett (2003) accounted for differences in cultures by way of a schematic of influences on cognitive processes (see Fig. 2) that has a direct relationship to the framework adopted in the present study. He referred to differences between the West and East Asia in their respective "habits of thought," which have developed from very different ecologies—ecologies, in this sense, meant not only in the metaphorical, sociocultural sense, but also in the sense of the physical environment and its relationship to the people.

Different ecologies, Nisbett contended, have led to divergent "economic, political, and social arrangements" (p. 32): the interplay among the terrain of China, the irrigation systems, and the cultivation of rice, particularly in southern China and Japan, has led to a collective mind-set that requires harmonious, cooperative relationships amongst neighbours. The ecology of Greece, in contrast, is more amenable to more individualistic pursuits, such as hunting, fishing, and trade, which do not require the same degree of cooperation.

The types of social structure typified here have led, in turn, to an outlook in Chinese society that perceives the interdependence not only of people, but also of things — hence to a certain *field-dependency*, in sociopsychological terms. On the other hand, differences in the Greek ecology afforded the inhabitants, rather than an attention to the environment, the "luxury of attending to *objects*, including other people and their goals with respect to them, without being overly constrained by their relationships with other people" (p. 36; emphasis added). Nisbett illustrated in this way the possibility that the "folk metaphysics" of these two disparate societies was influenced by the targets of attention: the environment or field for the Chinese, objects for the Greeks.

Nisbett pointed out that that folk metaphysics would have influenced epistemology, particularly those beliefs concerning the sources of knowledge. In the case of the Chinese, an attention to *field* would lead, indirectly, to beliefs that knowledge may be acquired by examining the complex and fluid interrelationships amongst events; the Greek attention to objects, however, would render it more important to consider such objects in isolation, to categorise them, and to deduce static rules for their existence and functions. More directly though, and more germane to the present study, Nisbett observed the direct influence that social practices may have on habits of thought. The use of logic by the Greeks could be perceived as a way of negotiating conflict—the classical Western emphasis on rhetoric and arguments supports Nisbett's view here. In contrast, the imperative of social harmony of the Chinese and its consequential spurning of conflict, its focus on dynamically interacting parts, would not have engendered a transcendental, dialectic approach.

In sum, Nisbett recognised a sequence of ecology influencing economy and social structure, which in turn influence attention and folk metaphysics, with the ultimate outcome in tacit epistemology and cognitive processes. This is not seen, however, as a rigid sequence, nor is it unidirectional. It does provide a flexible model for considering the interrelationship amongst national culture, everyday practices (as reflected, frequently, in a society's institutions, such as its schools), individual beliefs, and cognitive outcomes, such as transfer of learning. This model is further developed in the cultural matrix of social psychology (Fiske et al., 1998), which frames the investigation here.

The East-West distinction is, of course, not a new one, and continues to attract consideration. The relative influences of different cultures on cognition and the mechanisms for this, however, are now receiving greater attention. For example, according with Nisbett's views, Ventura et al. (2008), in a study investigating the Aristotelianism), influences the way in which one perceives and, hence, processes cognitively one's physical environment. Venture et al. referred to contemporary examples in their investigation, such as the perceptual interconnectedness of Japanese urban landscapes in comparison to Western ones.

2.4.3. Organisational Culture

However the culture of organisations—or, in this case, schools—may converge with national culture, the ensuing framework adopted for this study, the cultural matrix of social psychology, concentrates on consecutive areas of sociocultural influence in, initially, broad societal context and, subsequently, in the practices that reflect the mores of the societal culture in that society's institutions. It is important to note, in view of the discussion above, that Hofstede (2002) distinguished between national culture and organisational culture, observing the relative permanence and stability of an individual's core societal values to those engendered by an organisation, which are partial and transient.

A further reflection here is that an individual may simultaneously belong to more than one organisation, such as that of the workplace, that of a religious group, and that of a social club—or even that, in the context of this study, a student may experience cultural practices in one class, conducted by, for instance, an American instructor, and another in a class conducted by a Thai instructor. Students' beliefs may switch between cultural contexts in a way that resembles, in its mechanisms, personal epistemological models such as that of Muis et al. (2006) and Limón (2006), which see domain-general beliefs as the bedrock upon which more domain-specific beliefs are developed as a student progresses through the learning process. Although these models apply to disciplinary knowledge and beliefs, they may be equally applicable to cultural ones.

In organisational culture (as in domain-specific beliefs), the practices prevalent in the particular work or schooling context comprise the culture (or the belief system, in the case of domain-specificity), rather than do the inert core societal values. Thus, as Hofstede remarked, organisational cultures are more pliable that societal ones; change the practices, he argued, and one may change the culture, with the converse also being true.

While the reciprocal relationship between organisational culture and institutional practices is rarely disputed, some debate exists as to the relative influence of organisational culture and national culture on values. In the management literature, where writing as to organisational culture is the most prolific, Ralston (1995), for example, noted that there were three possible accounts for this relative influence: a *convergence* theory; a *divergence* theory; and a then-emergent *crossvergence* theory. The *convergence* theory favours the workplace culture as the dominant influence on values while the divergence theory perceives national culture as the major impellent. The *crossvergent* theory focuses on the interaction of both national culture and work ideology in creating unique value systems; it takes into account both macro- (such as core societal factors) and microcosmic predictors in the development of values (Ralston, 2008).

The ensuing framework adopted in this study, the cultural matrix (Fiske et al, 1998), combines the influences of societal culture and institutional ideology and practice on individual action; recognising the dynamic, bidirectional nature of these associations. In accounting for the interaction between these various factors, it presents a crossvergence view. In the model, however, the everyday cultural practices of the institution, whether the workplace, the home, or the school, are immediate to individual action such as learning outcomes. In this, the model, moreover, tends towards the convergence view, which is supported by studies in education, such as that of Ventura et al. (2008), that indicate that active involvement in a learning context has a greater influence on what Nisbett (2003) refers to as "habits of mind" than does passive immersion in societal culture. Nevertheless, societal culture is still seen as being only slightly more distantly associated with these everyday institutional practices, with the learning context—the secondary school—mediating this relationship, and thus being of more direct interest in this study.

While the study of culture has its origins in anthropology (Cheng, 2000), many of the driving concepts of organisational culture originate from the field of business management where explications, studies and theories, such as those of Kidder (1981), Ouchi (1981), and Schein (1992), have examined, in particular, the relationship between organisational culture, organisational climate, and workplace effectiveness. For these purposes, *culture,* by consensus, refers to "a system of shared assumptions, beliefs, values, and behaviours in an given group, community, or nation" (Cheng, 2000, p. 209); the role of beliefs in an organisation is central to this, particularly people's beliefs as to "what works and what does not" (Wilkins & Patterson, 1985, p. 267). Climate, shaped by culture, can be defined as the distinguishing milieu of each organisation that compounds the characteristics of the total environment (Tagiuri, 1968); according to Owens (2001), the terms *culture* and *climate* can be distinguished insofar as "culture refers to the behavioural norms, assumptions, and beliefs of an organisation. Climate, however, refers to perceptions of persons in the organisation that reflect those norms, assumptions, and beliefs" (p. 145). In this distinction, one can perceive the essence of a model that associates broader organisational culture—the sociocultural *inter*personal, in Vygotsky's (1978) terms—with the individual *intra*personal. As Owen further notes, the overall culture of an organisation can have additional, sometimes distinctive "subunits" of culture (p. 151).

The enquiry adopted by the business management literature into organisational culture was motivated mainly by an interest in the relationship between this culture and business effectiveness (e.g., Bond, 1991; Deal & Kennedy, 1982; Kanter, 1984). There is considerable difficulty in empirically supporting such a relationship, owing to the challenges in measuring organisation effectiveness, of classifying culture, and of controlling environmental variables in the workplace (Owens, 2001). As a result, admittedly, much of the hypothesised relationship between certain types of organisation culture and differing organisational outcomes suffers from a scarcity of empirical findings. Nevertheless, such investigation is on-going, with many of the concepts being adopted by the field of education, despite arguably greater difficulties in defining and measuring what are essentially intangible learning outcomes (when compared, for example, to the tangible products and profits that are the province of business).

Despite these difficulties in measurement, the enquiry into school effectiveness and the quality of education has become a major concern in the past few decades (Cheng, 2000). Interschool cultural enquiry was spearheaded by scholars such as Rutter, Maughan, Mortimore, and Ouston (1979), who investigated the relationship between secondary school ethos and effectiveness. More recently, Campbell & Hourigan (2008) have investigated the impact of institutional culture on two undergraduate programmes in the same country (Ireland), finding that cultural differences between these institutions impacted, and were impacted by, the perceptions of the lecturers and the students, thus had an effect on learning outcomes.

Cultural enquiry has also been led into comparisons between education institutions in different societal contexts, making cross-cultural examinations (e.g., Dimmock, 2000) between, for example, Western institutions and Chinese, or Southeast Asian, ones (e.g., Cheng, 1997, 1999). Many of the theoretical frameworks that are employed to investigate school culture in this manner recognise a hierarchy of culture from that of the society or nation, to that of the community, the school, and, ultimately, the classroom (Cheng, 2000; Kilmann, Saxton, & Serpa, 1985; Schein, 1992). These frameworks, useful in guiding cross-cultural investigation, attempt also to account for the relationship between these cultural contexts and the individual. Cheng (2000) comprehensively sums up: these contextual cultures "are the critical sources of ambient and discretionary stimuli that affect and shape school members' behaviour and performance. Some of these stimuli can directly affect school members' behaviour and attitudes and some can shape their values and beliefs and indirectly change their behaviour and attitudes" (p. 210). Cheng concludes that the more immediate context, that of the classroom, by these means, should "have more direct stimuli on teaching and learning effectiveness." In this, we have the beginnings of a sociopsychological model that includes, comprehensively, societal and institutional contexts, that of the classroom and its practices, and individual learners' manifestations of these practices, through stimuli and cognitive processes, through learning outcomes. One could safely surmise that, in a modern, Western-orientated education system, the transfer of learning would be central to such outcomes.

School culture. The field of education, taking its lead from the business literature, has attended to the educational institution, whether at the primary, secondary, or tertiary level, as an organisation, recognising that schools, too, have distinct cultures that may have an association to their effectiveness, particularly in terms of learning outcomes.

Many contemporary initiatives that focus on school-wide change are based largely on the research-supported assumption that organisational culture is associated with learning outcomes. Such initiatives include those of the Innovative Designs for Enhancing Achievements in Schools (IDEAS) initiative in Australia, which, in its model for enhancing outcomes, includes elements that may be subsumed by the concept of culture as discussed in this section. These elements include a strategic vision, community expectations, and workplace practices that are aligned across the organisation and contribute to a distinct and cohesive community with a strong sense of its own identity (Crowther & Andrews, 2006, Summer; Pilkington & Lock, 2013)—central features of a distinct culture. The success and sustainability of initiatives such as IDEAS is, thus, according to Fullan (2001, cited in Pilkington & Lock, 2013) dependent on the school's ability to "recapture"; to implement "real and permanent cultural change" (p. 93).

Because of their proximity to the undergraduate learning experience, secondary schools are the main interest of this present study. Brady (2008), for example, in constructing a cultural model to investigate school effectiveness, notes that secondary schools "are complex institutions whose organisational structures, programme delivery mechanisms, and institutional community members combine to produce distinctive minisocieties" (p. 1), replete with the features of any such culture, such as assumption-driven rituals, ceremonies and traditions. Brady and others have remarked on the significant effect that these cultures have on the individuals that inhabit them. Gaziel (1997), in an empirical example, investigated 20 secondary schools in Israel, having teachers in these schools complete a *Perceived Culture Inventory* and then making comparisons between the emerging cultural dimensions. He found correlations between variations in these dimensions and student achievement; in other words, perceived school culture explained differences between effective schools and "average" ones (p. 316).

In focusing less on "effectiveness" and more on the sociopsychological, cognitive elements of learning, Ventura et al. (2008), mentioned elsewhere in this discussion, similarly show how secondary school culture is related to these elements. In an acknowledgement of not only differing school cultures, but also of the influence of national culture on these secondary school contexts, Ventura et al. found that schooling in Western culture (in this case, Portuguese), promoted context-free processing, which accords with Hall's (1976) relativistic measure of incidents or messages within a culture as a continuum from high-context to low-context: Portuguese culture, being Western-orientated, would contain a greater incidence of low-context messages than would Thai culture, and this tendency would be reflected in the country's schools.

Of interest to the model (the cultural matrix) applied to the present study, passive exposure to the culture of a society or country could not, by itself, account for these differences; Ventura et al. found that active cultural exposure in the secondary school was crucial. This finding lends support to a model that examines learning outcomes (in the form of transfer, in this case) as they are related both to national culture and, more immediately, to secondary school culture. It also accords with Hofstede's (2001) notion that while the culture of countries provides basic values, it is relatively inert; the organisation culture, on the other hand, through its immediate practices, is more pliable and has a more direct effect on the individual. The findings concerning the immediacy of secondary school culture are, furthermore, compatible with Cheng's (2000) assertion that it is the learning context, through direct stimulus, that has the critical impact on learning.

2.4.4. Culture and Learning

Culture, on its various levels, has featured in many recent studies concerning learning, academic attainment, literacy and intelligence.

Nisbett (2009), for example, examined the connection between culture, on the one hand, and intelligence and academic attainment on the other. Although he recognised that genetics has a fundamental, predispositionary role in a child's intelligence, he drew on a plethora of studies to show how environmental factors, such as culture, can dramatically compound any such biological endowment. Interestingly, Nisbett also argued convincingly that the intellectual ascendancy of higher socioeconomic groups, of certain races, and of certain cultures is not a result of genes. Rather, it can be ascribed to environmental conditions in the home and school settings, and to cultural values.

Nisbett cites the role of cultural values in the superior achievement, particularly in Mathematics and Physics, of East Asians students: these groups have a tendency to "work harder" (p. 158), possess a resilient response to adversity and failure, and are familiar with, and accept, criticism. The culture, he writes, "demands... making the most of their natural intelligence" (p. 159). Nisbett's observations about the connection between culture, on the one hand, and intelligence and attainment, on the other, are of relevance to this discussion, as they are both concerned with the ability to solve problems—as is the transfer of learning.

Ventura et al. (2008), in their investigation of the relative influence of schooling environments more directly addressed elements of transfer of learning itself. They cited various tests, such as the Framed Line Test and the Rod-and-Frame Test (employed, respectively, by Ji, Nisbett, & Ping, 2000; and Kitayama, Duffy, Kawamura, & Duffy, 2003, both cited in Ventura et al., 2008) that indicate, in accord with others, such as Nisbett (2003), that East Asians are more "field dependent" and thus have difficulties divorcing a physical object from its frame, than are Americans. East Asians, hence, have a more holistic cognitive orientation that emphasises "relationships and connectedness among objects in the field" while Americans (and presumably other Westerners) tend more to "focus exclusively on the object and its attributes" (p. 79). This Western tendency of de-contextualisation is crucial to transfer of learning, because, as Pea (1987) observes, intelligence, and hence transfer, has long been defined by the ability of the learner to abstract knowledge and skills from the learning context—the capacity to move away from field-dependent knowledge use "where knowledge and skills resources are 'welded' to their initial context of acquisition" (p. 44).

What is important to this discussion is that while Nisbett's (2009) focus is on the broader community of the culture (and particularly on the influence of parents), Ventura et al. (2008) focus on the direct influence of the culture of the school on learners. In their comparison of the effects of literacy and schooling on participants in Portugal and Thailand respectively, the researchers investigated whether schooling itself, in conjunction with culture, has a significant influence on cognitive orientation. They found that such an effect could be observed in the Portuguese group, but not the Thai one, leading them to conclude that one of the elemental factors of transfer, the ability to abstract from context, is a result not only of "passive exposure" to Western culture, but also, crucially, of Western schooling. Although the researchers were not able to identify specific learning activities that contributed to the more analytical stance of Western school-levers, they speculated that the process of reading, especially, may be influential in its transmission of core cultural values.

The findings of Ventura et al. cause one to consider not only the influence of Thailand's broader culture on student entrants to an international college in Thailand, but also the critical role of the primary and secondary schooling environment on these learners. The conclusions of the study suggest that while a child may be raised in the broader Thai culture of the community, he or she may receive significant influences from a Western-style schooling, which may in turn incline him or her more towards the context-free processing that that favours transfer of learning (Pea, 1987).

This last point is significant, considering the context of the current study is an international college in Thailand, because while some students are admitted to the college from Thai public schools, most attended international schools, bilingual schools, Catholic schools, or schools abroad. An investigation of these differing influences on learning, and the transfer of learning, is clearly opportune.

Culture and transfer of learning. Much of the discussion to this point has been based on the extrapolation of transfer-related elements from more general conceptualisations of learning. While investigation into the relationship between culture, societal or organisational, has become widespread, not only in business but also in education, it is difficult to locate studies that have explored, in direct and specific terms, the relationship between culture and transfer of learning. Pea (1987), however, foreshadowed a full investigation of this relationship by observing that constraints on "appropriate" transfer are defined by culture through its customs and conventions, and that sometimes transfer may fail because of proscriptions that may vary across cultures (p. 48). Hence, in the context of a Thai university, a student may perceive it as inappropriate—even, discourteous—to question (possibly erroneous) dicta of a lecturer, as cultural mores of hierarchy and "face-saving" may proscribe such behaviour. Such a student, if he or she had previously been subjected to Thai public schooling, might perceive rote-learning as an appropriate form of learning as a result of being rewarded for such a strategy—this being anathema to Diener's and Dweck's (1978) sought-after mastery-orientedness.

Thus, the learners' cultural context, whether from the microcosmic sphere of the classroom or the macrocosmic of the community, may either facilitate or obstruct the transfer-conducive elements of personal epistemology characterised by, for example, Diener and Dweck. The desirable characteristics of a "mastery-oriented" learner, such as self-reliance and reflectiveness, are arguably more prevalent in individualistic, lower-context cultures than collective, higher-context ones.

While very few studies in education examine the direct link between culture and transfer of learning, contextual and sociocultural elements, as has been noted by Haskell (2002), are a significant focus in many workplace-related studies that evoke transfer of training of learning. Some recent examples include a doctoral thesis (Evans, 2012) that has examined transfer from the perspective of organisational culture. The study examines transfer of learning from, specifically, the workplace culture of the British civil service, concluding that the existing models are inadequate in accounting for the transfer of learning. Because informal practices and workplace subcultures reflect more accurately the cultural assumptions of the learners, the study indicates the dependence of transfer on a supportive informal ethos, rather than on imposed formal systems and management practices. It is apparent, in other words, that direct instructional practices and the formal contexts that support transfer of learning are insufficient. Although these instructional practices need not be supplanted, they should be considered as part of a whole that includes the addressing wider organisational culture.

Equally notably, Closson (2013), in the field of adult education, adopts an even more emphatic approach to cultural context: she recognises that while Baldwin and Ford (1988) famously advocate the role of the learner as one of their three elements for successful transfer of learning (see Section 2.2.4.), sociocultural elements such as culture, ethnicity and race are seldom investigated as factors relevant to the identity of the learner in the process of learning transfer. Closson proposes that these factors be acknowledged and that educators include "culturally resonant metaphors, case studies, and examples" (p. 66) during programme planning and then "analyse the environment and potential barriers that may exist for learning transfer." However, Closson does not articulate a link between cultural factors and the underlying mechanisms of transfer. Of course, it would be remiss to consider the relationship between culture and transfer of learning without considering transfer of learning itself as a cultural construct. Nevertheless, the limited literature on this relationship fails apparently to step outside the paradigm of learning transfer to consider it in this particular way.

In a cultural critique of the ascendancy of transfer of learning in higher education, Green, (2013) has observed that the transfer imperative has become stronger in recent years. Following the global economic failures of the 1980s, the economic imperative to justify tertiary education in terms of employment utility became much stronger (see also Louca, 2007): universities became increasingly engaged in rationalisation processes that were, in many ways, detrimental to the liberal arts missions of many institutions by emphasising, instead of the development of humanistic values and general thinking skills, specific transferable outcomes to the workplace.

Despite the centrality of transfer to Western education, many of education's goals are not quantifiable in terms of measurable transfer outcomes, particularly if one examines the purpose of education across different cultures. Green (2013) points out that these more value-orientated, non-quantifiable goals are not completely compatible with transfer goals in that they emphasise individual development—learning to *be*—rather than the stark utility of knowledge to an end purpose—learning to *do*.

However, in educational traditions in all regions of the world, learning to *be*, rather than on learning to *do,* is a cultural imperative. For example, in Nigeria, Fafunwa (1982), erstwhile Minister of Education of one of Africa's largest education systems, elucidated "seven cardinal goals of traditional African education" that include the importance of instilling in learners a respect for their elders, a sense of community, and an appreciation of their cultural heritage. In Muslim education, prominent educational Islamist Al-Attas (1979) has written of the centrality of "character-building based on the ideals of Islamic education" (p. 104). In Thailand, education was traditionally community based, and under the custodianship of Buddhist monks who not only taught the *dharma*, but through these teachings encouraged "compassion, friendliness, and love of peace" (Sirikanchana, 1998). Moreover, as Soudien (2011) has recounted, such values have found expression in the Western tradition: the values of "love" and "caring" appear in the classical discourse of Plato, of the Christian educational treatises of Hugo St John, and even in such an apparently disparate source as the didactics of Marx. Moreover, the American ideal of a liberal arts education, for all its emphasis on "strong and transferable intellectual and practical skills" (Association of

American Colleges and Universities, 2012), is fundamentally concerned, as with classical liberal education, with "producing mature and virtuous adults," expressed in more contemporary terms as developing "'good citizenship' and a sense of social responsibility" (Green, 2013).

In view of these differing goals, it becomes necessary to assess transfer of learning as *a* goal, rather than *the* goal of education. Furthermore, lest one becomes guilty of "epistemic violence" (see section "Beliefs constructs and learning"), one needs to assess not only the culturally "situatedness" (see Greeno, 1998) of the transfer-oriented learner, as previously discussed in this section, but also the appropriateness of transfer of learning itself as a cultural orientation (see Pea, 1987). This study, while mindful of this contextual orientation, operates on the central premise that if, in a globalised—and thus Western-inclined—world, transfer of learning is a key goal of education, then one needs to seek the qualities in the society, the culture, the institution, and the individual learner that, through their interaction, foster conditions that are supportive of such transfer. The focus on transfer of learning does not, in so doing, aim to deprecate or preclude other goals in education that may also have priority.

2.4.5. Culture and Learners' Beliefs

How, specifically, does culture induce these effects on learning? The major route is arguably through the learner's individual beliefs about knowledge and learning. From personal beliefs to culture, the focus merely shifts from individual values and beliefs to collective ones; from the specific to the systematic; and from individual agency to systematic influences on such agency.

Even though culture is notoriously difficult to explicate, most definitions will subsume collective values, assumptions, and beliefs (e.g., Hofstede, 2001; Schein, 1985) which are passed on to individuals within those cultures as "the correct way to perceive, think, and feel in relation to [certain] problems" (Schein, 1985, p. 9). In the field of cross-cultural psychology, in an influential article that strove to define culture as distinct from the sometimes interchangeably employed labels "society" and social system, Rohrer (1984) emphasised as central to his definition shared meanings; he repeatedly exemplified these meanings as beliefs, alongside values and norms.

To the anthropologist Barth (1995), culture could be described as a shared way of knowing; the interstices between the centrality of beliefs and of ways of knowing resound with the conception of personal epistemology, if one discounts the distinction between *shared* beliefs—culture—and *individual* beliefs—personal epistemology. While one should avoid the cultural determinist fallacy of assuming that individual beliefs are determined *solely* by cultural beliefs (Rohr, 1984)—*intra*cultural differences exist among individuals with regard to variables such as motivation, attitude, and cognition—it is, nevertheless, a small intuitive step from shared beliefs to individual beliefs.

Thus, culture arguably affects the way students perceive knowledge and their relative position as "knowers." A case can be made, therefore, that the key to an individual's personal epistemology (and related beliefs, such as those about learning) is the culture within which he or she functions. The influence of culture on learning beliefs, in particular, has support in the literature; for example, Jehng et al. (1993), in their study of university students, showed that these individual beliefs are produced by the culture, the context in which the beliefs are cultivated, and the activities involved.

That culture and learning context influence beliefs about knowing and learning is, moreover, evident in studies as to learners' epistemic beliefs that have been conducted in cultures and contexts other than those from which the assumptions and instruments of epistemic measurement originated. Originating from the US, the EBI that has been adopted in this present study, for example, is premised on five beliefs dimensions postulated by Schommer-Aikins (Schommer, 1990, 1994) that have had some support through factor analysis of the EBI through datasets collected in US student populations (Schraw, Bendixen, & Dunkle, 2002). However, analysis of data collected in different cultural contexts, using the EBI, such as in China (Chan et al., 2011) and Turkey (Cam et al. 2012), have yielded different factor structures, and fewer factors (three, instead of five, in both cases), suggesting that beliefs about learning and knowing are culturally situated.

Moreover, it is not only broader societal culture that has been demonstrated to have a relationship with these individual beliefs. Studies across institutions within the same broader societal context, but with different organisational parameters, have found differing epistemic belief systems among these groups. For example, Muis and Sinatra (2008) in analysing student responses to the EBI from institutions in North America, one in the US and the other in Canada, found some significant differences in the compared means between the groups in relation to the five dimensions of the instrument. Therefore, it may be arguable that while the broader societal culture has a constant and fundamental influence on individual beliefs, it is the more immediate organisational or institutional culture that may have the more direct effect, at least within the particular context that it is investigated—this would accord with the views of Cheng (2000), Hofstede (2002), and Schein (1992).

In investigating the role of institutional culture, limited support for a direct relationship between university students' secondary school background and elements of their belief systems was found by Fujiwara (2007). The study is of special interest here not only because of its broader contribution to understanding the relationship between institutional culture and learners' beliefs, but also because it was conducted in the same institution as this present study, MUIC. A two-way MANOVA ($N = 152$) was conducted to detect any differences in belief structures in Mathematics, as measured by a modified version of the Indiana Mathematics Belief Scales combined with the Fennema-Sherman Usefulness Scale (Kloosterman & Stage, 1992), among students grouped according to their secondary school backgrounds (local Thai school, local bilingual school, international school, or school abroad). The analysis indicated a significant relationship between secondary school background and one of the five emergent belief dimensions. This belief dimension concerned individuals' efforts in increasing mathematical ability.

In conclusion, in addition to the broad philosophical support outlined previously, one may find theoretical and empirical support for a relationship between culture and individual beliefs. This relationship may exist between societal or organisational culture and individual beliefs; it may also exist between these individual beliefs and behavioural or cognitive actions on the part of individuals. It makes sense, therefore, to examine the interrelationship between these spheres on a "meso" level, "linking macro and micro concepts to form integrated theories of organisations" as Fu et al. (2004, p. 285) have advocated. In this case, the macro-level consists of societal and cultural elements, and the micro-level individual beliefs. In such a meso-model, investigating these individual beliefs, rather than the direct cultural effects, on individual cognition or behaviour is useful: Fu et al., in their 12-nation study investigating the interrelationship of societal cultural values, individual beliefs, and managerial influence strategies, found support for "the potential use of such individual beliefs, in preference to existing cultural value schemas, as a more fine-grained means for predicting and explaining observed differences in individual behaviour across different cultural groupings" (p. 298).

This view by Fu et al. lends support to the approach of this present study. Rather that examining a direct link between culture and individual behaviour, beliefs about knowing and learning are examined in direct relationship to such behaviour in the form of transfer of learning. The underlying assumption as that the beliefs that the individual students hold are both intermediary to and immediate to such behaviour, an assumption that accords with the cultural matrix.

2.5. The Cultural Matrix of Social Psychology

The cultural matrix of social psychology, as articulated by Fiske et al., (1998) provides a comprehensive model that links together transfer of learning, learners' personal beliefs about knowledge and learning, and culture. It combines the conceptual elements that have been discussed in the foregoing discussion by providing, in the manner described by Nisbett (2003), for the interplay between societal structure (as influenced by ecology and economy) and, in turn, metaphysics, personal epistemology, and individual "habits of thought." It encapsulates both broader, societal culture (as defined and characterised by, most influentially, Hofstede, 2002) and organisational culture, which, as with societal culture, is concerned with values and beliefs, but which is also more directly concerned with everyday practice that enacts and symbolises these beliefs—"the way things are done around here." The cultural framework, furthermore, not only provides a means for understanding the interaction among different levels within a hierarchy of cultural influences—that of society or nation, that of the school, and, ultimately, that of the classroom (Chen, 2000), but also offers a means of examining these influences on the individual's thoughts and actions.

Fiske et al., in an effort to correct the "fundamental attribution error" and the "the tendency to characterise the self in terms of global attributes" (p. 915), synthesised increasingly strong arguments recognising the substantial dependency on cultural meanings and practices of fundamental psychological processes. They cited a plethora of evidence, moreover, that demonstrated that these psychological processes could differ substantially in other cultures from those in Europe and America— whence many of the universalistic assumptions as to the processes were derived (see also Hofer, 2008). They counter these assumptions with the basic premise of cultural psychology that "cultural practices and meanings complement and inform psychological processes, which in turn generate and transform these cultural practices and meanings" (Fiske et al., p. 916).

The cultural matrix was based on the axiom that "in order to participate in any social world, people must incorporate cultural models, meanings, and practices into their basic psychological processes" (p. 915). The model rests, moreover, on a recognition, similar to dialecticism, that it is not only these psychological processes that influence the cultural context, but also the cultural context that influences the psyche of individuals. Fiske et al., based on these assumptions, define the central problem of cultural psychology as "the question of how collective realities and each of the successively embedded systems enable, inform, and constrain human psyches." The present discussion has endeavoured, thus far, to illustrate, in broad terms, how the various elements of this study operate in their relationship to each other. The major areas of consideration have included that of the relationship between the cognitive and metacognitive processes of transfer of learning, on the one hand, and students' belief systems, on the other; the association between these belief systems and the classroom, as enacted through everyday ritual and learning experiences; and the relationship between broader, societal culture and that of the school. The matrix, thus, through the central question outlined here, attempts to incorporate all of these areas of enquiry.

In addition to framing these broad areas of enquiry, the use of the cultural matrix by this study underscores a growing awareness that one cannot, as was tradition in the subsumed theoretical spheres of both transfer of learning and personal epistemology, adopt a universalistic stance towards psychological processes and their manifestations in human behaviour. As Hofer (2008) has asserted, psychological enquiry is no longer assumed the province of elite Western institutions, which, in the past, applied findings based on research of their own student populations to other populations that might be vastly different in their values, beliefs, and practices. In this regard, the justification for the cultural matrix is provided by Fiske et al. (1998), who draw on a number of scholars, particularly since the 1990s, in demonstrating that "psychological processes depend substantially on cultural meanings and practices" (p. 915). They point to a large body of evidence that indicates that psychological processes differ among cultures; in this, they contrast such aspects as have previously been explored in this discussion, such as views of the self in society (collective vs. individualistic orientation) and on the relative dependence of the individual on others (independence vs. interdependence).

Unlike the models previously represented in this discussion, such as that of Nisbett (2003) and Cheng (2000), the cultural matrix is not merely a schematic of related influences. In the case of the cultural matrix, the authors gather conceptual and empirical support in an effort also to explain the mechanisms of these interrelated spheres.

Much of the focus in this discussion has been on the sociocultural environment. It must be emphasised, however, that Fiske et al., (1998) do not subscribe to a behaviourist view of the individual psyche being, at birth, a *tabula rasa*. In detailing the mechanisms of psychological development, Fiske et al., as is the case with Nisbett (2003), do not dismiss predisposionary or genetic factors in the development of the psyche; sociocultural context and biological factors are perceived as integrally-related and dynamic parts of individual development. In particular, Fiske et al. elucidate the manner in which *evolution* and *enculturation* contribute to the formation of the individual psyche.

Firstly, in explaining the manner in which children develop "culturally specific psyches from a common biological constitution" (p. 957), Fiske et al. posit a converse relationship in which the human propensity to construct culture has been shaped by evolution, and in which culture itself has guided evolution. They cite numerous theorists who discuss the notion that, in humans, social competence may guide natural selection (through participation in socially-condoned rituals and practices, particularly marriage and other rites of passage, than encourage social conformity). Fiske et al., recognising that social mores are relative, extend this focus to the cultural, pointing out that "the core of cultural competence is competence at coordinating social relationships" (p. 958). Furthermore, the delayed maturation of humans, when compared with animals, allows for a kind of extra-uteral development through family structures; this assists in arranging the psyche in a cultural manner.

Finally, concerning evolutionary psychology, Fiske et al. argue, in the manner of Chomsky's well-known view of language acquisition and Vygotsky's (1978) social interactionism, but drawing also on numerous other learning theorists, that learning is dependent on organisms being in prior possession of enabling structures: "no organism can learn very much—if anything—without a great many relevant, specifically focused constraints on constructible hypotheses. Learning requires implicit Bayesian prior probability distributions and theories of possible worlds, plausible dynamics, and credible causes" (p. 959).

Here Fiske et al. refer to linguistic principles developed by Chomsky (1965, 1980) and Pinker (1994) with regard to what they and other nativist linguists term *modules:* in the case of language, a module is "an evolved, motivated, highly structured proclivity for the acquisition of speech and grammar" (p. 959). Similarly, they argue, such prepared structures operate in spheres other than language that are socially construed, such as displays and perceptions of emotion, long-term heterosexual bonding, familial sexual taboos, and theories of objects and mind. Extending this to culture in general, Fiske (1994, in Fiske et al., 1998) reasons that these evolved human proclivities and prepared structures are a requirement, as in language, for the acquisition and utilisation of culture: "these are motivated, modifiable, biologically incomplete capacities to use the cultural models that are essential for mediating meaningfully coordinated, harmoniously communicative sociality" (Fiske et al., 1998). These capacities are labelled *mods,* which, as in the case of Chomsky's structural proclivities that may generate sentences, have the potential to generate "coordinating cultural models." While the authors admit that these concepts are speculative, it is important to note, nevertheless, that the cultural matrix, for all its emphasis on sociocultural influences, does not deny, as behaviourism did, the existence of genetically initiated proclivities in the individual psyche.

2.5.1. Enculturation

Fiske's (1998) concept of the *mod*, in the context of the cultural matrix, is closely related to that of *enculturation,* which is of more direct relevance to this particular study than the often-controversial theoretical speculation as to cultural evolution. Enculturation is a cultural-acquisition mechanism and can be defined as the development by a person of cultural competencies, such as values, knowledge of rituals, symbols and discourse, through immersion in a particular culture (Barry, 2007). The term most frequently refers to the development of one's own culture, as influenced by home and family, and is thus somewhat different from the related *acculturation,* which refers to learning of aspects of a second culture so as to facilitate individual functionality in that culture (Sam & Berry, 2010).

*En*culturation was thus considered more germane to the interactive and dynamic cultural areas that are subsumed by the cultural matrix; it evokes a holistic and "familial" approach to the development of primary cultural patterning that has an immediate relationship to the individual psyche than the secondary, relatively more "alien" processes, of *a*cculturation. The matrix conceives cultural influences, such as that of the home and that of the school, as integral and complementary, whereas acculturation models tend to allow for conflicting cultural influences (see, for example, Gudykunst & Kim, 2003; Kramer, 2012).

Fiske et al. (1998), in elaborating on the role of enculturation in the cultural matrix, considered the *mod*—an innate proclivity for a certain cultural model—as common to all humans, but as generating diverse cultural models. Drawing from Vygotsky's (1978) views of social interactionism, Fiske et al. (1998) saw the child as an agent who, through certain proclivities that direct motivation and exploration, actively constructs these cultural models through guided social interaction—such sophisticated construction, they argue, similarly to (Chomsky, 1959), would be impossible without a certain innate capacity towards this end (they also speculate as to the existence of a critical period for such enculturation). The child, through the guidance of caregivers, gradually perfects cultural models that facilitate social interaction within a certain cultural community. Fiske et al. (1998) provide a useful précis of their view of enculturation as follows:

> Beginning with their shared innate physics and theory of mind, by participating in the everyday activities of their cultures children develop culturally diverse and distinctive practices and beliefs about faxes, amulets, magic, computers, souls, software, ghosts, angels, ancestor spirits, viruses, witches, holograms, and gods, whose defining attributes are remarkable transformations and recombination of these initial preconceptions (p. 961).

The importance of participation in contextual "everyday activities" to the cultural development of the psyche is one that resounds with Hofstede's views (amongst those of others who have been discussed here) on the pliability and immediate influence of organisational culture on the individual. These routine practices are, moreover, integral to the home and school environment and, thus, the concept of enculturation is central to the view of learning developed in this present discussion. This view provides a common and substantial conceptual focus for the apparently diverse fields of study synthesised here: in transfer of learning, it subsists, for example, in Pea's (1980) notions of cultural appropriateness, and in personal epistemology, it finds expression, for example, in the views of Muis, Bendixen, and Haerle (2006) and others who examine the development of domain specificity through immersion in a field and guidance by experts in that field.

The concept of enculturation is closely related, moreover, to highly influential perspectives on socialisation in learning in general: Lave (1988) and Brown, Collins, and Duguid (1989), for example, in developing, respectively, related theoretical perspectives on situated cognition and cultures of learning, recognised the role of contextual "apprenticeship" in learning. Rogoff (1990, 1994), similarly evoked enculturation in conceptualising learning as a transformational process, achieved through guided participation in a particular learning context. Moreover, the concept informs views of learning communities and of guided discovery and learning (e.g., Bielaczyc & Collins, 1999; Brown & Campione, 1994) that remain current in discussions of effective learning (see, for example, Shernoff, 2013).

2.5.2. The Cultural Matrix and the Present Study

Barnett and Ceci (2002), in their review of the literature as to transfer of learning, noted "there is little agreement in the scholarly community about the nature of transfer, the extent to which it occurs, and the nature of its underlying mechanisms" (p. 612). Since this observation, there has been little conceptual development that improves this situation: the search for a generally accepted model for transfer of learning, one that would contribute to such an understanding, continues. The cultural matrix, adapted to the particular exigencies of transfer, may contribute conceptually towards such a model: it addresses the need, prominently articulated by Baldwin and Ford (1988), to include in considerations of transfer the instruction, the learner, and the environment; it accommodates—in a Vygotskian dialectic between the inter- and intrapersonal—sociocultural, metacognitive and cognitive approaches to transfer. Furthermore, it includes—in terms of Greeno's (1999) situatedness of learning—an acknowledgement of both individual agency and environmental systems and subsystems. Finally, it provides a conceptual framework that accommodates the associations among transfer of learning, learners' beliefs about knowledge and learning, and culture that have been synthesised in this conceptual review.

The cultural matrix is, therefore, philosophically and pragmatically, an appropriate starting point for developing a general theory of transfer of learning. It melds into dialectic the apparently disparate approaches that have commonly characterised investigations into the nature of learning. It is both a framework and a justification for this present study: it encapsulates comprehensively and cogently the concepts explored here and provides a model that, if empirically supported, may contribute to the general theory of transfer of learning that has been sought for over a century, the seminal exploration of Thorndike and Woodworth (1901a, 1901b) of this central concern of education.

Chapter 3
Research Methods

3.1. Research Purpose and Questions

The purpose of this study is to understand the interrelationship among undergraduate students' secondary school background, their personal beliefs about knowledge and learning, and their perceptions of transfer of learning. In order to achieve this, the researcher applied the cultural matrix of social psychology, as articulated by Fiske et al. (1998). Findings may contribute to a general theory of transfer, in addition to having practical policy implications for school-wide strategies that focus on the management of organisational culture.

The specific research questions were:

1. What is the nature of students' perceptions of the transfer of learning from the academic-literacy-based English Communication (EC) programme to the courses in the disciplines?
2. What is the nature of the relationship between students' perceptions of the transfer of learning from the EC programme and their personal beliefs about knowledge and learning?
3. What is the nature of the relationship between students' beliefs about knowledge and learning and their secondary school background ("culture")?

3.2. Conceptual Framework

This study is framed by the cultural matrix of Fiske et al. (1998), who, like Hofer (2008), decried the still-dominant assumptions of universality in Western-derived social psychology. Fiske et al. (1998) advocated the primacy of culture in considering the development of the individual psyche and its manifestations, recognising the comparative differences between West and East in relation to their respective orientations. In North America and Europe, for example, shared "implicit and unexamined cultural values and practices... emphasise individual rights, independence, self-determination, and freedom" (p. 919). Many other cultures, in contrast, "place a higher value on interdependence, and fostering empathic connections with others."

With regard to this study, the researcher recognises that the epistemic and related beliefs required for successful transfer of learning may be premised on individualistic values of learner autonomy and mastery-orientedness, as seen in the influential conceptualisations of Diener and Dweck (1978). These particular values have been advocated globally as desirable attributes—even as outcomes—in education. Yet, in many cultures, these same values may be anathema to those promoting social harmony and interdependence: a reliance on the teacher, for example, may be culturally condoned and, in such cultures, even the primacy of transfer of learning as *the* goal of education may be questioned.

On a broader level, the matrix proposed by Fiske et al. provides a comprehensive framework for conceptualising, systematically, the relationship between the sociocultural environment and the individual psyche. The matrix (see Figure 1) charts overlapping relationships between collective reality and sociopsychological processes, and between these processes and their manifestations in action.

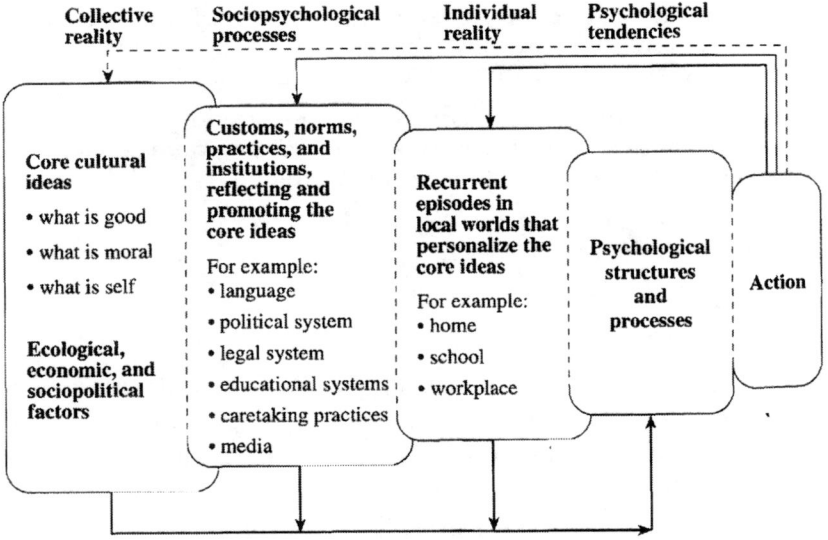

Figure 1. The cultural matrix of social psychology. Adapted from "Emotion and Culture: Empirical Studies of Mutual Influence" by S. Kitayama, and H. R. Markus (eds). American Psychological Association (1994).

To elaborate, there is bi-directional movement, starting on the collective level between the core cultural ideas (about morality, goodness and self) and ecological, economic and socio-political factors, and between these factors and the customs, norms and institutions reflecting and evincing the core cultural ideas (the language and the educational systems, for example). These, in turn, are reflected and manifested on the individual level through recurrent episodes "in local worlds," such as home, school and the workplace, that personalise the core ideas of the culture. Finally, the recurrent episodes are internalised in psychological structures and processes, which become manifested as "action."

The collective level of the matrix forms the broad perspective of this study, especially when reflecting on the values of Western society as compared to that of Thai. Because of the focus on transfer of learning in a formal educational system, the customs and norms that are most apparent in different types of secondary schools (for example, Thai state schools, international schools in Thailand, and schools abroad in Western countries) will be examined as these are thought to have an immediate association with undergraduate students' beliefs about knowledge and learning. These beliefs form, in terms of the matrix, the psychological structures and processes whereby sociocultural influences are converted into action in the form of transfer of learning—where, in Vygotskian terms, the *inter*personal is converted into the *intra*personal, together with its manifestations.

3.3. Participants

The full cohort of 186 students at that time enrolled in English Communication IV (EC4), the final required level of the English Communication (EC) programme, were invited to complete a numbered questionnaire. From those who chose to participate, eight typical cases were then selected based on the analysis of the questionnaires and invited to participate in semi-structured interviews. Students from EC4 were chosen for the purposes of this study because they were not too distant from their secondary school experiences (being in the fourth to sixth trimester of their undergraduate studies) while being sufficiently advanced in the EC programme to be familiar with the skills and knowledge that would be polled in the study. A final consideration in the selection of this group was the caveat by Burke, Jones, and Doherty (2005) that participants be in a position to perceive transfer to the target domain. Thus, the intended participants of this proposed study were considered suitable, as they had recently commenced courses in their respective majors beyond the required General Education levels.

3.4. Piloting the Study

Part of the questionnaire, termed the Measure of Academic Literacy Transfer (MALT), had previously been piloted in a related study (Green, 2008), which assisted in establishing the construct validity of the instrument.

In addition, the full composite questionnaire, as detailed below and as used in this study, was later piloted in order to establish reliability, to investigate any potential misunderstanding of the questionnaire items, and to adjust timing. A convenience sample of 16 students from a previous cohort, but at the same level and having similar demographic characteristics, was invited to participate in a test-retest sequence. The questionnaire was administered for a second time a month after the initial session to minimise the possibility of a practice effect, and data analysed for correlation to establish consistency and, hence, reliability (Rousson, Gasser, & Seifert, 2002). Any potential misunderstandings of individual items were elicited from the participants immediately following the administration of the first "test."

Preliminary interview sessions were held between an assistant and two participants in order to preview and, where necessary, revise the interview matrix.

3.5. Data Collection

Because of the impracticality of experimental designs in reflecting social reality, and because the overall aim of the study was to gain an understanding (*Verstehen*) of the application of a cultural psychological construction to a particular context rather than to explicitly test behavioural hypotheses in the manner prescribed by the traditional scientific manner, self-report survey methods were employed in the collection of data (Crabtree & Miller, 1999). This approach does not imply, however, any rigid ideological or ontological preference towards either qualitative or quantitative methods: while one may recognise that quantitative and qualitative approaches entail different ontological positions (for example, positivist for the former and interpretive for the latter), theoretical distinctions are often forsaken in the practice of research, becoming what Platt (1998) referred to as a reflection of "intellectual *bricolage* or *post hoc* justifications" (p. 275), being directed, instead "by quite other considerations, some of a highly practical nature." Thus, this researcher agrees with social methodologist Bryman (2012) in recognising that, often, the differences between quantitative and qualitative methods are polarised or exaggerated.

Accordingly, this researcher agrees that a dichotomy between these approaches is false (Lawrence, 1993): the distinction between behaviour and meaning; empirically tested hypotheses and grounded theory; and numbers versus words and are not as distinct as they sometimes appear (Bryman, 2012). The last of these, the distinction between numbers and words, is central to the perceived contrast between quantitative and qualitative paradigms; yet, social surveys of the kind employed for data collection in this study, while qualitatively motivated, use quantitative methods of analysis. The approaches are, thus, in fact, complementary (Field, 2009). The researcher should follow a pragmatic approach that is driven by the specific questions posed in the study and the contingencies arising in data collection and analysis (Onwuegbuzie & Leech, 2005).

While the differences between the qualitative and quantitative methods should not be exaggerated, the case for mixed methods should not be construed as a denial of potential issues. This researcher remains cognisant of the arguments against mixed methods research, which Bryman (2012) labels the "embedded methods" and the "paradigm" arguments, respectively. The embedded methods argument maintains that one, when making a decision to conduct either qualitative or quantitative enquiry, commits oneself to a single set of incompatible epistemological or ontological assumptions. Quantitative methods, by this argument, are bound by positivist notions and qualitative ones by interpretive.

In a similar manner, the paradigm argument holds that qualitative and quantitative methods are different, incommensurable paradigms. Bryman points out, however, that this separation, in the case of both arguments, is very difficult to sustain, and that, particularly in the case of the paradigm argument, the "contentions about the interconnectedness of method and epistemology... cannot—in the case of social research—be demonstrated" (p. 630). In any case, while the *analysis* of the questionnaire in this study is indeed quantitative and that of the semi-structured interviews qualitative, there is consistency in the manner of data *collection.*

Both are based on an interpretation of participants' perceptions and are, thus, ontologically consistent. Nevertheless, in the present study, mixed methods were employed in relation to data analysis in the pragmatic manner that Onwuegbuzie and Leech (2005) advocate. Primary emphasis was placed on the quantitative analysis of the questionnaire data, while the secondary stress was on the qualitative analysis of the data from the semi-structured interviews, which was employed to augment understanding and provide illustrative value to patterns emerging from the questionnaire data.

As mentioned in the preceding sections, data collection methods consisted of a three-part questionnaire (Appendices A, B and C) and semi-structured interviews (Appendix E). The relationship between the research objectives and the data collection and analysis methods is displayed in Table 1.

3.5.1. The Questionnaire

Any self-report questionnaire has a number of well-documented limitations, especially in accounting for all explanations of observed correlations and, in cross-sectional designs, in ascribing causality (Spector, 1994). However, being mindful of these limitations, a researcher may use this method to gather responses from a considerable number of participants in a relatively short period (Kirakowski, 1997) while providing assurances of both objectivity (Moser & Kalton, 1979) and confidentiality (Gilbert, 1993). It is also worth recalling Carroll's (2002) remarks that the use of a self-report questionnaire to investigate learning, especially the transfer of learning, may be justified by the prospect that the students themselves, rather than their instructors, may be the best evaluators of what transfer is occurring, and to what extent.

The use of a questionnaire examining participants' perceptions was also considered to be consistent with the ontological basis of this study, which develops a view in which the realities of students' learning performance are related ultimately to social constructs.

Table 1. *Research Questions and Corresponding Methods*

	Research Objective	Research Method	
		Data Collection	Data Analysis
1.	What is the nature of students' perceptions of the transfer of learning from the academic-literacy-based English Communication (EC) programme to the courses in the disciplines?	a) Measure of Academic Literacy Transfer (MALT) (Appendix C) b) Questions related to English Communication in semi-structured interview (Appendix E)	i) Exploratory factor analysis (EFA); descriptive statistics ii) "Hybrid" approach, both deductive and inductive used to confirm findings from questionnaire
2.	What is the nature of the relationship between students' perceptions of the transfer of learning from the EC programme and their personal beliefs about knowledge and learning?	a) Factors from the MALT juxtaposed with those from EBI (Appendix B) and examined for relationships b) Questions in semi-structured interviews relate to constructs in the EBI.	i) Pearson and/or Spearman correlation and linear regression model to ascertain the extent to which variance in the MALT is predicted by the EBI. ii) See above
3.	What is the nature of the relationship between students' beliefs about knowledge and learning and their secondary school background ("culture")?	a) Demographic Section in questionnaire (Appendix D) concerning secondary school background examined for relationship to EBI and MALT.	i) Secondary school types examined for differences using one-way ANOVA and/or Kruskal-Wallis test to determine differences in central tendency and distribution in relation to data from (a) EBI and (b) MALT; regression (mediation model) to predict variability;
	Note. EBI = Epistemic Beliefs Inventory. MALT = Measure of Academic Literacy Transfer.	b) Questions in semi-structured interviews examine respondents' high school backgrounds in relation to beliefs	ii) See above

Again, Carroll (2002) develops a theme that is common in cultural psychology: that, although individuals have some measure of agency in their development, they do not act in "settings entirely of their own choosing" (Cole, 1996, in Carroll, 2002, p.24). This is a perspective that is central to the conceptual framework of this research. The settings that Carroll refers to, rather than being comprised of brick-and-mortar and objective "realities," are composed of people, and more particularly, of people's perceptions, and thus, as Bronfenbrenner (1979, in Carroll) stresses, "what matters for behaviour and development is the environment as it is *perceived* rather than as it may exist in objective reality" (p. 24).

The questionnaire employed in this study prompted self-report responses in three areas related to the research question: students' epistemic beliefs; students' perceptions of their own transfer of learning from the English programme to their other courses; and finally, demographic details concerning cultural background as evidenced by nationality and type of secondary school. These respective parts were arranged in a sequence least likely to induce a fatigue effect, with the longest being first, and the demographic section, where participants were considered least likely to record inaccurate responses, last.

In order to improve the response rate, the questionnaire would be administered during scheduled class time, with the consent of class instructors.

Section 1 of the questionnaire: Students' beliefs about knowledge and learning. Although studies have shown that the measurement of epistemic and related beliefs is indeed possible, and that these beliefs have an important impact on various cognitive tasks (Schraw, Bendixen, & Dunkle, 2002), measurement through self-report questionnaires is notoriously difficult (deBacker, Crowson, Beesley, Thoma & Hestevold, 2008). Keeping in mind these potential limitations, three notable questionnaires have been developed: the Epistemological Questionnaire (EQ), the Epistemic Beliefs Inventory (EBI) and the Epistemological Beliefs Survey (EBS) (respectively: Schommer, 1990; Schraw et al.,, 2002; Wood & Kardash, 2002).

From the three instruments mentioned above, the second, the EBI (Appendix B), was selected for the purposes of this study because it is briefer and has shown greater reliability and validity (Schraw et al.,

2002; deBacker et al., 2008). The EBI is derived from much of the previous theorising on personal epistemology, especially that in the highly influential work of Schommer-Aikins. The instrument aims at measuring the relative "sophistication" of learners' epistemic beliefs based on five constructs: *certain knowledge, simple knowledge, omniscient authority, quick learning*, and *innate ability*.

In developing the EBI, Schraw et al. (2002) attempted to address a number of problems that had arisen during the course of the development of the belief dimensions. The first of these was that, in analyses including that of Schommer-Aikins (Schommer, 1990, 1994), leading to this development, the dimension of *omniscient authority*, although hypothesised, had not emerged as a factor, although the other four factors, *innate ability, certain, knowledge, simple knowledge* and *quick learning* had. Secondly, the researchers wished to develop a shorter, yet more reliable instrument than Schommer-Aikins's 63-item instrument—and one in which all the postulated beliefs dimensions would emerge. Schraw et al. (2002), in their validation study, administered both the 63-item IQ and their newly-developed EBI, together with a reading comprehension test. Both the EQ and the EBI were subjected to principal components and principal factor analysis. In conclusion, Schraw et al. found that while the EQ did not yield the five a priori factors, the EBI did. Factors yielded by the EBI, in addition, were more coherent. Both instruments, however, delivered internal consistency components that were similar—although neither indicated high reliability.

Thus, although no instruments purporting to measure epistemic beliefs are ideal, the EBI seems to perform better in its concordance to the beliefs dimensions postulated by Schommer-Aitins and supported by a large body of research (e.g., Curtis, Billingslea, & Wilson, 1988; Damon, 1988; Jehng et al., 1993; Kardash & Scholes, 1996; Perry, 1970; Presley, 1985; Schommer, 1990; Schommer, Crouse, & Rhodes, 1992). An additional potential benefit was that the shorter length of the EBI, coupled with its comparable reliability, might preclude the possibility of a fatigue effect, particularly when forming part of a composite questionnaire, as was the case in the present study.

The EBI has been criticised, for example, by Welch and Roy (2012), for its "lack of stability." Welch and Roy cite a number of studies in different contexts that have used either factor or principal components analysis to extract the underlying belief dimensions of the EBI, such as those of deBacker et al., (2008), Ravindran, Greene, and deBacker (2005) and Schraw et al., (2002) in the US, all extracting approximations of the five hypothesised factors; and those of Mü ller, Rebmann, and Liebsch (2008) and Sulimma (2009) in Germany, extracting four factors (*speed of knowledge acquisition*, *control of learning processes*, *source of knowledge*, *structure/ certainty of knowledge*) and two factors (*structure*, *source*) respectively. To these may be added other examples of analyses of the EBI that have been referred to elsewhere in this study: Chan et al. (2011) in China, yielding three factors (*innate ability*, *certain knowledge*, *simple knowledge*); and Cam et al., (2012) in Turkey, also three factors (*quick learning*, *innate ability*, and *certain knowledge*).

Critics such as Welch and Roy (2012) point to the inconsistency in the number and nature of the extracted dimensions across various studies as evidence of instability. However, this apparent instability is only problematic if one has a universalistic view of epistemology and its related belief structures—an approach that has been criticised elsewhere in this discussion (Section 2.4.5.) If one examines the outcomes, certain patterns are arguably present: for one, the extracted dimensions differ across regions and, thus, across cultural clines. Notably, the studies in the US, with some exceptions, such as that of Nussbaum & Bendixen (2003), which yielded three dimensions, *simple knowledge*, *certain knowledge*, *innate ability*), tend towards the five hypothesised belief dimensions, while those conducted elsewhere, in other cultural contexts, yielded a different number of factors and sometimes alternative dimensions. Rather than instability, this indicates the cultural nature of beliefs—a major premise that has been developed in the present study. For this reason, this so-called instability did not preclude the use of the EBI. Furthermore, rather than accepting the a priori assumptions of the original development of the instrument, the relative nature of beliefs and belief systems provided justification for conducting a principal components analysis of the data collected in the particular cultural context, both organisational and societal, of this study.

In addition to being subjected to subsequent principal components analysis to establish their validity in the current cultural context, the original questions of the 32-item EBI were subjected to Thai language translation—back-translation (this researcher had been unable to locate an existing Thai version of the EBI). The original English-language items appeared on the questionnaire, with a Thai translation of each item appearing beneath it. Finally, to answer research question 2, data from this section of the questionnaire were juxtaposed with those of Section 2 in order to seek correlations that addressed research question 2 (see Table 1).

Section 2 of the questionnaire: Students' perceptions of transfer of learning. The second part of the questionnaire (see Appendix C) aimed at measuring students' perceptions of the transfer of academic literacy knowledge from the English Communications courses to the disciplines and, thus, allowed the investigation posed by research question 1 (see Table 1). Existing instruments for measuring transfer, the Learning Transfer System Inventory (LTSI; Holton et al., 2000) and one investigating undergraduate transfer of learning to the workplace (Burke et al., 2005) were not deemed appropriate to the context of this proposed study. The former relates to outcomes produced by a short-term, unified, and relatively specific period of training, and the latter relates to a different transfer context (from an undergraduate degree programme to the workplace).

Because of the unsuitability of these other instruments to the participants and the context of this study, it was considered appropriate to use an instrument that had been designed by this researcher for previous, related investigations into students' perceived transfer of learning, conducted in the same context as the present study (see Green, 2008, 2015). This instrument was labelled the Measure of Academic Literacy Transfer (MALT). In it, participants were asked to indicate the extent of their agreement or disagreement to 14 items relating to academic-literacy knowledge taught in the English Communication series of courses at MUIC.

Although the framework of the MALT was initially derived from groupings of items developed by Burke et al. (2005) in their study of the transfer of workplace-related knowledge (their knowledge categories included *information handling and retrieval, communication and presentation, planning and problem solving,* and *social development and interaction*), the categories for the MALT were much more narrowly defined, as dictated by the more limited context. The individual Likert-type items were developed organically from the context of the EC programme. Thus, only two categories were developed—*reading and research* and *writing*— with the seven items under each category being derived from actual practice in the programme. Each category also included open-ended questions that would allow for supplementary qualitative analysis.

To enhance reliability, care was taken that the Likert-type items were not based on ideals of transfer, but on what the students reasonably and realistically could be expected to apply in their studies at college. Specifically, the MALT items were developed from the experience of the researcher in consultation with a panel of peers consisting of other experienced instructors in the programme. A lexis was drawn from the context of the programme, one that the students could be expected to comprehend easily through their exposure to it over at least three trimesters in the form of course outlines, class discourse and assignment rubrics.

The MALT had been previously been subjected, moreover, to a pre-pilot stage by a group of students of similar demographic characteristics to the participants of this study, with a group discussion being held immediately afterwards in which the pre-pilot participants were asked questions by the researcher to gauge their understanding of the items and to identify any problematic areas. No particular problems were reported. The instrument then formed part of a pilot study (Green, 2008) in which, in addition to the Likert-type scale indicating degrees of agreement or disagreement, an option was included in each instance to allow participants ($N = 10$) to indicate whether they had not understood the question. None of the participants selected this option for any of the items. The MALT was then employed as part of a full study ($N = 39$; Green, 2015) in which Cronbach's alpha was calculated for the entire MALT scale ($α = .84$) and each of the subscales, *reading and research* ($α = .67$), and *writing* ($α = .78$). (In this present study, however, these latter categories, while appearing in the structure of the questionnaire, were not retained following the principal components analysis, from which two new categories—or dimensions—emerged.)

Thus, using a panel of experts, a pre-pilot, and a pilot stage, and a fuller study, the prima facie reliability of the MALT was satisfactorily established. The MALT would be subjected to further statistical tests of validity in the course of the principal components analysis conducted in this study.

Section 3 of the questionnaire: Demographics. The demographics section (Appendix D) polled factors known to have an influence on personal epistemology, including age (although little variance can be expected here) academic achievement (Youn, Yang, & Choi, 2000), and gender (Bråten, Gil, Strømsø, & Vidal-Abarca, 2009). The data from the demographic section allowed for the investigation posed by research question 3 concerning secondary school background (see Table 1), but, where feasible, the subsequent data analysis could be controlled for the variables mentioned above. In addition, students' nationalities were polled, as a broad indicator of culture, to allow the collection and analysis of data supplementary to the research questions and the conceptual framework; the primary focus, however, was on the respondents' secondary school background.

3.5.2. Semi-Structured Interviews

In order to add illustrative value to the data collected from the questionnaire, further to validate the findings (Was & Wells, 1994), and to gain a deeper understanding of initial findings, the survey was supplemented by semi-structured interviews, conducted by trained interviewers who were not direct stakeholders in the EC programme. Subsequent to the analysis of the questionnaire, a purposive sample of eight students who reflected typical cases was identified. These students were then invited to participate in the interview. The interview matrix (Appendix E) included guiding questions and prompts from the three main areas of the research: secondary school background; epistemic beliefs; and perceptions of transfer of learning from the English Communications courses to the disciplines. Less obtrusive, and thus less likely to induce a response effect, audio recording was used in preference to video recording. Recordings were transcribed and coded as soon as possible after the actual interview.

One consideration was whether to conduct the interviews in English or in Thai. The issue of translation, however, is fraught with interpretational problems (see, for example, Filep, 2009); as the researcher had only basic Thai proficiency, the consequent use of translation would further distance him from direct interpretation of the data. A number of additional considerations supported the use of English:

- the cohort under investigation included a number of non-Thai speakers;
- MUIC was an English-medium college, and thus the participants were assumed sufficiently competent in English (each having an assessed level of English competence and having completed most components of the English Communications series of courses successfully), and
- the language of discourse for the EC program was English, ensuring a familiarity on the part of the students with many of the subject-related terms used in the interviews.

Selection and training of interviewers. For the purposes of the semi-structured interviews, it was considered inappropriate for the researcher to conduct the interviews personally. The first reason for this was ethical: as the researcher occupied a position of authority within the organisation that could have direct impact on the participants, an interview conducted by the researcher would raise the question of potential harm to the interviewees. The researcher was both an instructor in the EC programme and the programme director. As such, he was in a position to potentially influence the consequences for the participants of either non-participation or the providing of responses that might be construed as "incorrect." Although the researcher might make every effort to prevent such an outcome, the perceptions of such harm from the participants might conceivable cause some anxiety in prospective participants.

The second reason for distancing the researcher from conducting the interviews was to avoid a response effect, as he could not be considered a disinterested party. While, again, the researcher might make every effort to avoid influencing the responses of the interviewees, the possibility presented itself that he might do so inadvertently, whether by, for example, using leading questions or by issuing unintentional signals of approval for "correct" responses through, for example, expressions, or gestures. In particular, distancing the researcher somewhat from the interviews decreased the risk of a social desirability effect, a significant possibility in the MALT Section of the interview, where interviewees were asked to respond directly to questions about the EC programme and its purported role in providing academic literacy support to students engaged in disciplinary studies. Students, in this case, might have provided desirable responses constructed to reflect the EC programme in a positive light, and they might not have been as frank in providing feedback that they considered more negative.

Thus, for ethical reasons and in order to avoid a possible response effect, the researcher recruited two interviewers who, although somewhat familiar with the EC program, were able to operate in a more detached manner in interviewing the eight interview participants. The original intention was to employ these interviewers from amongst the ranks of senior (fourth-year students), but only one such student, Aimee, was deemed suitable because of her facility in communication and her knowledge of the interview process through her interest in documentary film-making. The second interviewer was Karen, a visiting lecturer and recent PhD graduate who had been teaching a single class in the EC programme for little over a month. As interviews had been the primary data collection method in her doctoral research, her knowledge in this was considered an asset, while her relatively short-term engagement in the EC programme allowed her a greater degree of detachment than was possible from the full-time instructors—or the researcher himself in his then-role as programme director.

Once the interviewers had been recruited, they entered a brief, intensive, training period, during which the researcher attempted to ensure effective interview techniques and encourage a degree of standardisation, which would contribute to the overall reliability of the research. The researcher acted as facilitator and coach, being familiar with the research design, its framework, and its conceptual underpinnings. Moreover, the researcher had had extensive experience in conducting interviews, being for several years an oral examiner for the International English Language Testing System (IELTS), as well as conducting numerous admissions interviews for the college over a nine-year period, and several recruitment interviews of new faculty members over a three-year period.

The training was conducted at the premises at which the interviews would take place, much of it in the intended interview room. Both interviewers, Aimee and Karen, were able to make themselves available over three consecutive Saturdays, the last of these sessions occurring approximately a week before the actual interviews were conducted. Each of these training sessions was of approximately three hours in duration, and covered topics such the research framework itself, types of questions and prompts, ethical interview conduct, means of encouraging and facilitating interviewee responses, and other interview-related techniques. The trainees were given the opportunity to review semi-structured interviews and then to practise their own interview techniques in a close simulation of the actual interviews, immediately subsequent to which they were asked to reflect and were given constructive feedback. They were also given the opportunity to use the recording devices that would be adopted for the actual interviews, to allow them to become completely familiar with these devices.

Although some of the material for the interview training sessions were compiled by the researcher, much of it was adapted from training materials developed by the University of Cambridge affiliated Research Consortium on Educational Outcomes and Poverty (RECOUP), who have published on online manual (Singal & Jeffery, 2008), part of which addresses specifically semi-structured interviews. Specific materials from this online manual that were used in the training are appended (Appendices F, G, and H).

To foster inter-interviewer reliability and to familiarise the interviewers with the interview matrix, the researcher introduced the trainee interviewers to the conceptual framework of the research. This was done in such a way so as to avoid transmitting to the interviewers any preconceptions as to the anticipated outcomes of the research. This was a means of avoiding the introduction of a *questioning bias* to the interviews. As part of this familiarisation process, the trainees were introduced to the dimensions that had emerged from the principal components analysis (PCA) of the EBI.

Partly as a familiarisation exercise and partly as validation of the conceptual interpretation that had guided the researcher in extracting the principal components from the EBI, the researcher prepared individual printouts of each of the EBI items that had been retained following the final iteration of the PCA (as presented in Table 3). The trainees were then asked to place these individual items into three cohesive groups, which they proceeded to do without any further prompting from the researcher (see Appendix I). The groupings were, with only one exception, identical to the factors that the researcher had interpreted from the PCA, providing external validation to the findings.

Once the training sessions had been completed, the interviewers were briefed to contact potential interviewees who had been identified as typical cases based on their demographic profiles and their responses in the questionnaire. This measure was taken further to address potential ethical concerns and to prevent potential bias; it was deemed appropriate that the researcher neither be in direct contact with the participants nor be immediately aware of their identities. The researcher, therefore, without having direct knowledge as to the personal identities of the participants, provided the interviewers with codes corresponding to individual cases, by means of which the interviewers were able consult a list of names and contact details and, thus, invite participants to be interviewed.

3.6. Ethical Considerations

As briefly mentioned in the previous section, the primary ethical consideration arose from the researcher's position as both an instructor in the EC programme and its director. However, this risk was counterbalanced by the benefits afforded by the unique situation that MUIC presented in examining the research questions. The college, besides being one of the only coherent international undergraduate programmes in Thailand, offered a unique opportunity for comparative research as it had an arguably greater degree of heterogeneity in student secondary school backgrounds and nationalities than any comparable institution in the country.

In terms of specific ethics risks, students might perceive that their responses in both the questionnaire and the semi-structured interviews could have certain consequences to their studies or their assessment, or that they might have an obligation to participate in the research.

Specific measures to offset ethical risks included ensuring, first, that participation remained informed and voluntary. Specifically, it was made clear that no consequence would arise from either participation or non-participation. Signed informed consent was required for interview participants (see Appendices J and K), and grievance channels outlined. Second, measures were taken to ensure that all data remained confidential and secure. Data from questionnaires would be stored in a locked cabinet or in a password-protected computer and would not be available to anyone other than the researcher, while the researcher distanced himself from direct involvement in interviewing participants in order to avoid perceptions of potential risk or bias, as outlined in Section 3.5.2.

3.7. Expected Outcomes and Significance

As a general theory of transfer remains elusive and existing contenders controversial (Helfenstein & Saariluoma, 2006), a study that examines factors integral to transfer may contribute to a general understanding of this phenomenon, which is central to formal education.

Explorations into learners' beliefs, including personal epistemology, as they influence learning are much more recent than explorations of transfer of learning. The proposed study aimed to respond, on a general level, to appeals to examine practical links between learners' beliefs about knowledge and learning and the manner in which these beliefs activate learning in general. This investigation was partly in response to appeals such as that issued by Lising and Elby (2005), who call for such research; more specifically, the study also attended to an apparent deficit in studies linking personal epistemology to *transfer* of learning.

Investigations into cross-cultural influences on learners' systematic beliefs about knowledge and learning are more recent still. Bråten et al. (2009), for example, urge that "questions concerning how knowledge and knowing are contextualised in different cultural contexts" (p. 556) should be more fully addressed in cross-cultural research. Moreover, the universalist assumptions of previous research into personal epistemology, which made universal presumptions based often on Western research, need to be challenged (Fiske et al. 1998; Hofer, 2008), which may, in turn, call into the question the primacy in education of transfer of learning itself, while giving impetus to more pluralistic goals.

A reasonable assumption is that, in a pluralistic system, transfer of learning will remain valid as one of education's main goals. As such, if findings suggested that the cultural psychological framework proposed by this research was valid, there might be implications for practice. An argument could be made for the supplementing of classroom-based strategies, such as that of Perkins and Salomon (1988), by school-wide strategies that focus on the management of organisational culture (see

Broad & Newstrom, 1992), employing, for example, approaches such as those of Schön (1983) and Senge (1990) in building organisational cultures of reflection, learning, and, in this case, transfer.

3.8. Projected Data Analysis - Pilot Study

A convenience sample of 16 students from a single class of EC4 participated in the pilot stage of the questionnaire. The pilot group, preceding the intended group for the full study by two trimesters, was similar in its demographic composition to that of the target group for the full study (by virtue of the students' then-current placement in the EC program and the general college curriculum). Similarly, situational conditions for administering the questionnaire were identical to that of the intended study (questionnaires were distributed during class sessions, following a briefing by the researcher for the purposes of informed consent). The only exception was that the pilot survey was completely anonymous, whereas the full study would use coded questionnaires so that typical cases might be identified for the purpose of interviews.

The pilot study was conducted in order to establish an estimate of the time required for students to complete the all three sections of the questionnaire and, more importantly, to investigate any potential impediments to reliability and validity of the questionnaire prior to conducting the full study. In terms of the second objective, the questionnaire was distributed on two separate occasions, a month apart, in a test–re-test sequence, with a paired-samples t-test utilised to determine whether there were any significant differences in response patterns between the two data sets.

Stage 1: Questionnaire. Complementing the qualitative methods used in data collection, data from the Likert-type scale items of the EBI and the MALT were subjected to quantitative analysis using SPSS v.21 and AMOS v.20. Statistical analysis was used to establish reliability and validity: principal components analysis (PCA) was employed to establish the factor structure of responses to each of these inventories, with confirmatory factor analysis (CFA) being conducted on the same data to assess the goodness of fit of the models derived from the PCA of both the EBI and the MALT.

The initial principal components analysis of the EBI and concomitant rotation methods ("oblimin") were chosen out of consistency to preceding analyses of the EBI (particularly that of instrument originators, Schraw et al., 2002) and from an effort to follow best practice. Specifically, PCA was adopted as being consistent with the study of Schraw et al., and with most of the other EBI analyses that followed (as discussed in Section 3.5.1.), and the oblique rotation method was employed as being both consistent with these previous studies and as compliant with best practice as determined by Costello and Osborne (2005) in their Monte Carlo study of these statistical methods. Moreover, the method of determining the appropriate number of components (scree test in conjunction with a parallel analysis) was also drawn from the recommendations of Costello and Osborne.

In investigating research question 1 (see Table 1), a descriptive analysis of Section 2 of the questionnaire, coupled with the PCA, was deemed sufficient.

With regard to the EBI (Section 2 of the questionnaire), the combined factor analysis was of particular interest, as some doubt may exist as to the cultural validity of the constructs proposed by Schommer (1994) (i.e., *certain knowledge, simple knowledge, omniscient authority, quick learning* and *innate ability*). If the PCA revealed a similar factor structure to Western studies involving the EBI, with data being clustered in a similar way around the subscales corresponding to the five constructs, then the EBI would be assumed valid, in its present form, for the purposes of the study. If, on the other hand, clustering were inconsistent with the proposed constructs, this might inform a discussion involving cultural comparisons of personal beliefs about knowledge and learning, and thus to a reformulation of the constructs themselves in a way that is more appropriate to the context of the current data set.

Whether the PCA revealed clustering that was consistent with the constructs of the respective inventories, or whether "new," conceptually and statistically coherent factors merged, it was intended that further data analysis of these two measures would proceed firstly by means of preliminary diagnostic tests, and then, if warranted, by means of a regression model to ascertain the extent to which variance in the MALT is predicted by the EBI, thus addressing research question 2 (Table 1).

Proceeding to the regression model, and to the contingent decision as to which variables would be entered into the analysis, would thus be dependent on prior diagnostic tests, both parametric and non-parametric.

The reasons, in this diagnostic phase, for conducting both parametric and non-parametric testing is that combining the methods in a complementary manner, rather than relying on each with its respective strengths and weaknesses, could indicate the feasibility of further, confirmatory analysis. For instance, while parametric tests tend to have more power, and thus more generalisability to a population, they are highly dependent on the vagaries of the distribution and its concomitant assumptions. Certain parametric tests, such as the ANOVA, are highly susceptible to the influences of outliers (Osborne & Overbay, 2004), and while efforts were made in this study to remove extreme cases in the data screening stages (as reported in that particular section) according to certain criteria, the possibility still existed that certain outliers that had not been so removed influenced the analysis.

In contrast, non-parametric tests, although less powerful than the former, are more robust to violations of assumptions of normal distribution, such as the influence of outliers, and thus allow less potential for error or misunderstanding (Bagdonavicius, Kruopis, & Nikulin, 2011; Corder & Foreman, 2009). Moreover, the non-parametric tests may reveal, in some cases, additional insights that the parametric tests obscure (Marmarelis et al., 2013). For these reasons, some statisticians, particularly in the life sciences (e.g., Glantz, 2005; Walker & Shi, 2014), have advised conducting both the parametric and non-parametric tests to fully explore the data. Walker, in Walker and Shi (2014), reports conducting both parametric and non-parametric tests on the same data to investigate whether they produce similar results: If the results are different, this is then an indication of the presence of influential outliers or other problems with the distribution. In this case, Walker reports giving credence to the non-parametric tests. In the same spirit, this study, while socially-based, adheres to the preceding advice: where, in the diagnostic phase, parametric tests (such as ANOVA) reveal a non-significant result, for example, and the non-parametric (such as Kruskal-Wallis) a significant one, the data would be subjected to the confirmation of a third test, in this case, linear regression.

Furthermore, if the preceding analysis, both in the diagnostic phase and in the confirmatory regression model, were to indicate a relationship between learners' beliefs and their perceived transfer of learning, the overall analysis would proceed to the demographic data in Section 3 would be used to divide the sample into groups, according to secondary school background. The data would then be subjected to appropriate non-parametric tests, such as the Kruskal-Wallis one-way analysis of variance or another appropriate non-parametric test to determine differences in central tendency in relation to data from either the EBI or the MALT, or both (depending on the outcome of the analysis of the relationship between these two data sets).

Initially, preliminary results that indicated a relationship among secondary school background, learners' beliefs, and perceptions of transfer of learning were to be further substantiated with a mediated regression model that would explore the validity of the conceptual framework presented by the cultural matrix and further specified for the purposes of this study. However, the feasibility of this analysis would be determined by the preliminary findings from the measures described above. Analysing the separate dimensions of the EBI, for example, in relation to both secondary school context and learners' beliefs would prove productive at a more advanced stage, provided the preliminary results justified such analysis. In addition to the data analysis detailed here that addresses directly the research questions, further secondary associations would be sought that might be germane in potentially informing the conceptual development of the cultural model, such as a possible relationship between primary nationality and beliefs.

Stage 2: Semi-Structured Interviews.
Sample selection. For the purposes of the analysis, purposive sampling was used; while the questionnaire was intended to frame the investigation and to investigate, in a general manner, the suitability of the model, an extrapolative purpose was not required of the semi-structured interviews. For this reason, random sampling was not used; rather typical cases were sought that could provide a complementary and somewhat deeper understanding of dimensions emerging from the analysis of the questionnaire, and that could exemplify the responses of the participants (Bryman, 2012).

As cultural differences related to the institution were considered of primary interest in their association to learners' beliefs about knowledge and learning, and to perceived transfer of learning, respondents were initially grouped according to their secondary school background, as provided in the demographic section of the questionnaire: to give a total of eight interviewees, at least one, and in some cases two, "typical" respondents were identified from each of the predetermined groups *state school in Thailand (n = 42), bilingual school in Thailand (n = 23), international school in Thailand (n = 56), school in Asia other than Thailand (n = 18)* and *school in North America, Europe, Australia or New Zealand (n = 24)*—no respondents indicated the remaining, open category, *other*. Descriptive analysis was then conducted to identify "typical" cases based on respondents' indications of the number of years they had attended their last secondary school, their age, their GPAs at both secondary school and college levels, their current trimester at MUIC, and their scores for both the EBI and the MALT (see Table 2). Where possible, "typical" cases were deemed those in which the medians (for categorical data) and means (for the EBI and MALT summed scores) converged. Ideally, therefore, a typical case from each high school group would conform to all of the characteristics for that group as displayed in Table 2.

Sometimes, however it was not possible to identify cases based on such a narrow convergence; in these instances, the parameters were broadened until cases that were as close as possible to the typical could be identified. In sum, all typical cases were in the age group of 19 - 21 and were in their sixth trimester at MUIC (in other words towards the end of the second year of studies) with the exception of most members of the group *school in Asia other than Thailand,* who were completing their fifth trimester. Other variations between the groups are reflected in Table 2.

Transcription of audio recordings. Bearing in mind the precept that researchers should "handle their own rat" (reportedly psychologist Bob Grice's advice, in Frost & Stablein, 1992) in order to familiarise themselves intimately with the raw data, the researcher personally transcribed all eight recordings. Although an effort was made to report as accurately as possible the words of the participants, a too-narrow transcription was avoided, as the effort and time necessary for the closest possible transcription was not deemed proportional to the intentions and possible outcomes of the analysis—this research focuses on an analysis of the content and does not purport to produce the results that would be desirable in, for example, a close linguistically-orientated discourse analysis (Dörnyei, 2007). It was also deemed desirable to facilitate reader accessibility and interpretability; an especially close transcription would frustrate this goal, particularly since all of the participants would be conversing in English as a second or additional language; although these participants would be functionally competent in English, a close transcription of every instance of an error would impede fluent communication of the ideas. Thus, a balance was sought between this pragmatic consideration and the advice of Bazeley (2011) that the transcription be sufficiently close so as to allow for some of the "emotional overtones and nuances of the spoken text" (pp. 44-45) and to "assist in communicating what actually occurred with a view to the purpose and the intended audience."

Table 2
Descriptive Statistics of Typical Cases for Each "Secondary School Background"

	State school in Thailand ($n = 42$)	Bilingual school in Thailand ($n = 23$)	Internat. school in Thailand ($n = 56$)	School in Asia other than Thailand ($n = 18$)	School in north America, Europe, Australia, or New Zealand ($n = 24$)
Age group	19 - 21	19 - 21	19 - 21	19 - 21	19 - 21
Time spent at last high school (yrs) (*Mdn*)	4.5	5	4	3	3
High school GPA (*Mdn*)	3.10 – 3.5	3.10 – 3.5	2.51 - 3	2.51 - 3	3.10 – 3.5
Current trimester at MUIC (*Mdn*)	6th	6th	6th	5th	6th
Current college GPA (*Mdn*)	2.51 - 3	2.51 - 3	2.51 - 3	2.51 - 3	3.51 - 4.00
EBI summed score (*M*)	- .13	- .14	.17	- .04	- .13
MALT summed score (*M*)	-.02	- .25	- .21	.08	.29

Guiding principles for analysis. Frequently, the interpretation and analysis of interview data begins with extremely close, line-by-line scrutiny of the text involved; this is particularly true of the grounded theory approach, whereby the data impels conceptual development. However, the initial impetus of this study was the a priori assumptions and structure of the cultural matrix of social psychology, a deductive approach to thematic development. However, As Fereday and Muir-Cochrane (2006) have noted, there may be a concern with rigour in a totally deductive approach: Schutz (in Fereday et al.), for example, cautioned against replacing the world of social reality with "a fictional, nonexistent world constructed by the researcher" (p. 2) and thus advocated essential postulates for research, including that the method and framework be clear and logically consistent; and that the model be grounded in the subjective meaning the action had for the "actor."

The inductive approach, therefore, has some advantages over the deductive one. However, while the inductive approach encourages rigour by allowing the data to drive the analysis, where the aim of the researcher is to confirm a hypothesis or test a theory, as Crabtree and Miller (1999) have recognised, rather than to conduct initial exploration through an immersion or crystallisation style, it is appropriate that the analytic process may be more structured, sometimes in the form a template that uses a code manual.

The template approach was considered appropriate, as the purpose of these semi-structured interviews was to exemplify and amplify findings from the questionnaire. Moreover, there already existed an overarching conceptual framework (the cultural matrix) whence the study had been designed, supplemented by the data extracted by the analysis of the questionnaire. However, in addition to the caveat of creating a fictional world, it was necessary to recognise the possibility that this approach might impede the discovery of novel, unanticipated insights (Crabtree & Miller, p. 165), and preclude the recognition of exceptions to assumed patterns. Thus, not desiring to dispense with the potential benefits of either an inductive (immersion/ crystallisation) approach and a deductive (template-based) approach—i.e., from a desire for both rigour and flexibility of interpretation—this researcher decided to pursue what Fereday and Muir-Cochrane refer to a "hybrid approach", adapting the steps that these writers followed in their study (see Figure 1) to one that is, arguably, more suitable for gaining the best possible advantage from both approaches.

While the principles of the hybrid approach have been considered appropriate to the rigour of this present study, the implementation was somewhat different. Therefore, while Fereday and Muir-Cochrane began by focusing on the deductive coding derived from their own theoretical framework, this study began with the inductive data-driven approach. As Figure 2 shows, the first three stages of the Fereday and Muir-Cochrane multi-stage approach involve developing the deductive codes. It is only in the fourth stage that these deductive codes are supplemented by data-driven codes, "guided, but not confined, by the preliminary [deductive] codes," (p. 7), thus expanding these codes, or, in some instances, deriving discrete data-driven codes.

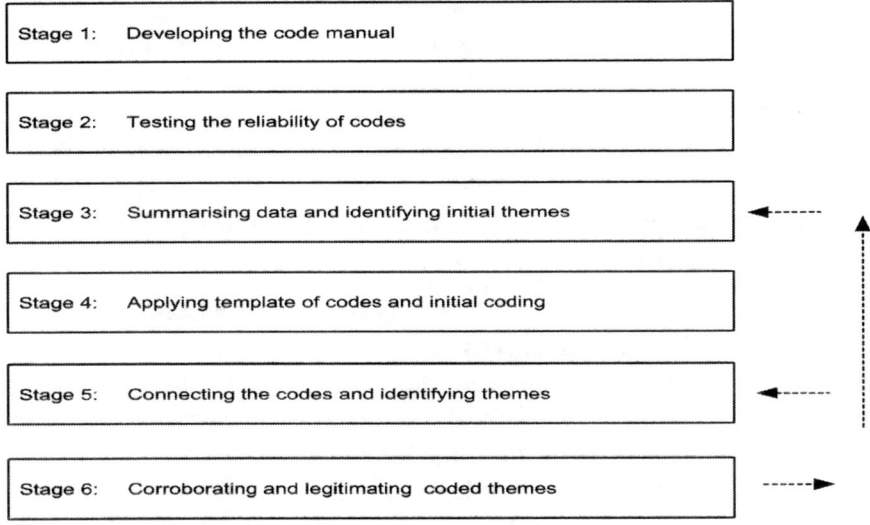

Figure 2. Stages undertaken by Fereday and Muir-Cochrane (2006) in coding the data. Adapted from Boyatzis, 1998 and Crabtree and Miller, 1999.

The hybrid approach, as outlined here, while allowing for these data-driven coding instances, retains the pre-eminence of the deductive coding template; it may this confine the development of discrete, data-driven themes to more of an extent than Fereday and Muir-Cochrane are prepared to acknowledge. It is difficult to depart from the template when it acts as a reference, both in its explicit form (in the preliminary codes stored in NVivo and readily accessible while performing additional coding), and as a conscious and unconscious reference on the part of the researchers. In order to address this potential problem, the analysis presented here began, instead, with the inductive, data-driven coding, derived as independently as possible from the pre-existing framework. Only once the initial themes had been so derived, were these juxtaposed to the template in order to refine the codes and identify potentially new themes as indicated by the data themselves (See Figure 3).

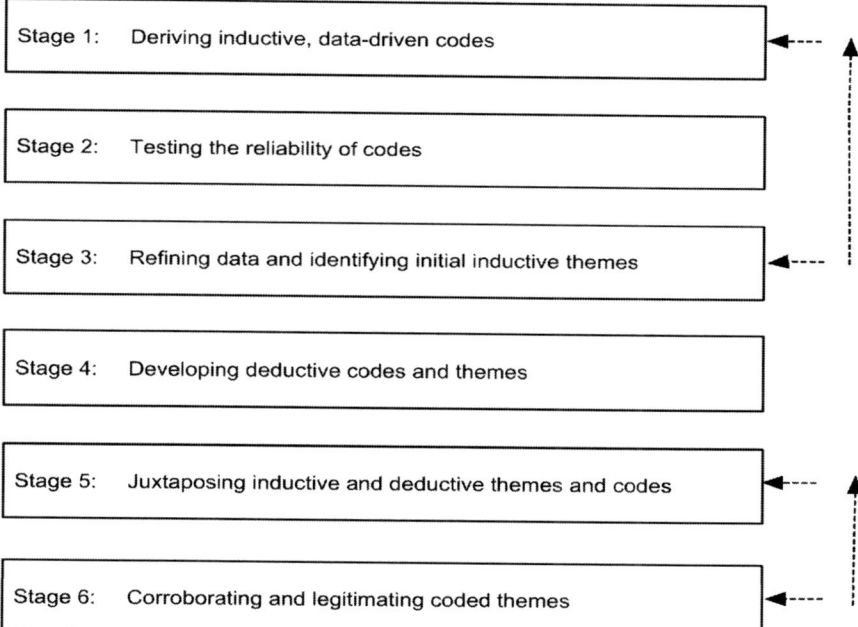

Figure 3. Stages of hybrid approach as adapted to this study.

This juxtaposition, moreover, contributed to the reliability of the overall analysis by adding corroborative between the data-driven codes and the template provided by the theoretical framework as modified by the principal components analysis and model testing of the quantitative data from the questionnaire. The deductive element involved the a priori development of a thematic template based on the theoretical assumptions and constructs underlying the interview matrix (Appendix E)—various secondary school backgrounds; the EBI constructs (certain knowledge, simple knowledge, omniscient authority, quick learning and innate ability); and the perceptions of transfer from the MALT—while the inductive element was the encoding and development of participant-driven themes arising from the discussions in the interviews themselves. These approaches were balanced using the adapted series of stages based on the approach of Fereday and Muir-Cochrane in a combined process that aimed to enhance the rigour and trustworthiness of the analysis.

Facilitating rigour of analysis. Integral to the hybrid approach outlined above, certain other measures were incorporated into the thematic analysis to improve the effectiveness of the research.

Because of the researcher's familiarity with the research context, it was considered particularly important to reduce the risk of *projection*, defined by Boyatzis (1998) as the "'reading into' or 'attributing to' another person something that is your own characteristic, emotion, attitude or such," induced "by familiarity with the phenomenon being studied and the source material, such as setting and type of qualitative information being collected" (p. 13). Although, as Boyatzis argues, certain levels of projection may be useful in understanding a situation, the risk is that the researcher may so project in order to gloss over ambiguities and gaps to the exclusion of other possible interpretations.

As disclosed previously, the researcher had a close relationship with the research setting, both as instructor and programme director, that had spanned over seven years., While efforts were made to mitigate the potential ethical ramifications of this by ensuring a certain distance between the interview participants and the researcher (he did not personally conduct the interviews, nor did he have direct knowledge of the identities of the participants), this familiarity with the research context also had possible implications for the kind of projection described here.

Boyatzis prescribes several measures for reducing the potential effects of projection. These include "developing an explicit code"; "establishing consistency of judgement"; and adhering "closely to the raw information in the development of the themes and code" (p. 13). To address the first of these, the development of an explicit code from the themes, whether through the deductive or inductive approaches already established here, the guidelines elucidated by Boyatzis were applied. Thus, where possible, five elements were included in deriving the final codes:

- labels;
- definitions of what each theme concerns (i.e., the characteristics or issues constituting each theme);
- descriptions of how to know when each theme occurs (i.e., how to "flag" themes);
- descriptions of any qualifications or exclusions to identifying themes; and
- examples, both positive and negative, to eliminate possible confusion when looking for themes (pp. x-xi).

Other than employing the explicit coding practices just described, efforts were made by the researcher to assess and apply consistency of coding. The solitary nature of the research work frequently precludes such collaboration. Fortunately, this researcher enjoyed the support of colleagues who were experienced in the research context. Thus, as described in the following section, the researcher was able to enhance reliability by coding the data, and then comparing the codes thus derived with those independently derived by a particular colleague who had several years' experience in the research context (namely the EC programme), but also had no direct relationship to, or awareness of, the conceptual framework developed in this study.

The two sets of working codes thus derived were then assessed for consistency, and final themes then developed from this. This development was through discussion, with certain codes being merged, other discarded, and some classified into themes.

Finally, reliability was sought through the adherence, where possible, to the raw data by the inclusion of the data-driven process of inductive theme development, as outlined in the previous section.

In sum, a number of efforts were made to enhance the rigour of the qualitative analysis. These included: an inductive element to ensure close adherence to the data; a deductive element to provide validation of the inductive element through juxtaposition to the theoretical framework and the questionnaire data; a transparent process of theme development that led to explicit coding; and a coding – re-coding process to assess consistency—and thus reliability.

Inductive identification of themes. The inductive analysis of the interviews began with pre-coding of the interview scripts. While the interpretational bias of the researcher is undeniable in extracting significant themes in this way, an effort was made to avoid imposing, in a formal structural manner, any preconceived assumptions and beliefs arising from the research framework and the assumptions derived from this.

While computer-assisted qualitative analysis software (CAQDAS), in the form of NVivo 10, was used in managing, and to an extent, analysing the data from the interview, much of this initial coding was paper-based, both as a personal preference on the part of the researcher, but also on the advice of Dörnyei (2007) who advocates the use of paper-based methods to complement CAQDAS, noting some potential problems in relying solely on the latter. These include (but are not limited to):

- *technological thinking:* the potential of CAQDAS to impede intuitive and creative thinking that assists an interpretational analysis
- *the coding trap:* a tendency to use the software to generate an overabundance of descriptive codes when the researcher is uncertain of his or her analysis and the emergent patterns
- *decontextualised coding:* while paper-based coding encourages the researcher to develop the codes in the context of the interview and the text, it is relatively simple to generate "increasingly fine categorisations" in CAQDAS that lose the perspective of the overall context (p. 267).

With this advice in mind, and in yielding to personal preference, this researcher began the inductive pre-coding with the transcription of the recordings. The researcher familiarised himself with the data and recorded in a journal (see Bazeley, 2011) any apparently significant keywords or phrases that raised nascent concerns, piqued interest, recurred in the data, or resonated with the assumptions of the researcher—an interpretational bias is inevitable to qualitative research, but, with awareness, may be a help, rather than a hindrance to this end (Dörnyei, 2007).

The interview transcripts were then printed; the researcher scrutinised the printed material and underlined key phrases and words that were evocative for the reasons mentioned before, or merely because they made "some as yet inchoate sense" (Sandelowski, 1995, in Denzin & Lincoln, 2003, p.783). Moreover, because culture was a central concern of the study, this pre-coding stage was informed by Spradley's (1977) advice that, because of each of these areas would potentially yield major cultural themes, the researcher should work to identify evidence of social conflict and cultural contradictions, indications of the manner in which participants negotiated social relationships and status differences, and participants' approaches to problem-solving.

This pre-coding phase proceeded iteratively, the researcher repeatedly highlighting, annotating textual fragments that were prominent for the reasons already indicated. The reading included the constant comparison of the instances from each iteration with those noted previously in both the transcription and proofreading stages. This assessment led, in turn to further reflection and first-level coding.

Once the pre-coding had been completed on hard copy, the researcher, after an interval of two weeks, used NVivo to conduct a similar activity in the preliminary analysis of the electronically-stored interview transcripts. This comparison of time-separated coding by the same researcher of the same data was considered useful in establishing reliability (Boyatzis, 1998, p. 10).

A further effort was made to augment the reliability of the inductive coding process by involving a colleague in independently developing data-driven codes (as seen described in the previous section), free of the theoretical assumptions that would exert an influence, whether consciously or unconsciously, on the initial coding efforts of the researcher himself. This colleague, although an experienced instructor in the EC programme, did not have direct awareness of the research framework or the specific research questions. The codes thus independently derived were compared and corroborated before being merged, reduced, and reclassified into a working list of codes.

Further comparisons were then made between the initial paper-based pre-coding and that of the electronic texts. Based on this comparison, nascent themes that consistently emerged were retained for purposes of final coding, with others reconsidered for their applicability, and in some cases being discarded.

Deductive identification of themes. The deductive template of ab initio themes was derived, in relation to the learners' beliefs about knowledge and learning, from the belief factors identified by Schommer-Aikins (Schommer, 1990; 1994) and included in the EBI (Schraw et al, 2002). Of the five belief structures identified by these authors – *innate ability, certain knowledge, omniscient authority, simple knowledge,* and *quick learning* – only those identified as valid by the principal components analysis conducted for this data set were retained. In some cases, these components subsumed items that would otherwise have been classified in the hypothesised structure of Schraw et al. (*omniscient authority*, for example, was subsumed by *certain knowledge* to create a broader conceptual category, *certain authoritative knowledge*, while *quick learning* was subsumed by *simple knowledge* – if knowledge is simple, one may assume that it will be rapidly learnt). Further details on these themes are developed in the relevant "Results" section.

The thematic template for participants' perceived transfer of learning from EC to the disciplines was developed from the framework guiding the MALT, consisting of the items representing transferable knowledge from the EC programme to the disciplines. These items had been contextually derived from the EC programme at MUIC (see Section 3.5.1), and were classified into two groups in accordance with the components extracted from the principal components analysis of the MALT: *critical, evaluative knowledge* and *rhetorical knowledge*.

Chapter 4
Results

The analysis projected in the previous chapter produced the following results, which are reported first in terms of the pilot study, then of the preliminary analysis of the questionnaire, through PCA and model fit of the EBI and MALT, then in relation to the thematic analysis of the open-ended questions in the questionnaire, and, finally, of the semi-structured interviews. These results, from both the questionnaire and the semi-structured interviews, are then applied systematically to addressing research questions.

4.1. Pilot Study

In considering both occasions of administering the survey, no participant was observed to complete the full questionnaire in fewer than approximately 11 minutes, and no student took more than 18 minutes to complete it. This observation was useful in considering the possibility of a fatigue effect and in providing accurate information on the time required to prospective participants of the full study.

The null hypothesis for the ensuing t-test (2 tailed) could be stated as follows:

The population mean difference between the paired values was equal to zero, while the alternative hypothesis would be:

The population mean difference between the paired values was not equal to zero.

Before proceeding with the t-test, it was necessary to test for outliers in the score differences, and for a normal distribution. A visual inspection of the boxplots of the score differences between both the EBI scores and MALT scores respectively for the first and second tests revealed no outliers, while a visual inspection of Q-Q plots for each of these score sets showed approximate normality, confirmed by the Shapiro-Wilk test, which returned non-significant values ($p > .05$) for both the difference between the EBI scores (.07) and the MALT scores (.78), thereby rejecting the null hypothesis for this test that the data were not normally distributed. Therefore, neither the assumption of the absence of outliers, nor that of normality was violated.

In comparing the scores for the EBI from the initial test (M = 88.75, SD = 8.68) and the re-test (M = 88.75, SD = 10.18), the results revealed that there was a no statistically significant variation (95% CI [-.09, 6.09], $t(15)$ = 2.07, p = .06, d = .52). For the MALT, the comparison between the initial test (M = 56.00, SD = 4.56) and the re-test (M = 54.75, SD = 6.78) similarly revealed a small, statistically insignificant difference (95% CI [-1.52, 4.02], $t(15)$ = .96, p = .35, d = .24).

The null hypothesis for the t-tests that the mean difference between the paired values was equal to zero could, therefore, not be rejected. Based on these results, it could be concluded that the questionnaire was stable over time and thus had prima facie reliability.

4.2. Stage 1: Questionnaire

4.2.1. Initial Data Screening

A total of 178 respondents (51.7% females; 48.3% males) from a possible 189 of the EC4 cohort (94%) returned questionnaires that were at least partially completed (further demographic data is reported subsequent to data screening, and as relevant to particular sections of the analysis). Data from these respondents were then screened to detect problematic variables and cases. Of Section 1 and 2 of the questionnaire (The EBI and the MALT respectively), a single respondent (Case no. 52) omitted Section 2 entirely, while the only missing datum in Section 1 was an omission by another respondent (Case no. 126) in a single item, EBI13. None of the variables in Section 3 of the questionnaire ("Demographics") displayed unacceptable levels (>10%) of missing data; as a result, no cases or variables were removed at this stage. The initial data screening then proceeded to the screening and testing of assumptions relevant to the particular analysis being conducted. Demographic data are reported as they pertain to each of these analyses.

4.2.2. The Epistemic Beliefs Inventory (EBI)

Data screening and testing of assumptions. As a preliminary to the factor analysis of the EBI, data were once again screened to detect outliers, and examined to explore the assumptions of normality, linearity, homogeneity of variance and co-linearity.

Box plots of all EBI items were scanned to detect cases with multiple outliers. Because the sensitivity of factor analysis to sample size had to be balanced with the potentially distorting effects of outliers, it was considered prudent to remove only cases that presented outlying data that amounted to more than 10% of the total number of items (such cases could be regarded as unusual and, thus, would not lend themselves to constructing a typical model). Only one case (Case no. 116), which presented six outliers, was, therefore, removed.

Once the atypical case had been removed, the distribution of the univariate data from each of the EBI items was examined by means of visual inspection of histograms and perusal of statistical measures of skew and kurtosis. Given that principal components analysis is not as sensitive to deviations from normality as methods such as maximum likelihood (Field, 2009), a skew or kurtosis z-score of greater than 3.29 ($p < .001$) was considered a cause for concern when considered in relation to a histogram. In accordance with this last standard, most items (63%) were sufficiently normal in their distribution. In terms of both the statistic and the visual inspection of the histogram, however, 12 items showed deviations from normality. Of these, four items (EBI 21, 24, 31and 32) displayed substantial deviation in addition to considerable kurtosis issues. These latter four items, in particular, were noted for possible removal of items during the principal components analysis.

More important than normality in factor analysis is the assumption of linearity because the common factor model is essentially an expression of a linear regression model (Flora, LaBrish & Chalmers, 2012). However, because of the impractical nature of generating a scatterplot matrix for all 32 items of the EBI, linearity was initially tested by visual inspection of a matrix of nine random IVs and DVs (EBI items 1, 4, 11, 12, 15, 18, 20, 25 and 27; and 3, 5, 9, 16, 19, 22, 23, 29 and 30, respectively). The resultant scatterplots were difficult, however, to interpret, as data points were so widely dispersed and showed no clear tendency. Linearity was thus tested, in the same random sets of items, by means of the "deviation from linearity" test available under ANOVA in SPSS. From 81 pairs, the statistical measure of 74 (91.35%) indicated no significant deviation from linearity ($p > 0.05$).

Homogeneity of variance was tested using the same sets of randomly-selected variables using Levene's test available under one-way ANOVA in SPSS (similar difficulties presented themselves in interpreting scatterplots). From 81 pairs, the test indicated that 70 (86.42%) were not significantly heterogeneous in their variance ($p > .05$).

The final assumption that was tested was that of the absence of co-linearity between variables. Iterations of all variables in the EBI were tested using the Variance Inflation Factor (VIF) in the linear regression analysis in SPSS. No co-linearity was detected, with the highest VIF being 1.58.

At this stage, despite some inevitable exceptions within the various tests (which were noted for further observation) the assumptions of assumptions of normality, linearity, homogeneity of variance and co-linearity were deemed sufficiently intact to proceed to the factor analysis of the EBI.

Principal components analysis. Principal components analysis (PCA) was selected as a method of exploratory analysis to reduce the dimensionality of the EBI for three main reasons. Firstly, PCA is less sensitive than methods such as maximum likelihood (ML) to deviations from normality (Fabrigar, Wegener, MacCallum, & Strahan, 1999; Field, 2009), even though the use of ML has been identified by some (e.g., Costello & Osborne, 2005) as better practice. Secondly, the primary purpose was to reduce the data in all the variables into a set of weighted linear combinations for the regression analysis to follow; PCA is an appropriate method for this (Fabrigar et al., 1999). Finally, as a secondary purpose was to validate the hypothetical structure of the EBI, it was desirable to adhere, to a reasonable extent, to the methods used by previous researchers (e.g., Bendixen , Schraw, & Dunkle, 1998; deBacker, Crowson, Beesley, Thoma, & Hestevold, 2008; Chan, Ho, & Ku, 2011) in the interests of replication and comparison.

In an initial exploratory analysis, generated to investigate the construct validity of the of the EBI in relation to the current data set, direct oblimin rotation was specified in SPSS on the assumption that factors would be at least somewhat correlated, as they tend to be in the Social Sciences. In particular, all the factors related to the common overall dimension of "personal epistemology." The analysis was set to extract 5 factors as corresponding to the hypothesised and subsequently validated structure of the EBI (Bendixen, Schraw, & Dunkle, 1998; Schraw, Bendixen, & Dunkle, 2002), these factors being *innate ability* (IA), *certain knowledge* (CK), *simple knowledge* (SK), *omniscient authority* (OA) and *quick learning* (QL). All EBI items were included in this particular analysis; a single missing value in EBI 13 was excluded listwise in relevant analyses.

The initial analysis revealed that the five "forced" factors explained 34.81% of the total variance for the current data set. An examination of the pattern matrix was difficult to interpret in terms of any of the hypothesised factors, with items from each of the original factors being highly interspersed, and only three of the extracted factors from the rotated solution showing any conceptual cohesion in terms of the hypothesised factors. Because of the inconclusive nature of this initial investigation, it was decided to commence de novo with a principal components analysis that would adhere to the procedures for investigating a new data set, allowing statistical analysis and interpretation, rather than preconceived notions of the underlying factor structure, to guide the extraction of statistically and conceptually sound factors for this particular set.

The "new" analysis was preceded by a diagnostic examination of the inter-correlation matrix of all 32 EBI items. Although a recommendation is that items with significant correlations ($p < .05$) below .3 be considered for exclusion (Field, 2009), this would have resulted in the elimination of most (23) of the EBI items. As such, only items with no significant Pearson's correlations above .2 were considered for removal from the analysis in this particular instance. Only two items were thus identified, EBI 21 and 24, these items previously having displayed substantial deviations from normality. The items were thus removed from further analysis.

A preliminary principal components analysis was then conducted on the remaining 30 items, with direct oblimin again selected as the rotation method (with no reason being apparent for factors to be uncorrelated). The overall sampling adequacy for the analysis was verified by the Kaiser-Meyer-Olkin (KMO) measure as being adequate (.64) (Field, 2009), while a similar analysis of individual items through the anti-imaging matrices revealed that 4 items, EBI 11, 22, 31 and 32, had a KMO adequacy measures below the threshold of .5 (EBI 31 and 32 had also previously shown high levels of deviation from normality). These items were therefore removed from the analysis at this point, resulting in an overall KMO statistic of .68; a re-examination of the anti-imaging matrices revealed, moreover, that all remaining individual items had adequate KMO statistics.

In this preliminary analysis, no set number of factors was specified for extraction; rather, further analysis would rely on both statistical and conceptual interpretation in order to arrive at a suitable number of coherent factors.

As to the methods of statistical interpretation of the number of factors, the researcher selected the interpretation of the scree plot along with parallel analysis. The latter, in particular, has been identified as "best practice" by Costello and Osborne (2005) and O'Connor (2000), who demonstrated parallel analysis to be more accurate than the frequently used Kaiser's Criterion, which specifies the somewhat arbitrary retention of factors having eigenvalues above 1. As a case in point, Kaiser's Criterion here yielded nine factors, while the point of inflection on the scree plot indicated (somewhat ambiguously) that a three-factor solution might be more appropriate (see Figure 4). This three-factor solution was confirmed by parallel analysis computed using 1000 permutations of the random data (using SPSS syntax developed by O'Connor, 2000), for which the raw data eigenvalues for three of the factors were of greater values than those of both the mean and percentile random data eigenvalues (see Figure 5).

As suggested by the scree plot and the parallel analysis, a subsequent principal components analysis was run with the same rotation options as before, but specifying three factors to be extracted. The analysis proceeded through a number of iterations, with items being removed on the basis of low final communalities, small loadings on "proper" conceptual factors, and conceptually incongruous loadings, until producing a factor structure that was both statistically and conceptually cohesive (see Table 2). In all, 17 of the original 32 items were retained (see Table 3). The final analysis produced a KMO of .66, with Bartlett's Test of Sphericity being highly significant at < .01.

The factors that emerged were consistent with three of the five originally hypothesised factors, *innate ability* (IA), *certain knowledge* (CK) and *simple knowledge* (SK). *Omniscient authority* (OA) was absorbed into CK, the blended factor (labelled "certain, authoritative knowledge") being retained as such, as, arguably, no conceptual incongruity exists between certain knowledge and omniscient authority: certain knowledge may be perceived as being both authoritative and deriving its certainty from authoritative sources. Similarly, items from *quick learning (QL)*, one of each, were absorbed by both IA and SK: for the former, the statement "Students who learn things quickly are the most successful" could be seen as a function of innate ability, while, for the latter, "If a person tries too hard to understand a problem, they will most likely end up being confused" is conceptually related to the relative complexity of knowledge. The three marker factors (IA, CK and SL) were consistent with the factors extracted from the EBI in studies by Nussbaum and Bendixen (2003) and Chan, Ho, and Ku (2011). None of the extracted factors for any of the iterations of the PCA correlated to any significant extent (all were below .1), giving a strong indication that the oblique rotation method was the most suitable for this analysis (Field, 2009, p. 668), and that three distinct dimensions had been identified.

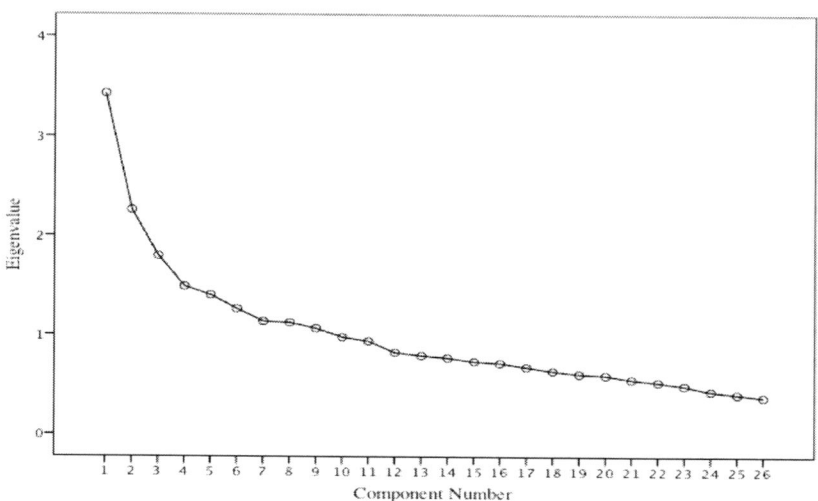

Figure 4. Scree plot showing initial extraction of Epistemic Beliefs Inventory (EBI) factors with related eigenvalues

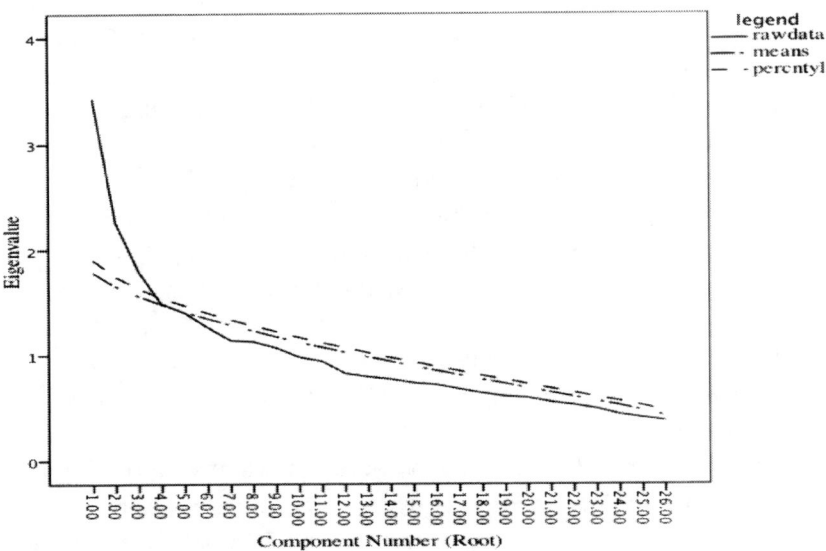

Figure 5. Graph showing eigenvalues of raw data ("rawdata") from initial extraction of Epistemic Beliefs Inventory (EBI) factors compared to means ("means") and percentile ("percentile") eigenvalues calculated by 1,000 permutations of random data from parallel analysis, generated using script from "SPSS and SAS Programs for Determining the Number of Components Using Parallel Analysis and Velicer's MAP Test," by B. P. O'Connor, *Behaviour Research Methods, Instrumentation, and Computers, 32*, pp. 396-402.

Table 3
Factor Loadings for Principal Components Analysis with Oblimin Rotation of EBI Scales (N=177)

	Rotated factor loadings		
Item	Innate ability	Certain, authoritative knowledge	Simple Knowledge
EBI5 Some people will never be smart no matter how hard they work. (IA)	**0.70**	-0.21	0.04
EBI15 How well you do in school depends on how smart you are. (IA)	**0.60**	0.22	-0.07
EBI17 Some people just have a knack for learning and others don't. (IA)	**0.57**	-0.12	0.11

Item			
EBI3 Students who learn things quickly are the most successful. (QL)	**0.56**	0.21	-0.06
EBI26 Smart people are born that way. (IA)	**0.54**	0.14	0.03
EBI8 Really smart students don't have to work as hard to do well in school. (IA)	**0.49**	-0.11	-0.11
EBI12 People can't do too much about how smart they are. (IA)	**0.49**	-0.03	0.23
EBI25 What is true today will be true tomorrow. (CK)	0.08	**0.58**	0.07
EBI19 If two people are arguing about something, at least one of them must be wrong. (CK)	0.22	**0.53**	-0.13
EBI23 The moral rules I live by apply to everyone. (CK)	-0.37	**0.53**	0.06
EBI4 People should always obey the law. (OA)	-0.14	**0.50**	-0.02
EBI7 Parents should teach their children all there is to know about life. (OA)	0.10	**0.49**	0.06
EBI20 Children should be allowed to question their parents' authority. (OA)*	-0.04	**0.47**	-0.02
EBI10 Too many theories just complicate things. (SK)	0.15	0.12	**0.75**
EBI13 Instructors should focus on facts instead of theories. (SK)	-0.06	0.17	**0.63**
EBI9 If a person tries too hard to understand a problem, they will most likely end up being confused. (QL)	0.13	-0.07	**0.60**
EBI18 Things are simpler than most professors would have you believe. (SK)	-0.14	-0.16	**0.52**
Eigenvalues	2.63	1.86	1.64
% of variance	15.47	10.96	9.67
α	.67	.50	.52

Notes. Factor loadings above .40 appear in boldface.

EBI = Epistemic Beliefs Inventory. Letters in brackets indicate factors originally hypothesised by Schraw, Bendixen & Dunkle (2002). * = Item reverse coded.

Table 4

Descriptive Statistics of Skew and Kurtosis for EBI Factor Scores

Descriptive statistic		Innate ability	Certain, authoritative knowledge	Simple knowledge
N	Valid	176	176	176
	Missing	1	1	1
Skew		.18	.02	-.25
Std. Error of Skew		.18	.18	.18
Kurtosis		-.47	-.35	.16
Std. Error of Kurtosis		.36	.36	.36

Note. EBI = Epistemic Beliefs Inventory.

It is also worth recounting here, as described in the previous section, "Selection and training of interviewers," that the research assistants involved in the interviews had participated in an activity that assisted in the conceptual validation of the three factors extracted by the PCA. Although the exercise was aimed primarily at familiarising the assistants with the research framework, it also provided an independent confirmation of the conceptual coherence of the three factors. Subsequent to the analysis reported here, the principal researcher printed out the items listed in Table 3, separated them, and placed them randomly on a work surface. The research assistants were then asked to divide the items by moving them physically into three coherent groups. Although the assistants were unaware at this stage of the nature of the factors and their labels, they grouped the items, without much difficulty and without any prompting, by the same factors that had emerged from the PCA (see Appendix H). Only one item caused the trainees some confusion: "You can study something for years and still not fully understand it." In generating factor scores, the regression and Anderson-Rubin methods in SPSS produced identical results; the skew and kurtosis statistics for these are reported in Table 4. Both the descriptive statistics and the histograms indicated that distributions were normal, with no significant skew or kurtosis issues.

Table 5
Good Fit Indices, Critical Values and Values for EBI and MALT

Index type	Index	Traditional cut-off value/range	Revised cut-off value	EBI	MALT	Comments on limitations or strengths
Absolute fit indices	Model chi-square (x^2)		> .05 (non-significant)	139.68 p = .07 df = 116	111.77; p < .01 df = 43	Assumes multivariate normality; Sensitive to sample size
	Normed chi-square (x^2/df)		Recommendations range from < 2.0 to < 5.0	1.2	2.6	Minimises impact of sample size
	RMSEA	0.05-0.10	< .06 (Hu & Bentler, 1999); < .07 (Steiger, 2007)	.03	.10	Considered as one of the most informative fit indices; Reported with PCLOSE
	PCLOSE (?)		> .08 (McQuitty, 2004); non-significant	.91	< .01	See above
	SRMR		< .05 (Byrne, 1998; Diamantopoulos & Siguaw, 2000); .08 acceptable (Hu & Bentler, 1999)	.07	.08	Resistant to varied levels of measurement in variables
Incremental fit indices	CFI	>= .9	> .95 (Hu & Bentler, 1999)	.90	.79	Useful even when sample size is small
Parsimony fit indices	PNFI		Not determined (higher value means more parsimonious)	.52	.55	Penalises for model complexity – values may be considerably lower than other indices; should report with other indices

Note: EBI = Epistemic Beliefs Inventory. MALT = Measure of Academic Literacy Transfer. Adapted from Hooper, Coughlan & Mullen (2008)

Table 6

Factor Loadings for Principal Components Analysis with Oblimin Rotation of MALT Scales (N = 166)

	Rotated factor loadings	
	Critical, evaluative knowledge	Rhetorical knowledge
MALT1 tell the difference between fact and opinion in a reading text.	**.85**	.34
MALT2 find the main idea of a reading text.	**.64**	-.04
MALT16 take care to use correct grammar and spelling.	**.57**	-.15
MALT10 write information from texts in my own words (paraphrase).	**.55**	-.04
MALT3 find problems in the reasoning (logic) of an argument.	**.52**	-.14
MALT4 find problems in the support (evidence) of an argument.	.36	-.29
MALT12 plan and organise my writing (outlines, drafts etc.).	-.18	**-.84**
MALT13 write a thesis statement for written assignments.	-.02	**-.66**
MALT15 structure my writing according to a pattern (compare/ contrast, classification, cause/ effect etc.)	.08	**-.66**
MALT11 back up statements with specific support (examples, expert opinion, facts, statistics).	.30	**-.50**
MALT14 write topic sentences to start paragraphs.	.25	**-.48**
Eigenvalues	3.36	1.41
% of variance	30.54	12.85
α	.66	.70

Note. Factor loadings above .40 appear in boldface.
MALT = Measure of Academic Literacy Transfer

Confirmatory factor analysis. The goodness of fit of the model extracted by means of the principal components analysis was examined by means of a confirmatory factor analysis using SPSS AMOS version 21. The sample was considered adequate for a one-time analysis as it conformed to the widely agreed on threshold of 10 cases per any defined variable specified in the model (Schreiber et al., 2006). The sample was 176 (following the removal of a previously specified case with a missing value), while the number of specified variables was 17, producing a ratio of 10.35: 1. Therefore, the result was insufficient to split the sample in order to test the stability of the model.

Maximum likelihood (ML) estimation was used for this analysis, as variables that had been considered to deviate highly from normality had been eliminated during the PCA. In considering goodness of fit, the following indices were considered, as recommended by Hooper, Coughlan, and Mullen (2008), following their review of the literature addressing these indices: chi-square (x^2) in relation to its degrees of freedom (x^2/df) and its probability level; the root mean square error of approximation (RMSEA) and its associated confidence level (PCLOSE); the standardised root mean square residual (RMSR); Comparative Fit Index (CFI); and one parsimony fit index, here the Parsimonious Normed Fit Index (PNFI). The resultant figures for the EBI factor model are compared to both traditional and more recently-advocated values for these indices in Table 5. The CFA of the EBI produced scores that reached the currently-accepted goodness-of-fit thresholds for the most of the reported indices, the exception being that of the CFI, which, at .90, equalled only the traditional cut-off. The path diagram for the model, with its concomitant factor loading values, is presented in Figure 6.

4.2.3. The Measure of Academic Literacy Transfer (MALT)

Data screening and testing of assumptions. The MALT was subjected to the same data screening and assumptions testing processes as the EBI. An inspection of the boxplots for each item revealed 12 cases with multiple outliers above the criterion of 10% of total items. As the MALT consisted of only 14 Likert-type items, a conservative approach was adopted in removing from analysis all cases with more than two outliers (Cases nos. 36, 44, 52, 68, 75, 81, 108, 109, 124, 133, 161 and 188). The resultant sample was 165. The data were then checked for normality of the univariate MALT items: substantial deviations from normality in the histograms of MALT 5, 6, 7 and 10 was confirmed by both skew and kurtosis statistics exceeding 3.29. The remaining 10 items, however, displayed sufficiently normal distributions.

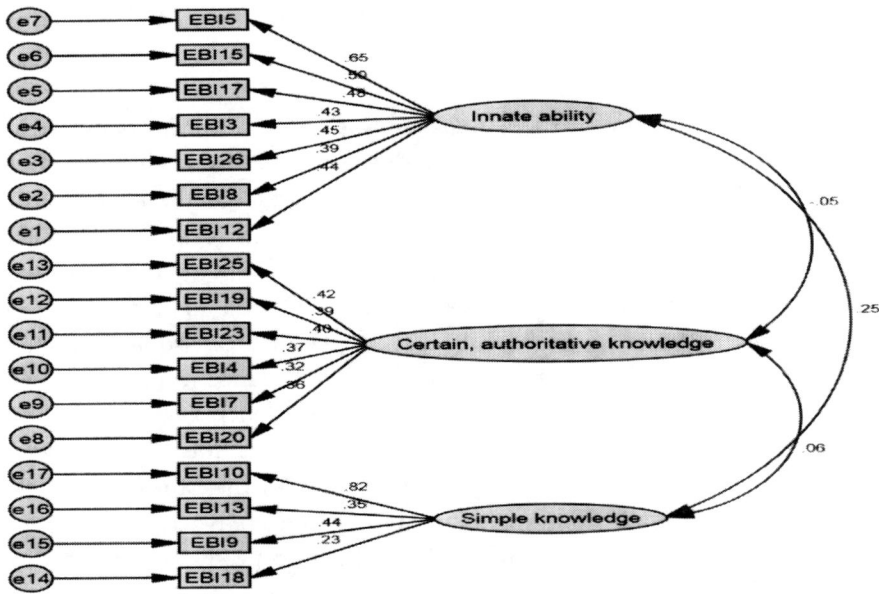

Figure 6. Confirmatory factor analysis model of three extracted factors from Epistemic Beliefs Inventory (EBI). EBI item numbers correspond to labels displayed in Table 2. Standardised maximum likelihood parameter estimates.

The MALT items were then tested for bivariate linearity; as for the EBI, the test of deviation from linearity available under ANOVA in SPSS was used for this. From 182 possible combinations, 150 (82.42%) showed no significant deviation from linearity ($p > .05$). It was noted that EBI 6, when entered as an independent variable, exhibited significant deviations from linearity with six of the dependent variables, substantially more than any other combination of variables, marking this item (as in its distribution, previously) as potentially problematic.

Again, to be consistent with the analysis of the EBI, the assumption of homogeneity of variance in the MALT was tested by means of Levene's test. Of the 182 possible combinations, 119 (65.38%) indicated no significant heterogeneity of variance ($p > .05$). Co-linearity was tested by means of the calculation of Variation Inflation Factor (VIF). No co-linearity was detected; the highest value for any combination of variables was 1.69

Although all assumptions were judged to have been adequately met, MALT 6 was removed from further analysis owing to both its substantial deviation from normality and its apparent non-linearity in relation to other variables.

Principal components analysis. In order to establish the quality of the data in preparation for the principal components analysis, a correlation matrix was generated from the remaining 13 MALT items. All items other than MALT 7 met the guideline of more than one correlation coefficient above .3 (Field, 2009); this item was removed from further analysis, as previous analysis had also indicated substantial deviation from normality.

Principal components analysis (PCA) was selected as the method of dimension reduction for the MALT as it was consistent with the analysis of the EBI, and as it had similar justifications (other than the validation of previously hypothesised factors). The rotation method selected was, again, direct oblimin, as factors were expected to be somewhat correlated. The preliminary analysis was allowed to proceed without specifying the number of factors to be extracted; the scree plot (see Figure 7) was difficult to interpret, with the single clear inflection point indicating one factor, and minor inflection points suggesting the possibility of up to three factors. A two-factor solution was indicated by parallel analysis, with this number of raw data eigenvalues being marginally greater than the random data percentile values (see Figure 8). Further analysis proceeded accordingly, with rotation options being retained, but specifying two factors to be extracted.

After a number of iterations, with decisions as to the retention of factors being made according to size of factor loadings and conceptual integrity (as for the PCA of the EBI), a conceptually coherent factor solution emerged that explained 43.39 of the total variance. The KMO statistic indicated adequate sampling at .74. Items clustered around conceptual areas that were termed "Critical, evaluative knowledge"—items that require making judgements and decisions—and "Rhetorical knowledge"—items that require the ability to organise ideas and information coherently.

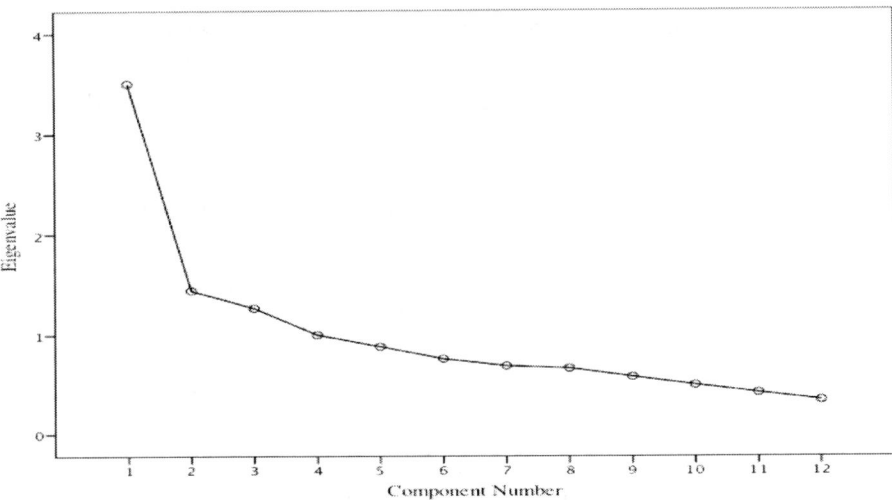

Figure 7. Scree plot showing initial extraction of Measure of Academic Literacy Transfer (MALT) factors with related eigenvalues.

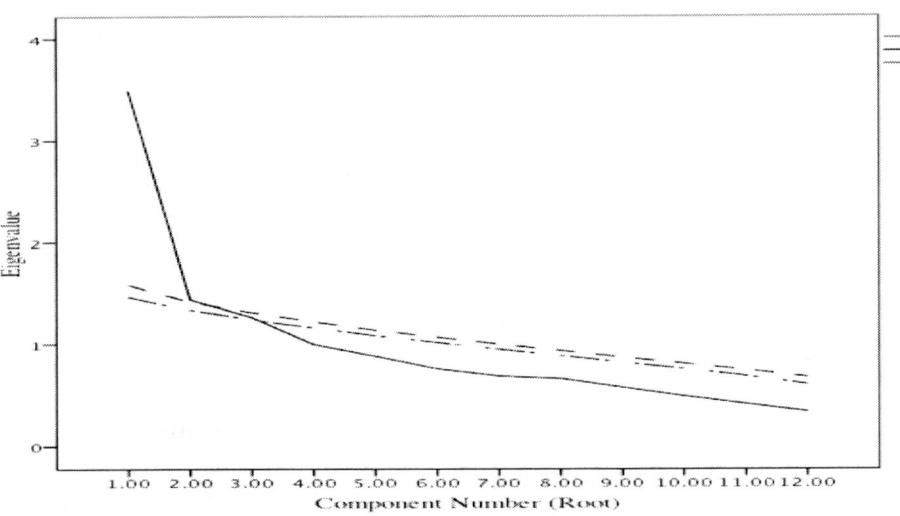

Figure 8. Graph showing eigenvalues of raw data ("rawdata") from initial extraction of Measure of Academic Literacy Transfer (MALT) factors compared to means ("means") and percentile ("percntyl") eigenvalues calculated from 1,000 permutations of random data from parallel analysis, generated using script from "SPSS and SAS Programs for Determining the Number of Components Using Parallel Analysis and Velicer's MAP Test," by B. P. O'Connor, Behaviour Research Methods, Instrumentation, and Computers, 32, pp. 396-402.

Alpha values for each factor are reported in Table 6. Regression and Anderson-Rubin methods yielded identical composite scores for each factor; an analysis of these scores (Table 7), together with visual inspection of the histograms revealed no substantial levels of kurtosis or skew.

Confirmatory factor analysis. As with the EBI, the pattern matrix derived by the EFA of the MALT was subjected to confirmatory factor analysis (CFA) using structural equation modelling as facilitated by AMOS version 21. As the number of cases per variable exceeded the threshold of 10 (Schneiber et al., 2006), the CFA was considered an appropriate method of analysis, with maximum likelihood (ML) also being deemed as a suitable method of estimation. Comparisons of the values so derived to commonly-accepted goodness-of-fit thresholds are reported in Table 5. Unlike the values derived from the CFA of the EBI, which indicated good fit when compared to most of the threshold scores, the analysis of the MALT produced values that were below the critical score for most of these indices (see Figure 9 for the path diagram of the model).

Table 7
Descriptive Statistics of Skew and Kurtosis of MALT Factor Scores

	Critical, evaluative knowledge	Rhetorical knowledge
N Valid	165	165
Missing	0	0
Skew	-.684	.023
Std. Error of Skew	.189	.189
Kurtosis	1.104	-.439
Std. Error of Kurtosis	.376	.376

Note. MALT = Measure of Academic Literacy Transfer.

Table 6

Factor Loadings for Principal Components Analysis with Oblimin Rotation of MALT Scales (N = 166)

	Rotated factor loadings	
	Critical, evaluative knowledge	Rhetorical knowledge
MALT1 tell the difference between fact and opinion in a reading text.	**.85**	.34
MALT2 find the main idea of a reading text.	**.64**	-.04
MALT16 take care to use correct grammar and spelling.	**.57**	-.15
MALT10 write information from texts in my own words (paraphrase).	**.55**	-.04
MALT3 find problems in the reasoning (logic) of an argument.	**.52**	-.14
MALT4 find problems in the support (evidence) of an argument.	.36	-.29
MALT12 plan and organise my writing (outlines, drafts etc.).	-.18	**-.84**
MALT13 write a thesis statement for written assignments.	-.02	**-.66**
MALT15 structure my writing according to a pattern (compare/ contrast, classification, cause/ effect etc.)	.08	**-.66**
MALT11 back up statements with specific support (examples, expert opinion, facts, statistics).	.30	**-.50**
MALT14 write topic sentences to start paragraphs.	.25	**-.48**
Eigenvalues	3.36	1.41
% of variance	30.54	12.85
α	.66	.70

Note. Factor loadings above .40 appear in boldface.
MALT = Measure of Academic Literacy Transfer

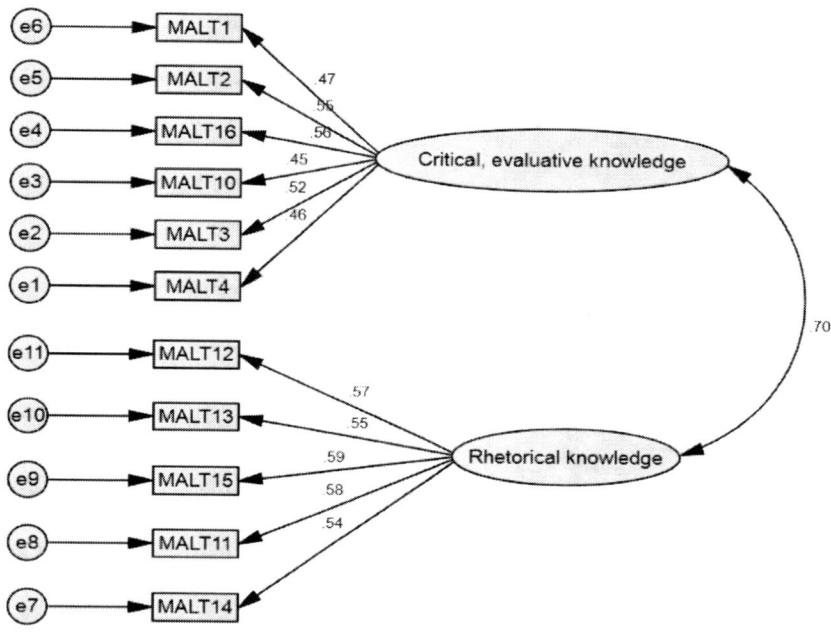

Figure 9. Confirmatory factor analysis model of two extracted factors from Measure of Academic Literacy (MALT). MALT item numbers correspond to labels displayed in Table 5. Standardised maximum likelihood parameter estimates.

4.3. Stage 2: Semi-Structured Interviews

This section describes the results of the hybrid thematic analysis that was projected in Section 3.5.2. This involved deriving inductive themes from iterative coding derived from the interview data, which were then juxtaposed to, and corroborated with, the deductive themes derived from the conceptual framework and from the quantitative analysis of the questionnaire data.

4.3.1. Deductive Themes

In the case of the students' beliefs, a template of a priori codes was developed from the theoretical perspective afforded by Schommer-Aikins and further developed by Schraw et al. (2002) in the form of the EBI. This a priori coding proceeded subsequent to the principal components analysis of the EBI Section of the EBI; thus, only the emergent factors identified as valid for this particular data set were retained. The three factors thus identified were: *innate ability (IA)*; *certain, authoritative knowledge (CAK)*; and *simple knowledge (SK)*.

Rather than retaining Schommer-Aikins's initial schema of "naïve" and "sophisticated" belief structures, the nomenclature advocated by (Muis, 2004) was adopted for the purpose of this coding (for the reasons given previously in Section 2.3.4.): "availing" (of transfer of learning) and "non-availing" [of learning]. Definitions and descriptors of each of the belief factors were developed from the conceptual base provided by Schommer-Aikins (M. A. Schommer, 1994) and (Schraw et al., 2002) with these applying to both availing and non-availing instances from the interview data (see Table 8).

For the a priori coding relating to students' perceived transfer of learning from the EC programme to the disciplines, the context- and practice-driven framework developed by this researcher for this particular study was used (see Section 3.5.1 for details). As for the section relating to students' beliefs about knowledge and learning, the factors extracted by means of the principal components analysis provided the primary codes: *rhetorical knowledge* and *critical, evaluative knowledge*. Again, definitions and descriptors were developed for these, as displayed in Table 9.

4.3.2. Inductive Themes

Although these inductive themes are reported here subsequent to the description of deductive framework, the actual coding of the semi-structured interviews began temporally before the application of the deductive themes. Thus, in the first instance, codes were developed in the manner described in Section 3.5.2; these were data-driven codes and were applied, as far as was consciously possible, without reference either to the research questions or to the conceptual framework of the study. The codes emerged from pre-coding developed from corroboration between this researcher and an experienced colleague who, although familiar with the context of the study, did not have primary knowledge of the contextual framework, and through iterations that involved classification, re-classification, merging and discarding of certain pre-codes. The final iteration of these codes is displayed in Table 10, as juxtaposed to the a priori themes.

Table 8a
Themes Developed A Priori Relating to Students' Beliefs about Knowledge and Learning (Theme 1)

Theme 1		
Label	Innate ability	
Definition	A continuum of "ability to learn in genetically pre-determined to ability to learn is acquired through experience" (Schommer, 1994, p.301)	
Descriptors	*Non- availing*	*Availing*
	Academic success or intellectual prowess as unattainable for those not born with natural intelligence or intellectual capacity	Success in learning or intellectual prowess attainable for all students, regardless of natural ability
	Rapid learning is equated with success	Learning as a gradual, potentially lifelong process
	Learning as product, rather than as process	Process, rather than product, orientated
	"Only geniuses are capable of... understanding mathematics [or whatever subject]" (Schoenfeld, 1988)	Understanding, even of "difficult" subject matter, is accessible to everyone with some effort

Table 8b
Themes Developed A Priori Relating to Students' Beliefs about Knowledge and Learning (Themes 2 & 3)

Theme 2		
Label	Certain, authoritative learning	
Definition	A complex continuum of "knowledge is absolute and handed down from omniscient authority, to knowledge is constantly evolving" (Schommer) and generated by all participants in the learning process	
Descriptors	*Non-availing*	*Availing*
	Knowledge as fixed, objective	Knowledge as fluid, ambiguous, subjective *and* objective
	Knowledge imparted by a single authoritative source	Knowledge from multiple perspectives, constructed by participants
	Absolute moral imperatives	Relative moral stance
	Law and morality as convergent (monist)	Law and morality as divergent (dualist)
Theme 3		
Label	Simple knowledge	
Definition	A continuum of "knowledge is compartmentalised to knowledge is highly integrated and interwoven" (Schommer)	
Descriptors	*Non-availing*	*Availing*
	Knowledge as reified, finite, context-bound	Knowledge as complex, abstract and nuanced
	Knowledge as a "mere basket of facts" (Anderson, 1984) Complete mastery attainable	Knowledge as relative Limitless depth, complexity and overlap

Table 9

Themes Developed A Priori Relating to Students' Perceptions of Transfer of Learning

Theme 1	
Label	Rhetorical knowledge
Definition	The ability to produce a structured, coherent and effective argument or explication of an issue, directed towards a particular audience or readership
Descriptors	Planning and organising a piece of writing; composing a thesis statement and topic sentences; constructing a cogent argument; using reasoning and support; effective and appropriate use of paragraphing; effective and appropriate use of rhetorical patterns (e.g., comparison-contract, cause-effect)
Theme 2	
Label	Critical, evaluative knowledge
Definition	The ability to make informed judgements and decisions as to the effectiveness, reliability or accuracy of textual information that contributes to a particular task
Descriptors	Identifying and distinguishing the main and supporting ideas in a text; distinguishing fact from opinion; identifying tone; identifying problems in reasoning (i.e., fallacies) and evidence; identifying and extracting crucial information from a text; identifying orthographic and/ or other errors in a text (one's own or another's); assessing the strength of an argument

Table 10a
Deductive Themes Derived From Template Juxtaposed to Inductive, Data-driven Themes (Beliefs)

Deductive Themes	Inductive Themes	
Beliefs (from PCA of EBI)	Primary category	Sub-categories
Innate ability	Innate ability	
Certain, authoritative knowledge	Attitudes to authority	Parents' authority
		Teachers' authority
		Other authority or law
	Knowledge certainty	Attitude to moral absolutes
	Source of knowledge	Level of dependence or autonomy
		Autonomous learning
		Cooperative learning
		Peer learning
		Teacher's role
		Group work vs. individual
Simple knowledge	Knowledge complexity	Knowledge as finite, reified
		Awareness of knowledge types
	Quick learning	
	Attitude to theory	

Notes. PCA = principal components analysis, EBI = Epistemic Beliefs Inventory. * denotes themes that are inductively derived and not convergent with deductive template.

Table 10b. *Deductive Themes Derived From Template Juxtaposed to Inductive, Data-driven Themes - Transfer of Learning & Cultural Background* (from PCA of MALT)

	General assessment of EC usefulness in other courses		
Rhetorical knowledge	Writing knowledge	Writing format	
		Sources and referencing	
Critical, evaluative knowledge	Discriminating main ideas, summarising and paraphrasing		
	*Transfer recognition after explication		
—	*Real world knowledge		
	*Unintentional transfer		
	*Transfer targets (classes)		
	Public speaking knowledge		
—	*Relative, contextualised beliefs and experiences	Contextualised beliefs	
		Cultural Comparisons and Experiences	
	*General metacognition	Learner self-awareness	
		Personal attributes	
Cultural background (from Demographic Section of questionnaire)			
Primary nationality	Geographic and/ or cultural origins		
Secondary school background	Secondary teacher attributes	Attributes of good teacher	
		Attributes of bad teacher	
		Teacher fallibility	
	Secondary student role	Students' role	
		Student participation	
		Relationship to teachers	
	Secondary learning context	Language of instruction	
		Class size	
		Activity types	
-	*Tertiary learning context	Perceptions of college teachers	
		Expectations of disciplinary instructors	

Notes. PCA = principal components analysis

4.3.3. Participants: "Cast of Characters"

Because one of the main aims of this research was to validate the cultural matrix as a model for understanding the transfer of learning, generalisable patterns, as identified by the questionnaire, assumed primary importance. It is equally important, however, to recognise that actual individuals, with their own personal backgrounds, preferences and idiosyncrasies, underlie any identifiable patterns from the general data. A number of these individuals, those that participated in the interviews, are identified here to "give them flesh," while at the same time preserving their actual identities by assuming pseudonyms (these pseudonyms are derived from a list of common Thai names – in one case, Chinese – and are not intended to resemble these individual students' actual names).

The brief biographies presented here are derived from the demographic data that the participants themselves provided, both through the questionnaire, and in the course of their respective interviews. In rare cases, student records were retrieved in to resolve conflicts in the data or to remedy omissions. This background information is presented here to assist in understanding these participants' relationship to many of the questions posed to them, and in investigating this background in relation to both their beliefs about knowledge and learning, and their perspectives on the transfer of learning from the EC programme to the disciplines.

Because these participants were selected from typical cases, with secondary school background being the only initial divisor, the characteristics that emerged with regard to age, cumulative GPA for both college and secondary school, the number of trimesters they had attended MUIC, and their scores on the selected EBI items were quite similar (for the ideals of selection, see Table 2, previously).

Bao-Zhi (20[1]) is of Thai nationality, but his parents are Taiwanese. He attended the Thai-Chinese International School for all five of his secondary school years, where his classes were conducted mainly in Thai, but also in Mandarin and English. He completed secondary school with a moderate cumulative GPA of 2.51 – 3 (on a four-point scale). He, like most of the other students interviewed, had not been an exchange student abroad. He was majoring in Environmental Sciences at the

---

[1] Denotes years of age at the time of data collection.

college, and at the time of the interview, he had completed six trimesters at MUIC, where his cumulative GPA (again on a four-point scale) was 2.73.

Kanokwan (19) is a Thai student who attended Bodindecha School (a public school with a bilingual programme in English and Thai) in Bangkok for four years before transferring, for her final year of secondary school, to Niva International School (predominantly English medium), also in Bangkok. She also spent one year as an exchange student in the USA before being admitted to MUIC. She reported her cumulative high school GPA as 3-10 – 3.5. At the time of in the interview, her major was Marketing (in the Business Administration programme), and her cumulative college GPA was 2.29. She had been at MUIC for five trimesters.

Tanawat (19) is of Thai nationality. He spent the final three years of his secondary school career at Assumption College in Bangrak (one of Bangkok's inner districts), which he identified as a "state/ government school in Thailand", but which is, at least nominally, a Catholic school, having been established the St Gabriel's Foundation, an institution of Catholic clergy. The school has a strong English programme. Tanawat's schooling before this is unknown. He attained a secondary school cumulative GPA of 2.51 – 3.00. He had not been an exchange student, and at the time of the interview had been at MUIC for five trimesters, enrolled in the Tourism and Hospitality Management major. His cumulative college GPA was 2.83.

Sirichai (22) is of Thai nationality. He had attended secondary school in Singapore for five years, which he did not name in the interview, where his instruction was in English, and reported a cumulative secondary school GPA of 2 – 2.25. He had not been on an exchange programme. At the time of the interview, he had been enrolled in the Tourism and Hospitality Management major for six trimesters, and his cumulative GPA was 2.10.

Sudarat (20) is a Thai national who spent the final three years of her secondary schooling at Assumption College in Thonburi, which, like its counterpart in Bangrak (see Tanawat, previously), was established by the St Gabriel's Foundation. As did Tanawat, Sudarat reported her secondary school as a "state/ government" school, as, unlike many Catholic-sponsored schools in Thailand, it does not purport to be a bilingual school. Nevertheless, like its counterpart, the school has a strong emphasis on its English programmes (Assumption College Thonburi, n. d.). Sudarat's previous schooling is unknown. She was not an exchange student, and she completed secondary school with a cumulative GPA of 2.51 – 3. At the time of the interview, she had been enrolled in MUIC for six trimesters, in the Tourism and Hospitality Management major. Her cumulative college GPA, then, was 2.91.

Thawatchai (21), of Thai nationality, completed the final three years of his secondary education at an international school in India, which he did not name in the questionnaire or the interview (his previous secondary school experience is also unknown); he reported a cumulative GPA of 2 – 2.25. He had not been on an exchange programme to any other country. At the time of the interview, he had been enrolled at MUIC for seven trimesters in the International Business major (Business Administration). His cumulative college GPA was 2.6.

Werawat (21), a Thai national, attended, for five years, Matthayom Watnairong School, which is self-described as an "English Program School" (Matthayom Watnairong English Program School, 2015) although Werawat himself, in the questionnaire, reported attending a bilingual school. This is possibly because he was enrolled as a student in the more English-language-intensive "integrated English program" of the school, which may approach the 80-percent-English-to 20-percent-Thai-language instruction common in bilingual schools in Thailand (as described in the introductory section of this study). He attained a secondary school cumulative GPA of 3.51 – 4. He had not participated in any exchange programme abroad. At the time of the interview, he had been enrolled in MUIC's Marketing major (Business Administration) at MUIC for 10 trimesters and had a cumulative GPA of 3.39.

Chatchai (20), reported his nationality in the questionnaire as "European, North American, Australian or New Zealand"; the interview, however, revealed that he was in fact of Thai nationality. He had attended secondary school in Thailand, India, and, in his final two years, New Zealand. He did not report his secondary school GPA range. At the time of the interview, he had attended MUIC, enrolled in the Marketing major (Business Administration) for six trimesters, his cumulative college GPA being 2.18.

In sum, the participants who were selected for the purposes of the interviews were quite similar in many of their demographic characteristics, as one would expect of a sampling selected based on typical cases. All were of Thai nationality, and between the ages of 19 and 22. Most had low- to high- average secondary school and college GPAs, with the exception of Werawat who had attained significantly higher grades than the other students in both secondary school and college. Most had also been at MUIC for five to six trimesters – with the exception of Werawat, who had attended for 10 trimesters – and were representative in their enrolments in their respective majors (Figure 10).

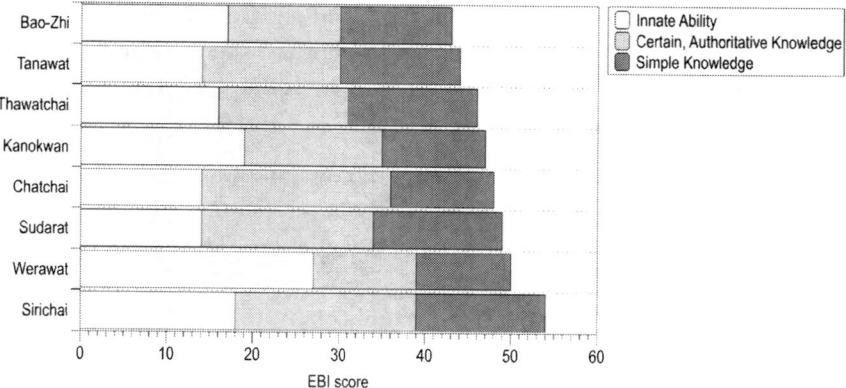

Figure 10. Scores of interview participants in EBI (Epistemic Beliefs Inventory), overall, and for the three dimensions extracted by the principal components analysis of the questionnaire data. Note that a lower score denotes a more availing ("sophisticated") belief system.

Again, because these participants were selected, as far as possible, from the convergent categories that identified them as typical cases, there was not a large relative difference among their overall scores for the EBI, although internally, for the three dimensions extracted by means of the PCA of the questionnaire data, there were some notable differences. For instance, while Werawat's overall EBI score is similar to that of the other participants, his score for the *certain, authoritative knowledge* (CAK) dimension is significantly higher (i.e., less availing or "sophisticated") than that of the other participants (his scores for the other dimensions are lower (and thus more availing) than those of the others[2].

---

[2] In the original conceptualisation and terminology of the EBI, low scores denote "sophisticated" beliefs and high scores "naïve" beliefs. For

In addition, while the eight participants were selected for the purpose of representation from the secondary school categories presented in the questionnaire (international schools; bilingual schools in Thailand; state or government schools in Thailand; schools in North America, Europe, Australia and New Zealand), all the participants, in fact, had experienced a secondary school career that was heterogeneous. Some, such as Bao-Zhi, while they had attended a single institution for their entire secondary school career, had experienced a milieu of cultures: international (read "Western") ideals of schooling, mixed with imported Chinese language and cultural values, together with the local Thai nuances: such was Bao-Zhi's experience. Others, such as Chatchai, had experienced remarkably different cultural and geographic contexts in the course of their secondary schooling: Chatchai had spent some years in a local Thai school before attending school in India, and finally in New Zealand for his final two years.

It should be noted that while these participants, in their secondary school backgrounds, did not reflect the ideals that were sought in investigating the cultural matrix as a model, they were arguably representative in their experiences of the heterogeneous backgrounds of students of international education, whether secondary or tertiary. Their voices would thus be useful in gaining the personal perspectives that were the intentions of the semi-structured interviews.

4.4. Addressing the Research Questions

Data from the questionnaire and the semi-structured interviews were analysed and applied to answering each of the research questions respectively.

4.4.1. Research Question 1: What is the Nature of Students' Perceptions of the Transfer of Learning from the Academic-Literacy-Based English Communication Programme to the Courses in the Disciplines?

Questionnaire. In order to address this question, an analysis of individual items of the MALT was required that retained measures of central tendency and indications of frequency and distributions at the raw-data level. For this reason, although the factors extracted from the

---

reasons given in a previous section, the value-neutral terms "availing" and "non-availing" (Muis, 2004) are substituted in this study.

principal components analysis (PCA) are preserved as subscales, with only their concomitant items being retained, scores are simply summed and averaged by each of these subscales in preference to utilising the weighted regression scores calculated during the PCA (which are more appropriately applied to the investigation of relationships among factors in subsequent analysis).

The non-refined method employed here is considered more appropriate in addressing the research question because it is a comparison of individuals' responses across these items that is of interest (DiStefano, Zhu & Mîndrilă, 2008), rather than a focus on the relationship between these and other factors for which refined methods, such as regression or Anderson-Rubin scores, are more suitable. Summed factor scores, averaged to preserve the scale metric, retain the variation in the original data (Tabachnik & Fidell, 2012) and are relatively simpler to interpret in this case, although they do not take into account the relative loading values of factors that would be used in examining the relationship between these and other variables.

Individual cases that had been previously removed during the data-screening phase (12 in total) were once again excluded for the purposes of this analysis as presenting generally exceptional sets of responses to the MALT, resulting in a sample size of 165.

Individual items and summed scales are presented in Table 11 below. For the purposes of reporting responses to individual items, median is used as the measure of central tendency, with range indicating dispersion, while the mean and median (the latter for the purpose of comparison) is calculated for summed scales, with histograms indicating the distributions.

The means of the summed scores for *critical, evaluative knowledge* ($M = 3.94$) and *rhetorical knowledge* ($M = 4.04$) show a tendency to agreement as to the transfer of these knowledge subsets to the disciplines. This general tendency is reflected in the medians for all the individual items subsumed by each of these subscales. Despite a relatively small standard deviation for each of the subscales (.51 and .55 respectively), however, not all respondents uniformly agreed to each individual item, as the wide range of responses in each of these items indicates.

Open-ended responses. The inclusion of the open-ended responses to the questionnaires was useful in adding some depth of understanding to the analysis of the otherwise confined responses to the Likert-type articles, and in allowing respondents some latitude in recording their own opinions. Open-ended responses to both the Reading and Research and the Writing sections to the MALT were considered.

Before the coding of the open-ended data from the questionnaire proceeded, items were scanned for invalid responses. Invalid responses were deemed those where there the respondent did not enter a response, where the respondent entered a response that did not directly or indirectly relate to the question, or where the respondent entered a closed response (such as "yes" or "no") to the open-ended question. These responses were eliminated before further analysis.

Reading and research.

In which course(s), other than EC, do you most use the reading and/or research skills listed above? After a number of coding iterations, responses to this question were classified by their stage of progression in the usual sequence of courses in a typical MUIC degree programme. Because the college follows the liberal arts education model that is common in the United States, students commence their progression with General Education (GE) courses, which, other than the English Communication (EC) courses, include Mathematics, and a broad selection from Foreign Languages, Humanities, Natural Sciences, and Social Sciences. Students will then move on to enrol in Core courses—typically courses that are common to the major area of study, regardless of the specialisation. Students will then progress to study Major Required and Elective courses. While this represents an overall sequence towards graduation, these course categories will, at times during the student's academic career, overlap: students, for instance, may be in the process of completing GE courses while being simultaneously beginning their Core courses. As such, these categories, while being comprehensive, are not mutually exclusive—respondents often reported transfer to more than one of these.

Table 11
Descriptive Statistics for MALT Summed Subscales and Individual Items

MALT Subscale	A	M	SD	Mdn	Rge	Min.	Max.
Critical, Evaluative Knowledge	.66	3.94	.51	4	-	-	-
MALT1 tell the difference between fact and opinion in a reading text.	-	-	-	4	4	1	5
MALT2 find the main idea of a reading text.	-	-	-	4	4	1	5
MALT3 find problems in the reasoning (logic) of an argument.	-	-	-	4	3	2	5
MALT4 find problems in the support (evidence) of an argument.	-	-	-	4	3	2	5
MALT10 write information from texts in my own words (paraphrase).	-	-	-	4	4	1	5
MALT16 take care to use correct grammar and spelling.	-	-	-	4	4	1	5
Rhetorical Knowledge	.70	4.04	.55	4	-	-	-
MALT11 back up statements with specific support	-	-	-	4	3	2	5
MALT12 plan and organise my writing	-	-	-	4	4	1	5
MALT13 write a thesis statement for written assignments.	-	-	-	4	3	2	5
MALT14 write topic sentences to start paragraphs.	-	-	-	4	3	2	5
MALT15 structure my writing according to a pattern	-	-	-	4	4	1	5

Note. α = Cronbach's Alpha, *M* = mean, *Mdn* = median, MALT = Measure of Academic Literacy Transfer.

Subsequent to the classification by stage, responses were also classified by subject area, which were determined not only by disciplinary grouping, but also by the academic divisions at the college: Business Administration; Fine and Applied Arts; Humanities; Natural Sciences; Social Sciences; and Tourism and Hospitality Management. Again, these categories were not mutually exclusive—a student who may be studying a GE Humanities course might be simultaneously enrolled in a Core course in Business Administration.

In total, the question elicited 140 independent, valid responses. Of these, nine respondents indicated that the reading and research knowledge they had developed in the EC courses was useful in all, or most, of their other courses, one student writing that "[in every subject]… for example, I have to read case studies to analyse the case and my lesson in class," and another commenting that "most of the subjects excepted for math, have to read a lot including do the research."

General Education courses were the largest group specified by respondents, with 66 respondents indicating the usefulness of the reading and writing skills to these courses. Next was the Core courses, with 60 responses, followed by the Major Required and Elective courses, which totalled 30.

Specific subject areas that were mentioned (whether from the GE, Core or Major courses) were as follows:
- Social Sciences (n = 58), particularly the Political Science, Psychology and Thai History courses;
- Business Administration (n = 52), particularly Essentials of Management, followed by Principles of Marketing;
- Natural Sciences (n = 14): Sustainable Development was prominent, in addition to various Chemistry and Biology courses
- Humanities (n = 12) – courses were widely dispersed but included Introduction to Logic and Philosophy;
- Tourism and Hospitality Management (n = 8), particularly Seminar in Service Management and Ethics in Hospitality Operations;
- and Fine and Applied Arts (n = 7), where no particular course predominated in the responses.

Notably, one respondent replied that the knowledge from the EC classes was useful in "none" of the other classes.

Not surprisingly, respondents commented, illustratively, that the knowledge from the EC courses was useful in other courses in which they were required "to write reports or presentation", "read books to in order to understand more about the content or information", or when a research project was required.

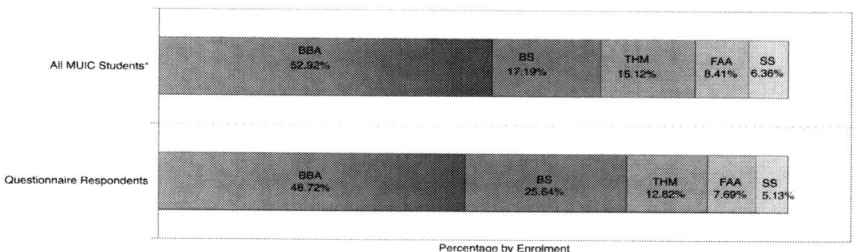

Figure 11. College-wide enrolment, by percentage, in various Majors: Business Administration (BBA) = 52.92%; Science (BS) = 17.19%; Tourism & Hospitality Management (THM) = 15.12%; Fine & Applied Arts (FAA) = 8.41% ; Social Science (SS) = 6.36%
Source: *Facts and Figures*, MUIC Computer System: Information Centre, 2012, Mahidol University International College.

What may seem incongruous at first glance, when one compares the overall enrolment of MUIC students in various majors, is that Social Science classes predominate. This preponderance might be explained by two main factors: Firstly, all students, regardless of Major, are required to enrol in a certain number of Social Science classes as part of their GE requirements. Secondly, these Social Science classes are closely related, in demands and content, to the EC classes. Not only do the reading and research tasks resemble those of the EC classes, but also the EC classes are thematically organised by social themes that are common to the Social Sciences.

In what other ways, if any, have your EC reading and/ or research skills helped you in other courses? This question generated 99 valid responses. After a number of coding iterations which involved the identification, classification, and (in some cases) re-classification of respondents' comments, four main themes emerged: *Information source processing knowledge* (n = 48); *Reading sub-skills*, such as reading speed and interpretation (n = 41); *Oral presentation knowledge* (n = 23); *Extracurricular* (or "real world") *knowledge* (n = 4); and *Content knowledge* (n = 1). Again, these thematic categories are not mutually exclusive, as the comments of respondents were not confined to a single area.

While this question sought to prompt responses that extended beyond the delimitations of the closed Likert-type items, many responses classified into the first two themes, *Information source processing knowledge* and *Reading sub-skills* duplicated or approximated these existing items. In terms of the former, students related, for example, how the knowledge from EC programme helped "me not to plagiarise and also help me to defend my opinion" and assisted in "in finding the best source for my essay," while in relation to the latter, they conveyed, for instance, that it "helps me to find the main idea of a reading text, fact or opinion."

Diverging comments did emerge, however: for *Information processing knowledge*, for example, one respondent commented that the EC courses were useful in that "they helped me be critical of knowledge that is presented to me." Interestingly, this respondent continued: "This is something that is not taught or valued in most other courses but is something that I view as important." This opinion suggests that there is sometimes a disjuncture between the EC courses and the others. Other respondents also mentioned the usefulness of critical thinking skills.

In the *Reading sub-skills,* an area that diverged from the Likert-type items was the time it took to read materials: "EC helps me in getting into the point in reading faster," wrote one respondent, while another replied that "EC helped me do the work quicker and easier". Many respondents felt, moreover, that their comprehension of reading texts had improved.

While the questionnaire was reflective of the focus of the study—on academic literacy skills—many respondents felt compelled to comment on the usefulness of the oral presentation knowledge they had gained from the EC classes. This response was not unexpected, as one of the courses in the EC progression, EC3, is a public speaking class. Thus, a third theme emerged that was extraneous to the transfer of reading, research and writing knowledge that was under investigation: *Oral Presentation Knowledge*. "EC3 course does not only help reading and research but also speaking skill, "commented one respondent, "I can get along with others well." Another respondent wrote "EC3 public speaking helped me with my presentations in my psychology minor courses"; many respondents agreed that this knowledge was useful in oral presentations in the other courses.

Gratifyingly, for an educator who has an interest in transfer beyond the classroom, a small number of students found extracurricular use for the knowledge gleaned in the EC programme, for example in "reading newspaper", in "free-time researching on interesting", "to work in the real world that most people prefer", or—one word—"responsibility."

While the EC courses are not content-based in the truest sense, they use the content of thematic themes as the vehicle to the process knowledge required for academic reading, research and writing: one respondent felt that the *content* of the EC courses was helpful in other courses: "The knowledge that you have been research for your essay can help you with some subject."

Finally, one respondent felt that the reading and research knowledge was not particularly helpful as "it's just common sense finding things."

Writing.

In which course(s), other than EC, did you most use the writing skills listed above? The responses to this question were coded and classified, similarly to the related question (above) in *Reading and Research*, by stage of progression (GE, Core, or Major required or elective courses) and by disciplinary area (i.e., Business Administration; Fine and Applied Arts; Humanities; Natural Sciences; Social Sciences; and Tourism and Hospitality Management). Once again, these categories were not mutually exclusive.

From 178 valid responses, eighteen respondents indicated that they had used the EC writing knowledge in all, or most, of their courses (e.g., "I think every course in MUIC requires the writing skill. For me, the writing skills are very essential for study"). However, the largest number of responses, by stage of progression, was generated in GE courses (n = 56), followed by Core courses (n = 48), and then by Major required or elective courses (n = 17). This pattern closely followed that for *Reading and Research*.

In *Writing*, the disciplinary areas, too, closely reflected the responses to *Reading and Research*. The number of responses per subject area was as follows:

- Social Sciences, 43, again with Thai History emerging foremost, with a diverse selection of other courses within the disciplinary area—courses that have "essay exams";

- Business Administration, 31—Essentials of Management and various marketing courses emerged foremost in this area;
- Humanities, 13—Art Appreciation, Health Education and Ethics courses were prominent here;
- Natural Sciences, 11—a variety of courses were indicated here;
- Tourism and Hospitality, 10—courses such as Ethics in Hospitality Management and Seminar in Service Industry emerged strongly in this area;
- and Fine and Applied Arts, 6, where a variety of specialised writing courses, such as Script Writing, were indicated.

Respondents indicated, naturally, that the courses that had written examinations or essays were the ones in which they were mostly likely to use the knowledge from the EC programme.

Three students responded that they had not found the writing skills useful: one of whom admitted that "I'm too lazy to do drafts and my grammar isn't bad to begin with," and the other of whom related that he or she had used "none of what I have learned or maybe I don't remember." This last statement might indicate that students are often unaware of the knowledge they transfer unless it is made explicit.

In sum, the GE Social Science courses, as those that are the most reflective of the EC classes, and as those that require the more intensive reading, research and writing skills, once again emerge as the leading areas of perceived transfer from the EC program.

In what other ways, if any, have EC writing skills been useful in other courses? This question prompted 75 valid responses, fewer than for the related *Reading and Research* section, possibly because the Likert-type items for this section were more comprehensive, and because respondents had already exhausted most of their responses—particularly those related to the oral presentation knowledge—in that previous section. After coding, classification, and reclassification, the following themes were extracted: *rhetorical knowledge* (n = 33), *written expression* (n = 18), *language control* (n = 17), *metacognitive knowledge* (n = 9) *quantity and rate of writing* (n = 5), *avoiding plagiarism* (n = 3), and *developing content* (n = 2).

Rhetorical knowledge related, for example, to structuring an essay and constructing an effective argument. Responses here reflected the Likert-type items quite closely, for example, "to write the introduction, and conclusion", "structuring and organising my work into paragraphs, counter-arguments, etc."

Written expression: A number of students reported that the EC writing skills had been useful in helping them express themselves in various ways. Illustratively, one respondent remarked that he or she knew "more how to translate my feelings into words," another that "EC has helped me to write essays in a more precise and coherent way," and a third that he or she could "write my major report assignment [so that] the texts are easier to understand

Language control: Although the EC courses focus on academic literacy and not on grammar in the sense of an ESL course, instructors, of necessity, give ad hoc guidance in language control issues. These also form a part of grading rubrics. Given this albeit secondary attention to grammar, many responses indicated that they had benefited from the EC courses in developing grammatical accuracy for application to other courses.

Metacognitive knowledge: This involved the ability to prepare, plan and reflect on writing assignments, or to generate ideas for these assignments. Respondents mentioned, for instance, "help to think while writing", "mind-mapped faster", or, converging with *rhetorical knowledge,* to be able to "criticise ideas, patterns: outline draft—make us to be careful before writing and ideas will be organised."

Quantity and rate of writing: Respondents commented on being able to "finish other assignments quickly", "waste less time", or "get used to writing a lot of research papers."

Other ways in which students reported having found the EC writing knowledge useful were in avoiding plagiarism and in developing content. Finally, perhaps again indicating the tacit nature of much of this knowledge, one respondent replied that "I don't know how, but it helps a lot!"

Student voices. The semi-structured interviews are reported here to illustrate the findings of the questionnaire, both from the MALT and the open-ended questions, and to provide further illumination.

General assessment of the EC programme. In their general assessment of the "usefulness" of the EC programme to their knowledge development, the responses of the interviewees accorded with the findings of the MALT and the open-ended responses of the MALT. Often, without prompting, the students interviewed could not be specific about what, in particular, they had found useful, but were of the general opinion that the programme had helped, to varying extents, in their further studies at college.

Kankowan, in particular, had found the EC programme useful in the writing and presentation knowledge the programme, as a whole, had afforded her:

> Aimee: Okay. Did you ever use anything you learnt from your EC ever?
>
> Kanokwan: A lot.
>
> Aimee: Tell me about that.
>
> Kanokwan: Most of... I think the most useful course from EC is EC3. Because I'm in the marketing major, so we use a lot of presenting. Like our projects is involve in presenting a lot, so I use a lot of skills from that. And also... EC1 and 2 and 3, I mean, and 4... we do, uh, a lot of writing which is what we have to do, like every single day... I think it's ...really... I think EC is the most useful course in MUIC. Like my sister, she graduated from here [MUIC], she said that EC is the most useful tool that she get from MUIC.

In addition to singling out the presentation skills in the EC3 class (a theme that emerged in the open-ended responses to the questionnaire and in the interviews, and discussed in more detail below) Kanokwan is effusive in her praise of the EC programme as the "most useful" classes at MUIC, and while the other interviewees are not quite as expansive in their esteem of the programme, the general attitude from all the interviewees was positive.

Students frequently expressed an awareness of the programme's aims to develop in them knowledge transferable to the other courses. They also made connections between the importance of English and the learning context: an international college. Frequently, they perceived uses for their EC classes that extended beyond the curriculum. Tanawat, for example, when asked by Aimee what he supposed the reasons were that students were required to enrol in the EC programme, responded as follows:

> I think it's to make everyone understand... the pattern of learning English in MUIC. Because... the freshman will come with different school and different skill of English, so... if they learn EC they have

to improve their skill. To be able to ... more effective to use in other classes... and in the public with communicating people.

Tanawat expresses here an opinion that the EC programme is instrumental in providing standardisation, as students enter the college with varying levels of English because of their varying school backgrounds. Interestingly, he perceives the goals of the programme not only in terms of their usefulness in other classes, but also to the "real world" goal of communicating with the public. Extracurricular transfer such as this is explored in a subsection below, as are somewhat unexpected responses. For instance, when Aimee asked Bao-Zhi to provide an example of how he had found the EC programme useful, he offered that the classes were a "spirit pusher," particularly given a hypothetical situation where he "was suddenly assigned to write a 2,000-word essay."

While themes such as this last—which emerged from the data rather than from the template—will be articulated here, more specific comments from the interviewees that directly inform the research framework are presented first.

Rhetorical knowledge. Labelled as the ability to produce a structured, coherent and effective argument or explication of an issue, directed towards a particular audience or readership, this knowledge is that which relates to the first of the components extracted by means of the PCA of the MALT. Although the rhetorical knowledge represented here was intended, in the design of the research and the MALT itself, to apply to the students' writing and the identification of similar features in the writing of others, students often referred to the public speaking skills of the EC3 class. In terms of writing, nevertheless, it was in this area (as with the open-ended responses to the questionnaire) that the interviewees perceived the most transfer occurring. This transferable knowledge related to writing knowledge such as formatting an essay according to a rhetorical pattern or composing a thesis statement and topic sentences, evoking a total of ten responses from seven of the eight interviewees. Illustrative of an awareness of the transfer of an amalgam of non-specified writing skills was that of Tanawat:

Aimee: Has it [EC] helped you at all in other courses?

Tanawat: I think it's helped me a lot, because um... actually I don't know how to write essays... in the proper way... and it... made me understand how to write and how to explain in the topic and things like that.

While Tanawat has a sense of the knowledge assisting him in writing essays and defining topics, at three of the interviewees were more specific by naming rhetorical patterns that they may use in courses other than those of the EC programme:

> Aimee: Has EC helped you in your other classes?
>
> Sirichai: Yeah.
>
> Aimee: Can you explain that?
>
> Sirichai: The skills of things like... compare and contrast... those kind of skills that I need to work... I recently work on my introduction to TIM [Tourism Industry Management] projects, I need to compare and contrast, so I can use the skills to do the projects.

Other than general writing skills, such as topic generation, or fluency and rhetorical patterns, the students frequently referred to the knowledge of citation and referencing conventions that they were able to transfer to other classes:

> Karen: What things have you been using?
>
> Werawat: Uh.... one of the most obvious examples would be references. How to write references and how to... make a clear... how to write an essay, for example, a paragraph... yeah. How to... for example, ERS[3] taught us how to, you know, write a proper English essay, right? I mean, prior to ERS, if I can remember correctly... even though I think I can write English, but these classes they improved me somehow, yeah... my English skills.

Many of the responses are illustrative of the complexity of the literacy knowledge that involves writing skills. Although studies like the present one, that focus on theoretical development, divide the knowledge into discrete packages, such as *rhetorical* or *critical,* or *referencing skills* and *rhetorical patterns*, this knowledge is, on application by the students themselves, seldom delimitable in these ways. Although some students can discern particular types of knowledge that they may apply to other courses, it is common to have students instead express a vague awareness of their existence or nature ("they improved me *somehow*"). The apparent difficulty in expressing precise applications underscores an

---

[3] ERS, English Resource Skills, is the remedial entry-level English course for students who are unable to meet the English language competency requirements for the default entry-level EC1 course.

observation by Carroll (2002) about the difficulty of measuring transfer of academic literacy knowledge because of its complex and non-unified nature. Nevertheless, when students themselves do perceive the nature of these types of knowledge (in the same terms as theorists or researchers do), they most frequently will invoke the knowledge that has in this study been classified as rhetorical, perhaps because, in its particular forms in this study context, it most closely resembles its targets in the other courses.

Critical, evaluative knowledge. In the template, this was defined as the ability to make informed judgements and decisions as to the effectiveness, reliability or accuracy of textual information that contributes to a particular task. Responses in this area from the semi-structured interview data were not as readily identified as in that of *rhetorical knowledge;* in fact, only one instance was readily discernible from the students' responses in the interview:

> Karen: Did any of your EC classes help you figure out main ideas?
>
> Sudarat: Yeah... it helped me for like when we... when we had to study EC, I had to read many research... for I have to summarise... and find what the research says about... okay, it helped me.

The ability to "figure out main ideas" and to summarise clearly involves evaluating information to make decisions in its application. However, Sudarat only assents to this type of knowledge upon being prompted by Karen in what can be construed as a leading question. In the course of in the interviews, the students seldom volunteered information that related to this type of knowledge, and to be fair, the interviewers rarely asked. A possible reason for this is that this type of knowledge, when compared to the more readily evincible rhetorical patterns, paragraphing or referencing is far more oblique—far more abstract and more related to metacognition than is the more practicable rhetorical knowledge. This raises at least two possibilities: one is that, as (Salomon & Perkins, 1989) have argued, the transfer of more abstract, metacognitive learning—high-road transfer—is more prone to failure than that which more closely resembles the surface features of its targets—low-road transfer. The second possibility is one upon which Carroll (2002) remarked in her study of the development of first-year composition: she argues that, rather than an actual failure of transfer, often students are not aware of their own development as writers, and hence of the transfer of this more abstract knowledge. The problem, therefore, is one of detection, rather than of failure.

Transfer acknowledgement after explication. That sometimes students are unaware of their development as learners or of the transfer of certain types of complex knowledge is a theme that emerged independently of the MALT framework. As has been previously remarked, students often had to be prompted to discern the transfer of knowledge from the EC programme to the disciplines. The need to prompt and probe in this regard was common in some of the interviews, as illustrated in the following exchange, in which the interviewer, Aimee, is prompting for further information on the transfer of knowledge to the other courses. At first Bao-Zhi, the interviewee, does not acknowledge using and particular knowledge from the EC programme:

> Aimee: You don't have, like, introduction, body, conclusion?
>
> Bao-Zhi: Oh yes, right, that too! …. And, yeah, it gave the basic skill of my essay writing, actually kept on improving throughout my EC classes.

It was often necessary for the interviewers to provide explicit prompts in this manner, to which the interviewees would assent, sometimes as if this transfer had just at that moment occurred to them. The necessity for explication by the interviewer recalls the advice of Salomon and Perkins (1989) that, in order to effect transfer, instructors should be explicit in their expectations, and not expect transfer to take care of itself (this latter approach being what they disparagingly refer to as the "Bo-Peep theory" of education). This counsel, of course, may be modified by Carroll's remarks to the effect that lack of detection does not necessarily equate with absence of transfer. At the very least, however, students may require explicit prompts and reminders in order to be aware of their knowledge development and transfer.

Public speaking knowledge. As in the open-ended responses in the questionnaires, a strong independent theme emerged that spoke to students' perceptions of the usefulness of the public speaking knowledge developed in the EC3 class. The focus of this study, as had been previously acknowledged, was on the transfer of academic literacy skills from the predominant writing and reading focus of the programme. It is apparent, however, that students regard the oral presentation knowledge from this class as extremely useful, perhaps because it most closely resembles the types of presentation assignments that they produce in other courses. Half of the interviewees (four out of eight) referred to this oral presentation knowledge. This portion of the exchange with Kanokwan, referred to previously, is representative:

> I think the most... useful course from EC is EC3. Because I'm in the marketing major, so we use a lot of presenting. Like our projects is involve in presenting a lot, so I use a lot... skills from that.

Other students, such as Tanawat, give the writing and oral presentation more-or-less equal significance:

> As I am majoring TIM, there would be a lot of presentations and many essays to do... so after I finish all EC, I... feel like I have ability to write essays and presenting more frequent and... more fluent.

Both Kanokwan and Tanawat are explicit in their perception that the usefulness of the oral presentation knowledge is owed to their majors, Marketing and Tourism Industry Management.

Much of the knowledge from the EC3 class that is transferable to the majors is consistent with the *rhetorical* and *critical, evaluative* knowledge that has been identified for the writing, reading and research skills that are the overall focus of the EC programme; students are encouraged to use the knowledge that they have developed in EC1 and EC2 in developing topics, researching, planning and organising their speeches. There is, however, other knowledge that is more particular to a public speaking class, as evinced in the following response by Thawatchai to Karen's probing for further information as to what he applies to the other courses:

> Tawatchai: And... in presentation also, I... I use, in EC 3, the speaking. Like... from... that class I think know what I should do in front of others more, because... before if I have to do like presenting in front of class, I feel like... I feel like so shy. And like I would be, like shaking. But from that class... I have to do it, like, every week, so I feel like common for me now to... speak in front of the class or to do a presentation.
>
> Karen: So do you remember any of the specific skills you were taught that you use?
>
> Tawatchai: Hmmm... like, I remember that in my first... in my first essay in EC 3, the first one that I speak in front of the class, I remember that... after my presentation end, one of my friend ask me

a question, and I... didn't hear it properly, so I said, like, "huh?" like this, it mean that I cannot hear you, I say like "huh?" and then that guy asked me again and I said "Huh? I can't understand," and I remember that the teacher told me that I should not do that... I should say like "Can you repeat the question again?" So that is one... small thing, but it would be helpful for me again.

Karen: Any others?

Other than confidence, fluency and public speaking questioning conventions, Tawatchai mentions practical techniques such as those relating to posture, gestures and eye contact. These are, in addition to the rhetorical and critical, evaluative knowledge that pervade the EC classes, intentional and explicit components of the instruction that students are expected to use not only in EC3, but also in the other classes, so that students mention these easily-identifiable and practicable skills is no surprise.

Unplanned transfer. The interviewees, at times, mentioned instances of transfer that were beyond the intended sphere of instructional expectations. These included Bao-Zhi's comment that his experience in EC acted as a "spirit pusher"—a motivator or expediter, perhaps—in cases where he was assigned essays on complex topics. Bao-Zhi expanded on this:

Aimee: What do you use specifically that you learned in EC that you use... for your... 2,000 word essays?

Bao-Zhi: Frankly speaking, it's just endurance... I don't think, like, normal Thai students would be able to write a 2000 word essay without this preparation. Yeah, it's good preparation for, well, worst case scenario.

Sirichai mentioned that a useful development from the EC classes was that he could type faster. These types of enablers, endurance and speed, while not forming part of the conscious instructional framework, should perhaps be given more attention in the development of the more conventional academic literacy knowledge that is under consideration here.

Transfer targets. From the responses reported thus far, it is apparent that students are often aware of the applicability of the knowledge developed in EC to their courses in their majors. The Tourism Industry Management and Marketing majors were prominent in the interviews because most of the students happened to be drawn from these majors;

this was more-or-less representative of the college enrolment, as has already been established.

The analysis of the open-ended questions of the MALT have provided an overview of the types of courses that were particularly availing of transfer, and the interviews reflected similar selections by the students. Prevalent were courses that included research assignments and presentations; these assignments, of course, closely resembled those in the initial EC context, so the transfer of learning—low-road learning—was easily effected. A representative response included this:

> Karen: So where have you used that [referring to referencing knowledge] ? What class are you using that in?
>
> Tawatchai: Yeah, in many class. Like in each and every research project, I have to write a reference list.... so the teacher can check that this information is from... the other website, not... not made up by myself. Like yesterday, I did a presentation about Spain... unemployment rate. So I have to find information from the internet, so I did the references, did the... "okay, this graph... I have taken this graph from this website, and he is the one who write this... who made this graph on this date or month or year," like that.

Similar, but more closely related to the public speaking knowledge that many students find useful, was this response by Werawat that followed prompting by Karen to provide examples of where certain knowledge from the EC programme had proved useful:

> Any classes I take... I just have... I just have marketing presentation; it's a new product development in class... at eight am, today, I, uhh... for example, the EC3 class I studied with Douglas [an EC3 instructor]... I think it's great... a great class, I really enjoy it. Like how... I learn from that class how to, like, make a proper gesture, how to present, you know, how to... make a speech... public speech, stuff like that, so I can adapt that kind of concept, like you don't move around when you make a presentation, you look... you look at the people's eyes when you talk to them, and gestures, and stuff like that. I... I think I kind of, yeah, I remember that, because I think I use that a lot, in other classes, so I think I remember them. And also... when writing report, essay, for example, like how you must have an... opening sentences and concluding ideas, stuff like that. I don't know if I can name them right, but, yes... those kinds of stuff.

This response is reproduced at length here because it is illustrative of much of the foregoing discussion: the awareness of an overall transfer of presentation and essay writing knowledge to certain types of contexts that resemble, at least in their activities, the EC one. Again, the type of transfer articulated is low-road; Like the other students, Werawat makes no explicit mention of the more abstract critical, evaluative knowledge that would constitute high-road transfer.

"Real world" knowledge. While the immediate and explicit purpose of the EC programme is to provide support, in the form of transferable academic literacy knowledge, to the disciplines, the ultimate aim of education, and thus all educators, is the "real-world" application of classroom learning. Instances of this emerged from the semi-structured interviews. Kanokwan, for example, reported that the EC knowledge had been of considerable use to her elder sister, who had preceded her at the college and was now employed: "She... works in ERM, which is the, like, the environment consulting something... Yeah, and she has to... write a lot of reports and present it to her boss and... uh... she said that she got all her skills from EC."

Finally, it should also be remembered that the EC programme is concerned not only with academic literacy knowledge, but also with the use English language in general as a means of communication, which is of considerable instrumental importance to the students who enrol in an international college. Tanawat, for one, expressed his awareness of his developing competence in communicating in English at large—also, of course a significant transfer in its own right.

Implications for the research question

While the MALT indicated a range of responses for the overall scale and each subscale, the trend of the responses in this measure was towards agreement to the transfer of learning; in other words, most participants perceived that they were applying knowledge from the EC programme in their courses in the disciplines.

Although similarly varied, most of the responses to the open-ended questions suggested that participants perceived that this transfer was occurring in courses that resembled the EC courses, especially in the assignment types, such as essays or class presentations. Participants perceived that it was mostly superficial knowledge, such as that related to rhetorical patterns or oral presentation knowledge, that they were applying in their major courses.

The nature of this transfer will be discussed in more detail, particularly in relation to the conceptual development of this study, in the final chapter.

4.4.2. Research Question 2: What is the Nature of the Relationship Between Students' Perceptions of the Transfer of Learning from the EC Programme and their Personal Beliefs About Knowledge and Learning?

Questionnaire. In order to investigate this question, the analysis of the questionnaire data explored associations between the EBI and MALT scales and subscales. This analysis was conducted initially by means of Pearson product-movement correlations in order to establish the existence of relationships and to explore their magnitude. However, as the parametric Pearson correlation failed to detect a significant relationship, the non-parametric Spearman correlation was also conducted to investigate a possible relationship, which it so indicated (for an explanation of the use of both parametric and non-parametric methods as diagnostic tests, see Section 3.8.). As a result of the significant relationship indicated by the Spearman correlation, a regression model was generated in order to confirm the relationship established by the MALT and the EBI and to establish the extent to which variance in the MALT was predicted by variance in the EBI. The regression scores that had been generated by the PCA of both the EBI and the MALT were used for the calculations involving the subscales, which consisted of *innate ability* (IA); *certain, authoritative knowledge* (CAK); and *simple knowledge* (SK) for the EBI; and *critical, evaluative knowledge* (CEK); and *rhetorical knowledge* (RK) for the MALT. Summed values of these scores comprised the scale values for the composite EBI (EBISUM) and MALT (MALTSUM) respectively.

Before generating the Pearson correlation matrix in the first instance, scatter plots were generated to facilitate an initial exploration of possible relationships, but also to indicate whether the a priori assumption of linearity between the variable sets was intact. A visual inspection of scatter plots, while indicating a negative associative trend in 10 of the 12 pairs, gave no indications of non-linearity; the association between each pair of variables, however, was negligible, as evidenced by the highly dispersed nature of the dots and the low coefficients of determination (R^2).

The necessary assumption of bivariate normality was indicated by an approximately normal distribution of the regression scores for each of the subscales and composite scales (although there was some leptokurtosis for CEK and, therefore, MALTSUM), as indicated by the histograms. Although bivariate normality does not always follow from normally distributed variables per se, this is frequently deemed adequate to satisfy the assumption (Bertsekas & Tsitsiklis, 2002). As the assumption was unidirectional—a low EBI score (more availing) would be associated with a higher MALT score (more transfer)—the tests for statistical significance were one-tailed. Results for the Pearson correlation are presented in Table 12.

Although the initial scatterplots had not indicated any non-linearity, the wide dispersion of data points and the weak associations did not allow, conversely, for a confident assessment of linearity. Moreover, although the distributions were accepted as approximately normal for the purposes of the Pearson product moment correlation, there is some debate in the methodological literature as to how robust the procedure is with respect to deviations from normality (e.g., Pernet, Wilcox, & Rousselet, 2012): leptokurtosis was evident on the composite MALT score, for example. For these reasons, and in order to avoid the possibility of Type II error, Spearman's rank order correlation was run, for purposes of comparison and confirmation, on the same matrix of variables. The only assumption required for this test is that the monotonic distribution that was evident from a visual inspection of the scatter plots. The results are displayed in Table 13. The variables pertaining to the research question, the composite EBI and MALT scores (EBISUM and MALTSUM) displayed a negative association in both analyses; this analysis was non-significant in the case of Pearson's correlation, and highly significant in the case of Spearman's.

Table 12
Pearson Correlations for EBI and MALT Scale and Subscale Variables

Variable	MALT CEK	MALT RK	EBI IA	EBI CAK	EBI SK	EBI SUM
MALT RK	-.34**					
EBI IA	-.13*	.02				
EBI CAK	.09	-.10	.05			
EBI SK	-.07	-.05	.02	.01		
EBI SUM	-.07	-.07	.61**	.60**	.58**	
MALT SUM	.58**	.58**	-.10	-.01	-.10	**-.12**

Table 13
Spearman Correlations for EBI and MALT Scale and Subscale Variables

Variable	MALT CE	MALT RK	EBI IA	EBI CAK	EBI SK	EBI SUM
MALT RK	-.37**					
EBI IA	-.15*	-.00				
EBI CAK	.03	-.05	.05			
EBI SK	-.06	-.09	.02	-.00		
EBI SUM	-.08	-.09	.60**	.59**	.52**	
MALT SUM	.46**	.60**	-.18*	-.12	-.13	**-.21****

Note. EBI = Epistemic Beliefs Inventory; MALT = Measure of Academic Literacy Transfer; CEK = Critical, Evaluative Knowledge; RK = Rhetorical Knowledge; IA = Innate Ability; CAK = Certain Authoritative Knowledge, SK = Simple Knowledge; EBISUM = Summed score for composite EBI; MALTSUM = Summed score for composite MALT; ** statistically significant at the .01 level (one-tailed); * statistically significant at the .05 level (one-tailed). The association pertinent for the purposes of the specific research question is indicated in boldface type.

In order further to confirm this association and to investigate its nature, these variables were further subjected to simple linear regression analysis. For this analysis, the assumption of linearity had already been satisfactorily established through visual inspection of scatter plots. Outliers were detected in three preliminary iterations of the regression analysis by means casewise diagnostics, which revealed four cases beyond the bounds of three standard deviations. In the interest of satisfying the assumption, and of producing a model, the relevant cases (nos. 23, 47, 62 and 82) were removed, and the regression model was again generated.

Independence of errors was indicated by the Durbin-Watson statistic (2.13), and the further assumption of general homoscedasticity was satisfactorily established by visual inspection of scatter plot for the residuals across the standardised predicted values. An inspection of a histogram and the normal P-P plot revealed, moreover, that the residuals were approximately normally distributed.

The linear regression model indicated that the composite EBI score (EBISUM) could significantly predict the composite MALT score (MALTSUM), $F(1, 158) = 10.68$, $p < .01$. The relative magnitude of the composite EBI score accounted for 6.3% of the explained variability in the relative magnitude of the composite MALT score, the regression equation being represented as: composite MALT score = .05 + (-.148 x composite EBI score). The model is represented in Figure 12.

Student voices. The non-parametric test, together with the regression model, indicated a significant relationship between students' personal belief systems and their perceptions of the transfer of learning from the EC programme to the disciplines. This relationship, however, was not as readily discernible from the interview data, owing to the nature of the sampling. Rather than seeking extreme cases with either relatively high or low scores in either the EBI or the MALT, the selection of cases proceeded by means of identifying typical questionnaire respondents from each "secondary school background" group. Representatives from each secondary school group were sought in order to explore the understanding of potential differences between these groups and their personal belief systems and, ultimately, their perceptions of transfer of learning.

In the analysis, these groups were similar in these characteristics (see 4.4.3); the typical cases were fairly homogeneous as a group of their own (see Table 2, previously), making meaningful comparisons unfeasible.

Despite these difficulties in exploring or confirming the relationship between students' personal belief systems and the transfer of learning (as directed by the research question), the interview data were useful in illuminating the composition and nature of the students' belief systems, as framed by the components analysis of the EBI. They also facilitated an understanding of students' metacognition beyond the beliefs dimensions and revealed a significant emergent theme as to the variability of these beliefs.

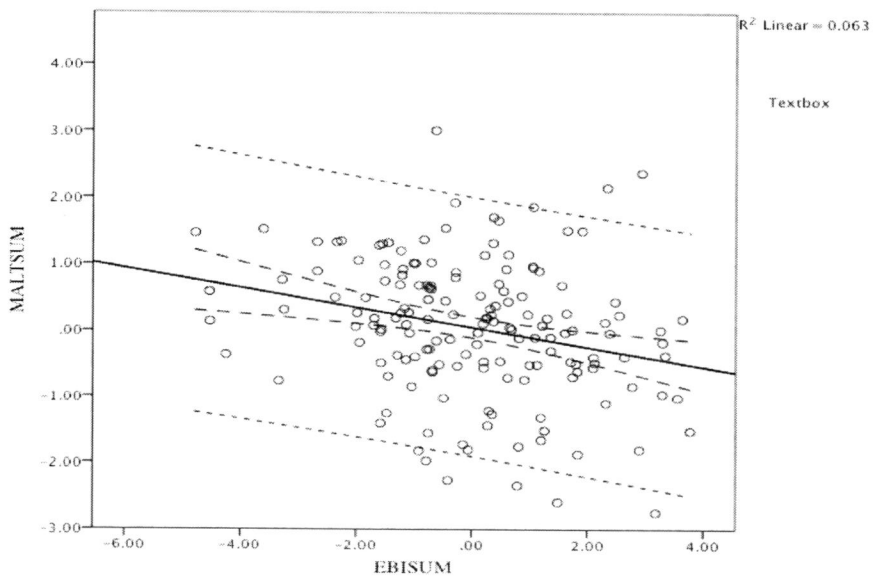

Figure 12. Scatter plot displaying linear regression of EBISUM as a predictor of MALTSUM, with lines representing confidence levels at 95% and predictive levels. EBISUM = Epistemic Beliefs Inventory; MALTSUM = Measure of Academic Literacy Transfer.

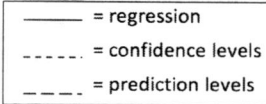

Innate ability. This was the first of the components that emerged from the PCA of the EBI and was consistent with Schommer-Aikins's (Schommer, 1990, 1994) hypothesised beliefs. It was defined as a continuum of "ability to learn in genetically pre-determined to ability to learn is acquired through experience" (p. 301). Because it is presented as a continuum, the researcher sought instances in the interviews that indicated either more or less availing beliefs as to *innate ability*.

While the interviewees had been selected based on typical descriptive statistics, including that of their scores in the EBI, this first dimension, as in the ones that follow, revealed some variability—along with a cultural nuance for which the original hypothesised dimension had not provided.

As with the other dimensions, interview questions aimed at *innate ability* prompted a minor number of responses that could be considered, in Muis's (2004) terms, *availing* of learning or, in the context of this study, of learning transfer. For example, when asked by Aimee as to who had the greater probability of succeeding, those with innate ability ("naturally talented") or those who were tenacious in their efforts, Kanokwan replied that "We all have the same chance, equal chance, to be successful. It depends," Kanokwan continued, "on how hard you work." While the initial question by Aimee presupposed the existence of innate ability, Kanokwan's response is clearly an espousal on her part of a belief that learning and the acquisition of knowledge is a factor of effort, rather than of innate ability. Similarly supportive of the function of effort was Sirichai's utterances in the following exchange:

> Aimee: Okay, so, what do you think about students who learn things quickly? Do you think that they are more successful than students who have to work harder to learn things?
>
> Sirichai: Mmmm.... not necessarily.
>
> Aimee: Can you explain?
>
> Sirichai: Well... If those who understand well in class, they might not practise, and... they might not be able to... um... remember what they learned in class well as those who... practise a lot.

Tanawat extended this view of the role of effort in successful learning outcomes, although, as in other instances, innate ability was presupposed by the interviewer (mostly as a result of prompts derived from the EBI itself):

> Aimee: How about... do you think that the ones who aren't that smart... do you think that you can work to become smarter? Or work to be at the same level as smart people? Or do you think that you can't?
>
> Tanawat: Yes, if you... ummm... if you... try enough, you can be like them, or maybe higher than them.

Tanawat ascribes this potential triumph of effort over innate ability to the motivation that those who are not born with such abilities possess in overcoming this potential limitation.

Views such as those of Kanokwan, Sirichai and Tanawat, while accepting the proposition of inborn abilities, are distinctly indicative of availing beliefs as to learning; rather than resigning themselves to a factor beyond their locus of control, they recognise the participatory role of the learner him- or herself in the acquisition of knowledge.

While other responses by the students, if placed on the continuum, could be revealing of less availing beliefs, they shared the attitude of these latter interviewees as to the role of effort. In other words, the students believed in innate ability but, at the same time, recognised the role of effort in academic or other success. Moreover, in the responses of a single interviewee, a less availing belief could emerge in immediate contradistinction to one that was highly availing. An example is in this account by Kanokwan:

> I mean, I'm not smart, but I study a lot. I...In our family, we all suck at math, so we have to, you know, keep practising and practising, like, unlike my friend, I study before an exam for, like, three weeks, before the finals and before every term, but my friend, he's really, really smart, so he study only... one day, and then he got like a perfect score, and then I got like... 70 or something like that. So I think... umm... everybody is not smart, so... but we can put a lot of effort to get there.

Thus, like most of the respondents, Kanokwan does not question natural predisposition, such as mathematical ability, yet she is unequivocal in recognising her agency in successful learning outcomes. Bao-Zhi (who, because of his relative ease in communicating in English and his greater willingness to elaborate on the issues, is frequently quoted in this analysis), displayed similar, somewhat complex, beliefs:

> Aimee: ... Do you think there's any case, or do you think that it's possible that some people, no matter how hard they work will never be smart?

Bao-Zhi, at this stage, requests some clarification on the question; Aimee endeavours to elaborate and give some examples, after which Bao-Zhi directs a further enquiry:

> Bao-Zhi: Wait... define "smart" first [laughs].
>
> Aimee: Good question. We'll start with that what do you think smart is?
>
> Bao-Zhi: Okay, I would say smart is in a sense, instinct, naturally born. I would call that smart.
>
> Aimee: Okay...
>
> Bao-Zhi: But "intellectual," I would just separate it from being smart again, because it's the ... understanding, of like...in the other, like, angle. It's like you don't try to compare... eh... IQ and EQ as such...so yeah, capability of each of the sides are both important, but then, well, if you want... but yeah... personally, I would define smart as the

instinctive sides, being naturally born and, yeah, these are the smart people.

Bao-Zhi is thus able to resolve the conflict between innate ability and effort by distinguishing between mental abilities that might lead to successful learning: "being smart" or "understanding" he perceives as innate; nevertheless, he believes success is not necessarily predicated on this innate capacity, but that this capacity is a factor in the facility of learning; later in the exchange he refers to the popular fable of "The Tortoise and the Hare" in elaborating on this point.

What also emerges from the extended exchange between Aimee and Bao-Zhi is a minor theme as to factors other than the individual's innate capacity or efforts that may account for success in learning. In the Thai cultural schema, in fact, selecting between these two possibilities might present a false dilemma because it does not take into account an additional external locus: that of the role of fate, fortune or predestination in determining an individual's success or otherwise, a compound factor that features highly in the Thai cultural cosmology. The Thai belief in predestination and fatalism are elaborated upon by Thai culture and linguistics scholar (Vongvipanond, 1994):

> A person's life is pre- programmed by "phrom" or Lord Brahman in Hinduism. The ups are considered "choke" or good fortune. The downs are "khroe" or bad fortune. Both imply man's inability to manage his own life independently (p. 8).

The challenges posed by such a conviction to a "modern education" have been recognised by writers such (Changkakoti & Broyon, 2008) and (Sirikanchana, 1998): the belief is self-evidently anathema to the more Western credence of mastery and agency on the part of the learner, and would, therefore, be considered, in the context of the EBI, non-availing. By extension, so would be the Thai belief in intercession by the spirit world.

Admittedly, an invocation of such an external locus is overtly evident in only one instance in the interviews; it appears, however briefly, in a further section of the exchange between Aimee and Bao-Zhi, as reported above, as to the factors of academic success:

> Aimee: Do you think there's such a thing as people who are naturally smart?

Bao-Zhi: Well, I believe that there are some people who are naturally capable of learning certain things faster than others.

Aimee: And do you think that those people end up being more successful later on?

Bao-Zhi: No... I don't because, uh, it requires skills and opportunity and... luck [laughs]. So, in the end, I would say...luck [laughs]

While Bao-Zhi appears to acknowledge the role of natural abilities, ultimately he believes that success is largely a product of good fortune. He elaborates on this by providing the example of the success of Microsoft co-founder Bill Gates, citing that he owed his success largely to being in an opportune position to benefit from "luck."

Although this sole mention of luck does not seem sufficient grounds upon which to develop a theme, the role of external loci such as predestination and intercession by spirits is not to be underestimated as a prevalent belief in Thai culture. Arguably, its sparse mention in the interviews is a result of their semi-structured nature; while there is some latitude on the part the interviewees in composing their responses, these responses are framed by the questions of the interviewers. The questions are, in turn, framed by the a priori assumptions of the research structure—in this case, the EBI—and of the presuppositions of the interviewers. However, in the context of this research—an international college in Thailand—some Thai students present manifestations of this belief. For example, over the ten-year period of his employment at MUIC, this researcher has observed, during the examination period, the increased frequency of visits by students to a spirit shrine located on the premises of the college. Some students seek intercession in providing a successful outcome to the examinations. In this cultural context, therefore, this theme deserves some consideration. By extension, such culturally-specific factors should be integrated into schemes of belief dimensions in particular cultural contexts.

Certain, authoritative knowledge. The second of the components to emerge from the PCA of the EBI, this set of beliefs did not represent the original hypothesised dimensions. Schommer-Aikins hypothesised two discrete dimensions here: *omniscient authority* and *certain knowledge,* but the PCA did not support separate dimensions. Instead, as reported earlier in this section, items related to *omniscient authority* were subsumed by *certain knowledge* to form a new dimension, labelled *certain, authoritative knowledge*. The two original dimensions were conspired congruous to each other as both concerned the ultimate sources of knowledge (see 4.2.2), and the combined component was defined as a continuum of "knowledge is absolute and handed down from omniscient authority, to knowledge is constantly evolving" (Schommer) and generated by all participants in the learning process.

In analysing the interview data, instances derived from sub-themes involving the sources of knowledge, its certainty, and students' attitudes towards authority were, as in the case of the other beliefs dimensions, examined for more or less availing beliefs.

It should be clear, because extreme cases were not presented here, that none of the students who were interviewed exemplified either an availing or non-availing stance towards certain, authoritative knowledge. Their comments are instructive, nevertheless, in understanding the beliefs of the students in the specific research context of this study.

Among the less availing views were those that viewed the teacher as the ultimate source of knowledge. Chatchai, for example, when asked whether he became frustrated when the teacher did not provide "the right answer," replied "I prefer doing it myself first and then after that, if I couldn't do it anything, I prefer teacher to... teacher to give answer straight away." This account exhibits an awareness of one ideal of the autonomous learner—the classroom, instructor, nevertheless, remains a "fall-back." In a reply that is related to the role of the teacher, but also expresses a faith in the certainty of knowledge, this following exchange is also enlightening:

> Karen: Have you had the experience where teachers give you a question that really doesn't have an answer?
>
> Sudarat: I don't. I don't face with this situation but I... the teacher always asks the question, that I can't answer because I don't know, but there is the right answer, but I don't know. I never... I never see the question that there is no answer.
>
> Karen: But you do see questions where there is an answer but you don't know what it is?
>
> Sudarat: Yes.

The idea that the teacher might ask a question to which there is no particular "right" answer seems alien to Sudarat's experience. In Sudarat's perception, the absence of an answer indicates her ignorance, rather than the absence of a clear and certain answer. In fact, in what follows, she expresses a dislike for teachers who do not provide the "right answer" when she is, in her view, ignorant of it:

> Karen: How would you feel if she [the teacher] didn't give the answer?
>
> Sudarat: If she... if she did not give the answer I think, for me, I will don't like her... or he...
>
> Karen: So you want to have the answer?
>
> Sudarat: Yes. Because we are the student, we need to know the answer from the teacher, but if the teacher didn't give the answer, and... and how do we get the answer from? So the teacher should give the answer to the student.

Thus, Sudarat voices a strong belief in the role of the teacher as the source of knowledge that is transmitted from the teacher to the student, a non-availing belief that is contrary to more availing beliefs of participatory knowledge construction.

Other non-availing beliefs were expressed in relation to moral certainties and absolutes, particularly concerning the nature of truth (an imminent inquiry that is at the heart of the philosophical origins of epistemological enquiry). A few instances, notably these below, were unequivocally less availing:

> Aimee: What about other truths... like, do you think there are truths that could be true for you that aren't true to other people?
>
> Sirichai: I don't think so.

Aimee continued to probe Sirichai, enquiring as to whether he believed certain people were entitled to their own version of the truth. Sirichai affirmed the more absolutist view:

> Sirichai: Because... if like... how do I say? ... If no matter what the world believe in, there's always a truth. So it depends on [unclear].
>
> Aimee: Alright, so you believe that there is one truth that everyone lives by?
>
> Sirichai: There is a truth... no matter what they believe in.

Such unequivocally non-availing beliefs were, however, the exception. More commonly, other interviewees made at least some concessions towards a relative notion of truth, while not completely rejecting the belief in an absolute:

> Karen: So there can be more than one version of the truth?

> Tawatchai: The truth, I think there can be one version of the truth, but... it depend on... the perspective. But the truth; I think there is only one version of the truth.

In addition to these less availing beliefs regarding the source of knowledge and moral, many of the interviews displayed what many would consider obvious considerations to authority, but with even greater ambivalence. What was remarkable in many of the responses here was a sense that questioning the authority of parents, teachers or others was somehow "wrong" or, in Tawachai's words, "disrespectful"—but only, perhaps, in the Thai cultural context. The passage below represents a common theme that emerged here:

> Aimee: Okay. How about just... how about... your parents, for instance? Would you ever consider questioning your parents?
>
> Sirichai: Well... most of the time, it's more of like, discussion not questioning... if I have doubt too.
>
> Aimee: Alright, so you have found a way to do it, where you don't have to like...
>
> Sirichai: Yes... my family has a tradition that those who have higher authorities are always right, so if we kind of... like adjust it... and make it discussion rather than questioning.

The first pattern that this passage illustrates is the awareness of a tradition, particularly strong in Thailand and many other Asian cultures of unquestioning respect for elders and others in authority. To many Western commentators (including Hofstede), the idea of unquestioning authority often implies a distance in the relationship. However, this sense of distance is belied here by this sense of familial "discussion," rather than of the questioning of authority. While, as some have said, there are no equals in Thailand, and relationships—parents-offspring; teachers-students; employers-employees—are governed by client-patron transactions (see, for example, Baskerville, 2003; Pagram & Pagram, 2006; Sirikanchana, 1998; Wyatt, 2003), these are not conducted at a distance; authority is not detached, either substantially or emotionally, from daily realities.

Instances such as these, which indicated a familial integration of authority into everyday interactions and activities, commonly emerged in the interviews—not only with respect to parents, but also to teachers. These relationships are often very intimate; this may reveal an acceptance of authority as being more closely assimilated into "the way of things" than it is regarded to be in the West. One, may, therefore, speculate on the reason for the failure of Schommer-Aikins's *omniscient authority* dimension to emerge in any of the factor analyses in Asia (including this one): to adopt a common metaphor, it is so closely interwoven into the fabric of society that attempts to separate it as a separate strand are futile. The West, on the other hand, with its tradition of more egalitarian values, has long had a preoccupation with scrutinising authority and its manifestations, a focus which arguably leads to its formulation as a discrete set of values and beliefs, as in Schommer-Aikins's conceptualisation.

In this study, the authority dimension is subsumed by the dimension *certain knowledge*. Furthermore, while the discussion of this dimension, thus far, has focused on less availing beliefs in this particular dimension, it should be noted that, in this particular group of interviewees, instances of *more* availing beliefs were more common. Bao-Zhi, in particular, was the most forthcoming in terms of more availing beliefs as to the sources of knowledge; an exchange is presented as length here because it is revealing of a complex understanding of the uncertain nature of knowledge and an acceptance of ambiguity:

> Aimee: Do you think there is a right or wrong answer to some of the big questions in life?
>
> Bao-Zhi: Hmmm... do you have any examples?
>
> Aimee: Something like... [long pause] Can you think of a big problem in life? Whether or not—
>
> Bao-Zhi: Were we created? [Laughs]
>
> Aimee: There you go.
>
> Bao-Zhi: Let's say I am entertained... entertained... by both sides of this thesis. I can think that I am created... and what I am what I am right now...and I can also think... that, uh...through different kinds of evolution like the survival of the fittest, we finally what we are today due to like this... changes in the climate and every single factors that shape what we are which doesn't make us more important than any other creatures at all. So, yeah... I can just think like I am created just like any other creatures. They are not important.
>
> Aimee: So, for you, do you prefer to think those two things? Are you okay with the idea of entertaining those two thoughts without making a conclusion?

Bao-Zhi: Yeah, I don't ...okay let's say that...well let's say I'm shaken by the facts that I learn. Well now, just a couple of week ago, we just... I just learnt one of our [indistinct] or something was a plant eater, then became a meat eater; it's very confusing. But then uh... still I enjoy the changes over time and the knowledge that scientists put a lot of effort in trying to explain it. It's still... let's just say it's a piece of me, influence.... and I also enjoy these religions' way of... uh... interpreting God's messages and... their customs, although we have a lot of these extreme people trying to discriminate others, there are also these people who's [sounds like "sinful"] and help the poor... umm... I would say it doesn't matter if we know what (unclear) to look at, at the moment.

Aimee: So... you're okay living in the ambiguity of not knowing... not exactly knowing what to believe, but entertaining all ideas together.

Bao-Zhi: Because when you think about for like the case of knowledge versus information, it... doesn't matter, uh, what they are as long as we, uh, enjoy our life right now.

Bao-Zhi's overall score for the EBI was lower than that of the other interviewees (see Figure 14, previously), and the passage reflects this more availing disposition; Bao-Zhi is not only comfortable with the uncertainty and mutability of knowledge, but he seems to relish both the ambiguities (he is "entertained" by it) and the development of knowledge that accompanies scientific enquiry.

Other students, notably Tawatchai, Sudarat and Werawat, also indicated more availing beliefs as to the knowledge uncertainty. Sudarat recognises the mutability of knowledge here:

Karen: Do you think knowledge stays the same or... do you think it changes over time?

Sudarat: It changes over time.

Karen: How does it change?

Sudarat: Time change, people change, knowledge change, technology change, so everything change... for me.

Werawat also recognised the changeability of knowledge. While demonstrating a preference for his opinions above that of others, he conceded that the views of others might alter his stance on a particular issue:

Karen: If there's a question that's posed, do you think that people need to agree with your answer, if there's different answers?

Werawat: [Sighs] Well, it might be kind of... narcissistic, but I would prefer it... if people agree with my answer I think, yeah. But I can also change my view, I think... if the answer...the other answers can really prove me otherwise.

Karen: So you're open to the idea... that your knowledge can change?

Werawat: Yeah.

This not only demonstrates more availing beliefs with regard to the *certain, authoritative knowledge* dimension, but also a willingness on the part of Werawat to reflect on his own learning—in itself availing behaviour. Other students also displayed, in their responses a propensity for reflection on learning, and this metacognitive conduct is developed in a later subsection.

As far as the *certain, authoritative knowledge* dimension was concerned, many of the interviewees demonstrated, in addition, more availing beliefs in relation to moral certainties and the nature of truth. These views were characterised by a relativistic stance, as in these exemplars:

Aimee: Are there any truths that should stay the same for everyone?

Kanokwan: I don't think so, no.

Aimee: So like everyone has their own...

Kanokwan: Yeah, they have their own right to believe what they want.

...

Aimee: Okay, and in your mind what is the definition of the truth?

Bao-Zhi: Hmm...[long pause] Well, whatever that person think to be right in his head. That's the truth.

Bao-Zhi, again, is the most articulate in voicing an availing belief in the nature of truth, as he continues, in response to Aimee's questions and clarification regarding the existence of an absolute moral truth:

Aimee: Do you think there is such a thing as an absolute moral truth that applies to everyone?

Bao-Zhi: Wait...an absolute what?

Aimee: An absolute moral truth that applies to everyone.

Bao-Zhi: No, I don't think that because... let's say it's like beliefs...in religions. These beliefs involve... these beliefs would form er... okay, all these beliefs were developed from, like, different kinds of environments. One belief that can become useful here doesn't necessarily become useful... yeah... on the other side. Basically what people believe do not... match all of the time, especially because they will develop different beliefs for a different purpose. So yeah, I don't think... [trails off]

Interestingly, Bao-Zhi's explanation of beliefs developing in particular environments, or contexts, and for different purposes is not only indicative of availing beliefs, but also reflects one of the main premises of this study, as framed by the cultural matrix.

A number of availing beliefs were also apparent in some of the students' responses to questions concerning their relationship to and views about authority, particularly pertaining to teachers or other societal authorities. Chatchai, for example, did not perceive teachers to be an infallible authority and source of knowledge, and, indeed, seems to counsel a certain amount of indulgence in the manner in which students address a teacher's mistakes as to fact:

> You know, sometimes we need... to give teacher... teacher can make mistake, everyone can make mistake, and... he... she not very good at teaching, but we have to give her time to develop her teaching.

While some of the students who were interviewed reported being comfortable, under certain circumstances, with questioning the teacher in class, no similar availing instances were apparent in their relationships with their parents. Instead, what emerged was the kind of qualified response, reported earlier, that Sirichai offered: from tradition, Thai students would not question their parents, although this was acceptable, according to Sirichai, in other cultural contexts.

In less intimate scenarios, with regard to the law and broader societal authority, more availing beliefs re-emerged, such as the positivist separation of law from morality inherent in the response by Tanawat:

> Aimee: When it comes to the law do you think that people should always obey the law? Like government law, national law?
>
> Tanawat: No.
>
> Aimee: Can you explain why not?
>
> Tanawat: Because some... some... situations that are our emotion, about what you feel about that situation, it is wrong according to the law only because... sometimes you feel that it's not bad but the law says bad.

Such instances speak not only to a belief in the fallibility of authority as the source of knowledge, but also to the vulnerability of the code, as a body of knowledge, to reproach and criticism.

In terms of related, more availing beliefs as to this dimension, what also emerged were views of students themselves as autonomous learners or, at least, active participants in the learning process. Knowledge was not always imparted from "on high," but also came from independent inquiry, and successful students were, in some cases, viewed as those who were prepared to develop knowledge outside of the classroom.

Simple knowledge. This was the final belief dimension to be yielded by the PCA of the EBI. The component that was yielded by the PCA of the EBI was consistent with Schommer-Aikins's original dimension by this name, although it also absorbed an item from one of the discarded original dimensions, *quick learning*. *Quick learning*, arguably, is conceptually consistent with *simple knowledge* (see 4.2.2); if knowledge is simple, one may assume that its acquisition would be relatively rapid. The dimension was defined as a continuum from "knowledge is compartmentalised to knowledge is highly integrated and interwoven" (Schommer), and again, more availing and less availing instances were identified from the interview data.

In what may be regarded as adducing less availing beliefs to knowledge, the students commonly expressed opinions as to the instrumental nature of knowledge. This view of knowledge reified as an instrument is akin to the "basket of facts" approach in that it recalls the related metaphor of a box of tools that are to be used in specific contexts. In fairness, this is a view that is sponsored by the shift to economic utilitarianism that has become common in tertiary education; students are encouraged to consider the transferability of knowledge to the workplace, and the classical Western ideal knowledge for its own sake is frequently eschewed (see Green, 2013).

Thus, while students interviewed here were tolerant of theory, they were so only to the extent that this theory could be applied to certain contexts. In expressing his view of the position of theory in learning, Sirichai, for example, opined that "[learning] should be hands on, rather than... I mean, teaching [of theory] is necessary, but hands on is required, so I think it should be 40 percent teaching and 60 percent hands-on." Bao-Zhi, who had expressed more availing beliefs in relation to the *certain*, *authoritative knowledge* dimension, concurred with this view, expressing, in his more articulate manner, a certain boredom in being subjected mostly to theory:

> Aimee: Why would you feel bored?
>
> Bao-Zhi: Well, actually like, okay, for someone like me, I would be more excited to actually know how these theories can be used. So, usually the facts, will, you know, show us like how they... yeah, how the real action of these theories... uh... instead of like just... showing us... how things work...well usually that's quite difficult for me.

The views expressed by Sirichai and Bao-Zhi were reflected, to greater or lesser degree, in the comments of most of the interviewees who were queried as to their attitudes to the teaching of theory in the classroom. Of course, these beliefs, while tending towards the less-availing side of the continuum, were not totally divorced from the more availing view that knowledge, being fluid and flexible in nature, might be abstracted from certain contexts, and that it might be applied across various domains. However, such a view, which would invoke high-road transfer, was not immediately apparent in any of the responses.

Thus, while the majority views were located (as reflected by the EBI scores) somewhere in the centre of the continuum, an unequivocally non-availing opinion as to the difference between fact and theory emerged on one occasion. Aimee enquired of Tanawat as to what his view was on the difference between facts and theory. Tanawat replied that "theory is... something you make up, and a fact is the truth." This sentiment was repeated by Tanawat:

> Aimee: Okay, so if we say that... do you like teachers who present several competitive theories and let their students decide what's best?
>
> Tanawat: I think presenting facts is more... reasonable, because it really happened. It's not just theories.

The sentiment is remarkable in that it indicates a belief that theory is fantastical and unrelated to reality or truth; not a view that is compatible with the kind of abstraction that Perkins and Salomon (1988), for example, see as predicating high-road transfer. Further in the conversation, Tanawat expresses a clear preference for simple knowledge:

> Aimee: Do you agree that too many theories just complicate things?

Tanawat: Yes. [Both laugh].

Aimee: Can you explain...? You already did explain a little on this...

Tanawat: As I said about many theories at the same time, it make people confused. What... What is come together, why it has to come together, or anything... Why there have to be this theory or why... why... they can be used to apply... and everything will mixed up in your head.

As was evident in the previous section concerning *certain, authoritative knowledge*, a recurring theme throughout these interviews was the ambiguity of beliefs invoked by students' awareness of cultural context, particularly with regard to how the students were *supposed* to perform, or what they were *supposed* to believe because of their membership of a certain cultural group:

Karen: Okay. Do you like it in a classroom where the teacher... gives a theory, but not necessarily the facts? Do you like to explore theories in the classroom... without really the facts?

Werawat: I think... I prefer facts more than theories. For me, I think I have a kind of Thai student mindset...

This theme, arising from cultural comparisons and awareness of expected or—reminiscent of Pea's (1989) conceptualisation of "situatedness"—appropriate beliefs or behaviour, is one that will be explored in a subsection below.

In contrast to the clearly unavailing beliefs that have been illustrated above, some of the students espoused much more availing beliefs in relation to the complexity of knowledge. While some students expressed a preference for simple, uncomplicated learning, others, such as Chatchai, acknowledged that knowledge was complex at times, and learning difficult and long-term:

Karen: Is it okay for you to struggle for an answer?

Chatchai: Yes.

Karen: So you don't have to have the answer right now?

Chatchai: Yes, because, I mean, talking about facts, you need to do some research, it's not like you read the news, only one page and then can answer everything. Sometimes is read... read the news only one place, cannot answer the whole answer, you need to compare whether the... the news is true or not, you need to... find more information.

Tawatchai, too, reports being comfortable with theoretical knowledge:

> Karen: how do you feel in a class where there's a lot of theory being... umm...looked at? Are you comfortable with theory, or do you have to have hard facts all the time?
>
> Tawatchai: Mmm... I am okay with theory, I think.
>
> Karen: Can you think where it's been like that, where there's been a lot of theories?
>
> Tawatchai: Yeah...in the Microeconomics.
>
> Karen: Tell me about that.

Tawatchai at this point proceeds to list several economics theories and give some brief explanations. The interview continues:

> Karen: And you're okay with that kind of learning?
>
> Tawatchai: Yeah, I'm okay with that.

Similarly, Bao-Zhi, again consistently with his low score for this dimension of the EBI, expresses a sense of enjoyment—"fun"—in exploring conflicting and complex concepts. First, he asserts that the boundlessness of knowledge, then he distinguishes between different types of knowledge:

> Bao-Zhi: I believe that knowledge is limitless. Although I don't consider...okay, I don't think information is knowledge.
>
> Aimee: Okay, explain that?
>
> Bao-Zhi: So okay. Information let's say it's just like facts. We just keep on knowing a lot of facts it doesn't mean that we understand... like the way how it is supposed to work and even whether... this information is useful or worthy of understanding or not and still it depends on our application. Are we going to apply it to anything then? It's just information.
>
> Aimee: What about knowledge? What is knowledge then?
>
> Bao-Zhi: Knowledge, I would say, it's like....er... let's say it's like our understanding on ...umm, let's say the process, on it's application, on when do we need to know more and when we need to... be satisfied... with what we know. Let's say that...uhhh...knowledge is more...is more...okay to me it's more of like... it's like...I'm trying to use more words...

Bao-Zhi, after pausing for thought, begins to elaborate on the difference between the folklore of certain "indigenous tribes," and the information that is needed to perform in a modern context, such as the stock market.

In his conceptualisation of knowledge, he seems to distinguish fact from understanding, information from wisdom, thus displaying what could be considered a highly availing system of beliefs that is antithetical to the idea of "simple knowledge."

In this dimension, thus, some relatively wide variation on the *simple knowledge* continuum was evident. However, while some students, such as Tanawat revealed a greater number of instances of less-availing beliefs, and those such as Bao-Zhi displayed more-availing beliefs, these were by no means consistent within these students' interviews. The examples here, as in the other EBI dimensions presented in this discussion, are not intended to present students such as Bao-Zhi as more "sophisticated" or Tanawat as "less"; they are intended to illustrate, rather, the nature of the beliefs themselves as expressed by these particular students in this particular cultural context.

Other metacognitive factors. The analysis of the semi-structured interview data was guided not only by the deductive themes derived from the a priori framework, but also attentive to inductive themes that could not be reasonably subsumed by the deductive ones. Thus, while the dimensions of *innate ability, certain authoritative knowledge* and *simple knowledge* were derived from the PCA of the EBI, a related, but independent theme that emerged from the initial coding of the interview data was that of metacognitive factors that could not be considered *beliefs*.

The relationship between beliefs and metacognition has been elaborated upon earlier in developing the conceptual framework for this study (see 2.3.3.): Firstly, epistemic beliefs, in particular, can be considered to have metacognitive dimensions; secondly, a number of studies have established a strong association between epistemic beliefs and learning outcomes; and finally, transfer of learning—particularly high-road learning—is predicated on metacognitive activities on the part of the learner, such as reflection and mindful abstraction of principles. Greater evidence of metacognitive behaviours on the part of a learner can, therefore, be considered availing of learning transfer.

Some of the interviewees evinced this type of availing metacognition, which, in these intances, is indicated by a learner's self-awareness of the learning process and learning roles. At times, a certain degree of metacognition was indicated by references by the students to their own characteristics as learners. Chatchai, for example, when asked by Karen as to the role of students answering questions in class, admitted to a preference to not answering himself "because I mean I'm a... I'm a shy person. I don't like to answer in the class, so I just watch them answer," or, when pressed, giving very short answers "because I feel so shy... I think I might be wrong or something." Tawatchai expressed a similar awareness of himself as a shy person. Werawat, on the other hand, reported that if "I really have to... you know, categorise myself, I think I will be more into like, the talking type." He also, in response to Karen's questions as to his attitude to students playing an active role in the classroom, admits that he is "just lazy."

Such self-awareness, while not fully encompassing the kind of active higher order thinking that constitutes the ideal—for example, monitoring, organising and revising—is nevertheless indicative of a learner who is willing to reflect.

In other, rare instances, interviewees displayed an awareness of the development as learners, often from what could be considered less availing beliefs to more. Bao-Zhi, as is apparent throughout this section, is again representative of this understanding and awareness of his development as a learner. In response to Aimee's questions about the types of classroom activities he experienced in his secondary school, he gives some examples of participatory learning experiences. Aimee then enquires as to his feelings about being involved in these activities, to which he responds:

> I loved that actually. Actually at the time... hmm... I did not feel that way, actually; at first I felt really nervous, well, because none of the other teachers actually encouraged students to do activities as much. So yeah, at first I think I have to admit, at first I actually not like it at first but then I started to like it after I feeled it myself improve... in the process.

Also revelatory of this level of self-awareness of his development as a learner is this passage, in which he reports the development of his beliefs about knowledge:

> Aimee: Do you agree that too many theories complicate things?
>
> Bao-Zhi: [Short pause] In a way, yes. But then... umm... how shall I put this...? Uh.. well...I came to realise that it's actually necessary to know more theories in order to... work better, I mean understand things better. Because like, you know, the facts is amazing, is cool,

but then, in the end, you need to understand the theories in order to understand how they actually works.

Relative beliefs. Other than non-belief-orientated metacognition, an additional inductive theme was yielded by the interview data. This theme was derived from the ambiguity of some of the interviewed students that revealed itself in their answers to the questions probing the belief dimensions.

Despite this ambiguity already being referred to in the responses of two of the students as to the EBI beliefs dimensions, it emerged strongly enough throughout the interviews to merit independent attention here; it is furthermore, potentially revealing of the belief systems of the students in the particular cultural and institutional context of this study. The theme was characterised by an awareness of the cultural plurality of learning contexts and behaviours.

One invocation of this theme was through an awareness of the supposed characteristics of Thai students (implicitly in relation to students from other cultures. Werawat, as already mentioned in the subsection "Certain, authoritative beliefs," for example, when questioned by Aimee as to his preferences in relation to "fact" or "theory" expressed his preference for "fact" based on having a "Thai mind-set." Sirichai, also as mentioned earlier, mentioned that his family had "a tradition that those who have higher authorities are always right." His elaboration here, to his American interviewer, can be taken as an awareness that such a tradition is culturally based and might not apply in other contexts. This awareness is in distinction to the classic "fish-in-water" metaphor commonly employed in considerations of national culture (e.g., Hammerich & Lewis, 2013). A fish is so inured to the water it swims in that it is no conscious knowledge of the medium—so it is with people and the culture into which they are born. Students such as Werawat, however, have been sensitised to a consideration of their own culture by exposure to that of others.

There were other instances of more explicit acknowledgement of cultural differences. Often, these contextual comparisons will relate directly to the learning context across the different cultures to which the students have been exposed during their secondary school careers. Chatchai, in considering the learning environment in New Zealand to that in

Thailand, for example, makes a comparison between the learners in the two cultures:

> Just, I mean... teenager in there [in classrooms in New Zealand]... is very good when they are studying. But when we go to the class, we talk, talk, talk and talk when the teacher starts to talk, they will all shut up and... quiet and concentrate... concentrate on their study... so that made me... study better, but it's not like in Thailand, like somebody who's still talking when the teacher is talking...

Kanokwan makes similar comparisons when she raises differences between her experiences as an exchange student in the US and those in Thai schools. She cites some superficial differences, such as the smaller (and thus more manageable) class size in the US, and the relative standards—"you have to do everything [in the US] to like perfection." As other interviewees did, she also espoused a belief that education elsewhere, as in the US or New Zealand, was "way better," and the teachers there more effective. In a reflection of the vestiges of the rote-learning system in Thailand, Kanokwan cites an example of a teacher in Thailand who "just sat there" while requiring Kanokwan, as the "head student" of the class, to copy text from the textbook to the board, so that the other students in their turn could "copy them down, and that's it." Similarly to Chatchai, Kanokwan compared the students in the US to those in Thailand, before returning to reflect briefly on the teachers:

> Everybody, like, really paid attention to the class and the teachers is, like, put a lot of effort into teaching, unlike the schools that I'd been before. So like... so it was a huge difference, yeah.

Kanokwan provides this as a reason, in response to Aimee, for her changing views about learning. From, this, one may conclude that changes in educational context across national cultures is, at least, a transformative experience for some students.

Before her exchange experience in the US, Kanokwan had attended two other secondary schools, one being a Thai public school, and the other an international school in Thailand. In a view endorsing an assumption in this study, she stated that the international school that she had attended in Thailand was "kinda like in America."

The ambiguity of beliefs and awareness of different contexts did not extend solely to comparisons of national culture or institutional settings, however. Three of the student interviewed expressed beliefs that certain subjects demanded certain types of knowledge. Concerning the certainty of knowledge, for example, Karen questions Sudarat as to her feelings about not being provided with a "right answer":

> Like, if the common sense... like, if the question is about Math... okay, we have to answer the exactly answer to the teacher, but if the... question is about...like, "What do you think, blah, blah, blah, blah?" Okay, it is my opinion, so I can answer in many ways: no right or wrong.

Such a view is reflective of the subject-related conceptualisation of domain-specific and domain-general beliefs about knowledge. A possibility exists that relativistic views about cultural setting might be similarly considered. This view as to culture-related domain-specificity and the adaptability of learners to varying cultural contexts will be discussed in the next section.

Implications for the research question. The non-parametric Spearman correlation and the subsequent regression model indicated a significant, small-to-medium negative relationship between the summed EBI and MALT scores. This suggested that lower scores (more-availing) on the EBI were related to, and predicted, higher scores (more transfer) in the MALT; alternatively put, more-availing beliefs were associated with higher perceptions of transfer of learning from the EC courses to the disciplines, and less-availing beliefs with lower perceptions of transfer.

The data from the semi-structured interviews were illustrative of the nature of the beliefs themselves; in this, the interviewees expressed a variety of beliefs, both more-availing and less-aviling, within the deductive themes derived from the EBI components. Emerging inductively from the interview data, general metacognition was also evident, as was a theme that related to ambivalent beliefs and an awareness of cultural context.

The findings as to the relationship between students' beliefs about knowledge and learning and the transfer of learning, in addition to the nature of these beliefs in this study context, will be explored more fully in the final chapter.

4.4.3. Research Question 3: What is the nature of the relationship between students' beliefs about knowledge and learning and their secondary school background ("culture")?

Questionnaire. The most appropriate manner of examining this question statistically was through one-way ANOVA, again deeming the composite scores from the EBI (EBISUM) to be continuous variables and thus amenable to parametric testing.

Because this particular enquiry was intended to lead ultimately to an examination of relationships between the three sets of variables, the EBI, the MALT and students' high school backgrounds, cases that had been excluded in both the initial components analysis of the EBI and of the MALT, and for the linear regression analysis of the composite EBI and MALT scores, were excluded for this particular analysis (N = 164). Of these, two respondents had failed to report a value for "high school last attended," and were therefore excluded from analysis, resulting in an N of 162. A case with a missing value in the EBI (Case no. 126, for EBI 13) was also excluded listwise from the analysis.

For one-way ANOVA, it was necessary to test three assumptions: firstly, that no outliers existed in the data; secondly that the data were approximately normally distributed, and thirdly that there was homogeneity of variance between the relevant variables. Box plots were generated in order to examine the first of these assumptions; these revealed two outliers (more than one box-length distant from the edge of their respective boxes) in two groups of the independent variable, "school in North America, Europe, Australia or New Zealand," (Case no. 23) and "bilingual school in Thailand," (Case no. 44). As these were not extreme outliers (no more than three box-lengths away from the edge of the box), and as these were relatively small subsamples (n = 24; n = 23, respectively). However, because the one-way ANOVA might not be the most powerful or robust test in this situation—it might not detect a true difference in the means, as outliers reduce the chance of rejecting the null-hypothesis (Wilcox, 2012)—a Kruskal-Wallis non-parametric test would also be conducted for the sake of comparison.

For this, and all related analyses, both parametric and non-parametric tests were employed: because the presence of outliers, for example, might have influenced parametric results, a significant result for the corresponding non-parametric test may have provide justification to re-administer the parametric test after the removal of potentially high-leverage outliers (for further justification for using both parametric and non-parametric tests, see Section 3.8.1).

Table 14

Measures of Central Tendencies for Analyses of Variance between Cultural Factors (Secondary School Background and Nationality), and EBI and MALT Scores

Cultural Factor	EBI			MALT		
	M	SD	Mdn	M	SD	Mdn
Type of secondary school last attended (N = 162)						
State/ government school in Thailand (n = 42)	-.13	1.90	.11	-.02	.91	-.08
Bilingual school in Thailand (n = 23)	-.14	1.90	-.38	.25	1.10	.19
International School in Thailand (n = 55)	-.17	1.73	.20	-.21	1.24	.09
School in Asia other than Thailand (n = 18)	-.04	1.77	-.29	.08	1.07	.18
School in North America, Europe, Australia or New Zealand (n = 24)	-.13	1.68	-.02	.47	1.11	.27
Primary nationality of student (N = 164)						
Thai, Malaysian, Laotian or other Southeast Asian (n=147)	.06	1.74	.19	.13	.99	.17
Chinese, Japanese, Korean or other East Asian (n = 6)	-.46	1.25	-.44	-1.13	2.03	-2.03
Indian, Pakistani, other subcontinental Asian, or Middle Eastern (n = 7)	-.72	1.82	-.75	-.54	.98	-.48
European, North American, Australian, New Zealand 9 (n=4)	-1.02	3.09	-.67	1.00	1.84	-.21

Note. EBI = Epistemic Belief Inventory, MALT = Measure of Academic Literacy Transfer, M = mean, SD = standard deviation, Mdn = median. Confidence level for the mean = 95%. Figure after "/", as in "n = 55/ 56," indicates subpopulation for MALT. Results are not statistically significant (p>.05)

In this particular analysis, data were approximately normally distributed, as assessed by visual inspection of Q-Q plots, and as confirmed by Shapiro-Wilk values, which were non-significant for each of group of the independent variable, "state/ government school in Thailand", "bilingual school in Thailand", "international school in Thailand", "school in Asia other than Thailand", "school in North America, Europe, Australia or New Zealand" ($p > .05$). None of the respondents had selected the final category, "other," so this group was eliminated from further analysis.

These prior assumptions having been met, the one-way ANOVA was processed. The Levene statistic generated in this process was non-significant ($p > .05$), indicating that the further assumption of homogeneity of variance had not been violated.

Although the output indicated a difference in means among the groups (see Table 14), the result of indicated that the difference was not statistically significant, $F(4,157) = .24, p = .92$.

Because of the presence of outliers, and because, moreover, it is an appropriate procedure when the number of cases for each group of the independent variable are unequal (Kraska-Miller, 2014), the Kruskal-Wallis test was then conducted for the sake of comparison. The Kruskal-Wallis test, similarly to the one-way ANOVA, indicated that differences in the distributions among the groups were not statistically significant, $\chi^2(4) = .43, p = .98$

Because neither test for an association between students' secondary school background and their personal epistemology as measured by the EBI, produced a statistically significant result, the enquiry was extended, while remaining within the scope of cultural background, to search for a significant association between the students' nationalities and their personal epistemology.

Extension a): Investigating the relationship between students' primary nationalities and their personal epistemology. This analysis ($N = 164$) proceeded in the same manner as the preceding series of tests: assumptions were tested, a one-way ANOVA run, and the Kruskal-Wallis test administered for the sake of comparison and consistency. One outlier (case no. 44) was detected in the box plot for the group "Thai, Malaysian, Laotian, or other Southeast Asian, and two in "Chinese, Japanese, Korean or other East Asian". As these were not extreme outliers (no more than three box-lengths from the edge of the box), they were retained in the ensuing one-way ANOVA. The distributions of data were again approximately normally distributed, as assessed by visual inspection of Q-Q plots, and as confirmed by Shapiro-Wilk values, which were non-significant for each of group of the independent variable ($p > .05$). Levine's test (as produced by the one-way ANOVA procedure) revealed a non-significant result, ($p = .18$), indicating that the further assumption of homogeneity of variance had not been violated.

Although the output again indicated a difference in means among the groups, as indicated by Table 14, this difference was not statistically significant, $F(3,160) = 1.19, p = .31$.

While the medians across each of the national groups were somewhat different, the Kruskal-Wallis test, like the parametric one-way ANOVA, indicated that differences in the distributions were not statistically significant, $\chi^2(3) = 2.21, p = .53$.

As the investigation thus far had not revealed significant associations between either students' high school backgrounds or their primary nationalities and their EBI scores, it was decided to further investigate a direct relationship between both of these variables and the MALT.

Extension b): Investigating the relationship between students' secondary school backgrounds and the MALT. For the first analysis, that of high school background and the MALT, a visual inspection of the box plots indicated one extreme outlier (case no. 23). Once the extreme case had been eliminated from further analysis, a number of groups displayed non-extreme outliers: "State/ government school in Thailand" (case no. 78); "International School in Thailand" (cases no. 47 and 61); and "school in North America, Europe, Australia, or New Zealand" (cases no. 36, 58 and 84). Visual inspection of Q-Q plots and Shapiro-Wilk statistics for each group revealed adequate normality with a single exception, "International School in Thailand." In general, however, the assumptions were deemed to have been adequately met in order to run the one-way ANOVA, with the added safeguard, for comparison, of the Kruskal-Wallis test as in previous instances. Data transformation was not considered feasible in terms of the bivariate data.

The Levene statistic generated in the course of the one-way ANOVA indicated that there was no significant homogeneity of variances. Once again, however, the differences in the means of the groups for "High School Type" were statistically non-significant, $F(4,157) = 1.81$, $p = .13$. The Kruskal-Wallis test, similarly, indicated a non-significant result, $\chi^2(4) = 5.28$, $p = .26$.

Extension c): Investigating the relationship between students' primary nationalities and the MALT. The analysis then proceeded in a similar manner to an investigation of the relationship between students' nationalities and their mean scores on the MALT. The box plots for each group identified a single extreme outlier (case no. 62), which was removed prior to further analysis, which then revealed one group, "Thai, Malaysian, Laotian or other southeast Asian," with four non-extreme outliers (Cases no. 1, 59, 78 and 84). An inspection of Q-Q plots, corroborated by the Shapiro-Wilk statistic, revealed adequate normality for all but one group, "European, North American, Australia, New Zealand," which showed borderline significance ($p = 0.4$) for non-normality. (See Table 14, previously, for n for each of the groups reported).

The Levene test run in conjunction with the one-way ANOVA in this particular analysis was significant ($p = 0.003$), indicating a violation of the assumption of homogeneity of variances. Although the standard one-way ANOVA indicated statistically significant differences in the means ($F(3,160) = 4.73$, $p < .01$), the violation of the assumption of homogeneity of variances necessitated the interpretation of a robust test, Welch's ANOVA, which had been run concurrently with the standard one-way ANOVA. Welch's ANOVA indicated that the group means were not significantly different, $F(3,7.390) = 1.316$, $p = .22$. The Kruskal-Wallis test corroborated the statistical non-significance of the difference between the means, $\chi^2(3) = 6.46$, $p = .09$.

Extension d): Redefining "secondary school background" and "primary nationality." As the possibility existed that the failure of the initial tests to detect a significant relationship between students' beliefs and their culture was a result of a mis-categorisation of the groups comprising "secondary school background" and "primary nationality," the investigation proceeded to tests that examined simpler binary categories that corresponded to the simpler Asian-Western divide that exists in much of the literature (see, for example, Nisbett, 2004). For "secondary school background," this entailed condensing the groups *state/ government school in Thailand*, bilingual *school in Thailand*, *international School in Thailand*, and *school in Asia other than Thailand (n = 18)* into a single variable, "Asian schools," with the remaining group, *school in North America, Europe, Australia or New Zealand* constituting the second group, "Western schools."

Similarly, for "primary nationality," the groups *Thai, Malaysian, Laotian or other Southeast Asian, Chinese, Japanese, Korean or other East Asian*, and *Indian, Pakistani, other subcontinental Asian, or Middle Eastern* were designated "Asian," while "Western was assigned to *European, North American, Australian, New Zealand*.

As each independent variable now comprised two groups, independent-samples *t*-tests (rather than the previous ANOVA) were run in order to investigate the relationship between these variables and the summed scores for, respectively, the EBI and the MALT. In addition, or, in some cases, as an alternative (where dictated by non-normality or insufficient sub-sample size, for example), the non-parametric Mann-Whitney test was administered for the sake of both confirmation and of consistency with previous procedures.

The relationship between "secondary school background" and the EBI. Tests for assumptions in this case revealed that no extreme outliers existed for either group, although a non-extreme outliers was present in the group *Asian schools* (case no. 44) and *Western schools* (case no. 23). As in previous analyses, these were retained. No significant non-normality was detected either by a visual inspection of the Q-Q plots or by the Shapiro-Wilk test (*Asian schools, p* = .16; *Western schools, p* = .12). There was homogeneity of variances in the values for the groups, as assessed by Levene's test (p = .38). The independent samples *t*-test, however, revealed that the differences in the means (see Table 15) between these to groups in their association to the EBI was non-significant (p = .75)

The Mann-Whitney test also produced non-significant results (p=.90; see Table 16).

Table 15
Results of t-tests and Descriptive Statistics for EBI and MALT Scores by Revised Secondary School Background

	Secondary School Background						95% CI for Mean Difference		
	Asian Schools			Western Schools					
	M	SD	n	M	SD	n		t	df
EBI	.01	1.80	140	.13	1.68	24	.65, .90	.32	162
MALT	.02	1.04	140	.47	1.11	23	.95, .01	2.00*	161

Note. CI = confidence interval, EBI = Epistemic Belief Inventory, MALT = Measure of Academic Literacy Transfer, M = mean, n = subsample size, SD = standard deviation * = results (two-tailed) are statistically significant ($p < .05$).

Table 16
Results of Mann-Whitney U Tests and Descriptive Statistics for EBI and MALT Scores by Revised Secondary School Background

	N	Mdn		U	z
		Secondary School Background			
		Asian Schools (n = 140)	Western Schools (n = 24)		
EBI	164	.01	-.02	1,651	-.14
MALT	165	.05	.25	2,004.5	1.44

Note. EBI = Epistemic Beliefs Inventory, MALT = Measure of Academic Literacy Transfer, Mdn = median, N = total sample, U = Mann-Whitney U statistic, z = standardised test statistic. Results are not statistically significant ($p > .05$).

The relationship between secondary school background and the MALT. Extreme outliers (no. 62 for *Asian schools*; no. 23 for *Western schools*) were removed, resulting in a normal distribution as assessed by visual inspection of the Q-Q plots and confirmed by the Shapiro-Wilk tests (*Asian schools*, $p = .14$; *Western schools*, $p = .26$). The assumption of equality of variances was also met, as assessed by Levene's test ($p = .1$). The *t*-test in this instance revealed that the differences in the means (see Table 15) were significant ($p = .04$): the mean summed MALT score for respondents who had attended Asian schools was lower than that of those who had attended Western schools.

Although the median of the summed scores for the MALT was also lower for Asian schools than that for Western schools (see Table 16), the Mann-Whitney test for the same total sample returned non-significant results ($p = .08$).

The relationship between nationality and (i) the EBI, and (ii) the MALT. As the sample size for the group *Western* was insufficient (n=4) for meaningful assumption testing in examining the association between the revised nationality scores and both the EBI and the MALT, only the non-parametric Mann-Whitney test was employed in examining these relationships.

Table 17

Results of Mann-Whitney U Tests and Descriptive Statistics for EBI and MALT Scores by Revised Nationality

	N	Mdn		U	z
		Primary Nationality			
		Asian (n = 160)	Western (n = 4)		
EBI	164	.01	-.67	249	-.76
MALT	165	.11	-.21	205	-1.24

Note. EBI = Epistemic Beliefs Inventory, MALT = Measure of Academic Literacy Transfer, Mdn = median, N = total sample, U = Mann-Whitney U statistic, z = standardised test statistic. Results are not statistically significant ($p > .05$).

Because of the disparity between the subgroups in terms of sample size, it was difficult to compare distributions; moreover, the test returned non-significant results for both the EBI ($p = .45$) and the MALT ($p = .22$) (see Table 17).

Mediated regression model. Although previous analysis had shown a statistically significant relationship between the composite EBI score and the composite MALT score, it appeared from subsequent analysis that there was no such relationship between either students' secondary school backgrounds or their primary nationalities and either the EBI or the MALT. As such, initial plans to run a mediated regression model to investigate the extent to which students' personal epistemologies mediated the relationship between their background cultures and the MALT were deemed unfeasible at this stage and, therefore, abandoned.

Student voices. As with the subsection that, through the questionnaire data, explored the association between students' perceptions of transfer of learning and their beliefs concerning knowledge and learning, the analysis of the data from the semi-structured interviews in this subsection did not reveal any conclusive relationship between these beliefs and their secondary school backgrounds.

In a larger sample, generating a coding matrix in NVivo that compared coded references across the secondary school attributes of the interviewees to availing and non-availing beliefs within the themes might be revealing. However, in this case, the number of interviewees was small, with only one to two representatives to each of the high school groups.

In addition, while the questionnaire had identified respondents according to the last secondary school attended, the students selected for the interviews revealed that, in many cases, their secondary school careers had not been homogeneous. While two of the students, Bao-Zhi and Werawat, had been each been in a single school for the entire five years of their secondary education, the six other students had each had a varied high school experience, moving within Thailand from, for example, a Thai government school to an international school (each entailing different cultural values), as was the case for Kanokwan); or even internationally, as for Chatchai, who had begun his secondary education in Thailand and then transferred to India before spending the final secondary years in New Zealand. In gaining this varied and multicultural experience, the students were arguably typical of many of the students who enter international education. Students who remain in a local Thai public school for the entire duration of their secondary school career are more likely to attend the regular Thai programmes at local universities than they are to enrol in an international college such as MUIC.

As reported, then, the secondary school backgrounds of the students did not conform to the ideal assumptions underlying the research question, which aimed to investigate the association between students' secondary school backgrounds and their beliefs about knowledge and learning. Nevertheless, similarly to previous section concerning the relationship between students' beliefs about knowledge and learning and their perceptions of transfer of learning, the students' responses in the interviews provided insights into the nature of their cultural backgrounds and the values and beliefs that were informed by these backgrounds.

"They will develop different beliefs for a different purpose."
The contextual comparisons and ambiguities in the subsection exploring students' beliefs were as prominent in the interviews as the deductive themes derived from the EBI—*innate ability*, *certain*, *authoritative knowledge*, and *simple knowledge*. In contrast to the development of these themes, the inductive derivation of the theme relating to cultural relativity was guided by Spradley's (Spradley, 1977) advice that inductive cultural themes could be yielded by evidence of social conflict and cultural contradictions, indications of the manner in which participants negotiated social relationships and status differences, and participants' approaches to problem-solving (see Section 3.8.1).

Evidence yielding culture-related themes has already been recorded in the subsection relating to students' beliefs. It included instances of cultural awareness (at least of purported national characteristics), as in Werawat's supposition about a "Thai mind-set" in relation to his preference for facts over theory, and reflections on apparent distinctions between cultural context, as in Chatchai's implied comparison of students from New Zealand and Thailand and Kanokwan's appraisal of the US high school she had attended as an exchange students and the

Thai public school she had attended earlier in her secondary school career. Supplemental to cultural awareness and comparisons of different cultural contexts was the consciousness of the application of different kinds of knowledge to different subject settings. An example of this was Sudarat's assertion that, in having supplying a single correct answer, Mathematics was different from subjects in which an opinion was required.

Instances of cultural ambivalence were particularly evident in the students' attitudes to authority. This applied to teachers, with some students, notably Kanokwan making explicit comparisons between the manner of Western teachers and their Thai counterparts in responding to challenges to their authority from the students. Kanokwan suggests that while Western teachers accept and even encourage these challenges, this is "unlike the Thai teachers, they... they think they're the one who know the most so 'You guys have to... believe me,' something like that."

This ambivalence towards the authority of teachers was extended to that of parents. Other than Werawat's acknowledgment of the "tradition" in Thailand of not questioning one's parents, Kanokwan acknowledges the role of situational context:

> Aimee: Do you think it's okay for children to stand up to their parents at any time?
>
> Kanokwan: In Thailand, no.

In Kanokwan's response is an implicit acknowledgement that certain norms are culturally relative and by no means universal.

On a more metaphysical level, Bao-Zhi expresses an awareness of the relativity of beliefs themselves when questioned by Aimee as to whether absolute moral truths apply universally:

> No, I don't think that because er... let's say it's like beliefs in religions. These beliefs involve, er, these beliefs would form er... okay all these beliefs were developed from like different kinds of environments. One belief that can become useful here doesn't necessarily become useful... yeah... on the other side. Basically, what people believe do not... match all of the time, especially because they will develop different beliefs for a different purpose.

Bao-Zhi's response is reproduced here not only because it is illustrative of students' awareness of cultural relativity, but also because it resonates with the conceptual framework of this study. Beliefs, in short, are developed in particular contexts for particular purposes.

One may speculate as to how this cultural relativity or ambivalence may be related to existing models of beliefs; a further reflection by Bao-Zhi in relation to absolute truth is illuminating in this respect:

> There's this quote from my father. He says, like, don't forget where you came from. So, okay, I define this message as like …well… okay… I think I my bloodline came from most of Taiwanese, but I was raised in Thailand, so I also like adopt these Thai beliefs. So, like, his message is…like…just don't forget like … the country I came from. Let's just say that he thought I was the kind of person who… is responsible to a certain extent in certain stuff and.. well he believed in good side in me. So he… that's why he said that, so I keep like what's good of me and try to learn from others while uh…yeah.. keeping certain good things the same.

Bao-Zhi seems to reflect a willingness to adapt to various cultural contexts, but, to retain, simultaneously a sense of his "home" culture. This view may be analogous to models of domain-specificity and -generality that have been explored in relation to subject domains in the introductory material of this study.

The theme of contextual ambivalence and relativistic cultural awareness, therefore, demands some independent attention in considering the relationship between students' backgrounds and their beliefs.

Implications for the research. The analysis of the data from the EBI and the demographic section of the questionnaire did not support a relationship between students' beliefs about knowledge and learning and their secondary school backgrounds. A subsequent extension of this investigation into associations between other aspects of students' cultural backgrounds, such as nationality, similarly did not yield a significant relationship. However, the failure of this particular study to detect such a relationship does not necessarily signify that this relationship does not exist. One might reflect, for example, that many students in international schools do not have the homogeneous secondary school backgrounds assumed in the design of this study.

One might further reflect on the cultural ambivalence and relativity that emerged as a theme from the semi-structured interviews, and the manner in which this may relate to any failure to detect a significant relationship. This consideration, among others related to the conceptualisation and "measurement" of culture, is continued in the final chapter.

Chapter 5
Discussion and Recommendations

This chapter elaborates on the findings of the research in the context of the research framework. It considers the limitations of the investigation before deriving a conclusion from the findings and their relationship to the conceptual development of the study. The implications for theory and practice are considered, and recommendations for further research made.

5.1. Discussion

The aim of this section is to discuss further the findings of the research, particularly in terms of key concepts and theories that were explored in the introductory chapters. First, the discussion will consider the validation of the two instruments incorporated into the questionnaire, the EBI and the MALT. It will then elaborate on the key results that emerged from the application of the questionnaire to the research questions, as augmented by the data from the semi-structured interviews. It will also address the limitations of the research and the findings. Finally, the findings will be related to the conceptual framework of the research—the cultural matrix of social psychology.

5.1.1. The Validation of the Questionnaire

Analysis of the EBI. Prior to applying data from the EBI to the framework of this study, it was considered necessary to examine its validity in relation to the current data set. Not only was this desirable in enhancing the reliability of the findings, but it also accorded with the assumptions of the research framework that beliefs and culture are closely related.

In terms of the first concern, a number of methods, as reported in previous chapters, were used to enhance the reliability of the instrument. In sum, before the PCA and CFA were conducted, both the EBI and the

MALT, as components of the full questionnaire, were piloted by a group of 16 students who, in an interview that was conducted immediately after the first administration of the questionnaire, reported no impediments to understanding any of the items. In a further effort to enhance the construct validity of the instrument, each item appeared both in the original English and Thai translation. This translation had been subjected to professional translation and then independent back-translation by a bilingual Thai language lecturer at MUIC, with the results being corroborated by this lecturer and the researcher and potentially problematic items revised.

A month after the questionnaire had been administered to the group of 16 students, it was re-administered, and results compared by means of a *t*-test. The *t*-test revealed no significant differences between the two tests, thus establishing the stability of the questionnaire and its components.

Of greater interest in its relation to the research framework and its implications to the discussion that follows is the factorial analysis, both through PCA and CFA, which followed the full collection of data for this study. This analysis was considered crucial to the study for reasons provided by writers such as Fiske et al. (1998) from whom the framework of the study—the cultural matrix—is adopted, and Hofer, who is an established authority in the conceptual development of personal epistemology. These theorists argue for a culturally relative interpretation of psychology. Hofer (2008), in particular, noted that many of the seminal studies in psychology were conducted in the US, often at elite universities. It would be specious, Hofer argued, to apply these findings unquestioningly to different cultural contexts—the underlying assumptions of these findings needed to be questioned and considered in relation to these contexts. Fiske et al., being concerned with cultural psychology, made a similar argument relating to the field in general while Hofer proceeded to direct her attention more specifically to the relationship between culture and epistemic beliefs.

It is in accordance with these relativistic views of the relationship between culture and psychological constructs, in general, and beliefs about knowing and learning, in particular, that the five initially-hypothesised beliefs dimensions of Schommer-Aikins (Schommer, 1990, 1994)—*innate ability, simple knowledge, omniscient authority, certain knowledge, quick learning*—were not adopted at face value in the present study.

It was noted, moreover, that, beyond the validation of the EBI conducted by Schraw et al. (2002), the instrument seldom yielded a dimension-structure consistent with the initial hypothesis; this was true particularly in instances when the instrument has been used in cultural contexts other than that of the US. Analyses conducted in Turkey (Cam et al., 2012) and China (Chan, Ho, & Ku, 2011), for example, had generated three-dimension solutions.

While, for the sake of thorough investigation and comparison, the PCA in the present study was initially conducted retaining a five-component structure, this structure proved to be statistically and conceptually unsound in relation to the present data set. Instead, the subsequent iterations (using "oblimin" and corroborated by means of scree plots and parallel analysis) indicated, similarly to the studies cited above, a three-dimension solution, with 17 of the original 32 items retained. While these dimensions shared conceptual elements with those of Schommer-Aikins, certain items that were originally hypothesised under the separate dimensions *omniscient authority* and *quick learning* were subsumed by the remaining dimensions, which were labelled, in deference to the original, *innate ability*; *certain, authoritative knowledge*; and *simple knowledge*. The CFA confirmed a satisfactory model fit in relation to most indices consulted (x^2: p = .07; x^2/df = 1.2; RMSEA = 0.3; PCLOSE = 9.1; CFI = .90). In addition to the statistical fit, further support for the conceptual validity of the structure of the dimensions came from an exercise in which the trainee-interviewers were asked to group the 17 retained items of the EBI into coherent groups (as reported in a previous section). Although the trainees had no foreknowledge of the EBI or its underlying hypothesis and received no prompting from the researcher, they grouped the items in a way that was consistent with the dimensions that emerged from the PCA.

The first observation resulting from this structure as it emerged from the PCA and CFA is that beliefs about knowing and knowledge (*certain, authoritative knowledge* and *simple knowledge* are distinct from beliefs about learning (*innate ability*), which supports the argument of Hofer and Pintrich (1997) as to the distinction between epistemic beliefs and beliefs about learning (see also Wang, Zhang, Zhang, & Dadong, 2013).

Thus, from an exclusivist perspective of personal epistemology, the version of the EBI that emerged is not, despite its name, limited to measuring epistemic beliefs; it also measures beliefs about learning. This view is consistent with that of the study, which does not purport to examine epistemic beliefs in isolation, but rather as a complex that can be studied in relation to both culture and transfer of learning.

The second observation is that the factor structure differs from that of the original analysis of Schraw et al. (2002), which, in a US student population, extracted the original five dimensions as hypothesised by Schommer-Aikins (Schommer, 1999, 1994). The divergent factor structure in the present study is consistent with different factor structures yielded by analyses in different cultural contexts, such as those of Chan et al. (2011) and Cam et al. (2012). Thus, the factor analysis conducted here, when considered in relation to analyses conducted by other researchers in diverse cultural contexts, provided further support for the view that cultural context and beliefs were related.

Of particular interest in considering the dimensions that emerged, in this case, from the EBI, is that Schommer-Aitkin's dimension of *omniscient authority* failed to materialise as an independent dimension in this analysis—or, as far as is evident, in *any* instance of factorial analysis of the EBI conducted in Asian populations. This failure is despite the well-examined hierarchical nature of many Asian societies; as Chan et al. (2011) observe, researchers often interpret the results of studies of Chinese populations in relation to the Confucian tradition of conformity and respect for tradition. Wang et al. (2013), in their validation of the EBI, perceived as problematic the failure of an *omniscient authority* dimension to emerge from a Chinese population. As it is with Chinese culture, so it is with Thai: one would expect an independent *authority* dimension to emerge.

That an authority dimension does not emerge is a paradox, but one that may be explained by the integrated, unconscious nature of control and authority in many aspects of Asian culture. Evidence indicates that Asians "would be less susceptible to... illusions of control than Westerners, as well as less concerned about issues of control altogether" (Nisbett, 2004, p. 101). Developers of EBI, Schraw et al. (2002), seemingly contrived, from their own admission, to adduce the *omniscient authority* factor from EBI, despite this dimension not emerging from

Schommer-Aikins's own studies. This contrivance possibly reveals a Western preoccupation with issues of control that is not shared by Asian cultures. Control tends, perhaps, to be embedded as an essential property, rather than as a discrete function, of other factors in Asian cultures. The issue of authority as culturally relative will be discussed further, as an extended case in point, in the subsections below.

Analysis of the MALT. Similarly to the EBI, the MALT was subjected to measures that would establish its trustworthiness. Other than being employed in other studies independently of the EBI (Green, 2008, 2015), which indicated the validity and reliability of the scale as a whole (see Section 3.5.1.), the MALT was subjected to the pilot study reported in the section above, where it was a component of the questionnaire as a whole. As was the case for the EBI, the pre-test—test design of the pilot study assisted in establishing the stability of the MALT as a component of the questionnaire as a whole.

In the first study, using what came to be called the MALT (Green, 2008), none of the respondents reported any misunderstanding of the items; this was considered significant since the MALT items, unlike those of the EBI, had not been translated into Thai. The assumption was that the students who participated in the MALT, having had exposure to the discourse of the EC courses for a number of trimesters, would be familiar with the terms and types of knowledge presented in the instrument. In the more recent study (Green, 2015), analysis of the instrument produced a Cronbach's alpha coefficient of .84—an indicator of good reliability, although, admittedly, the small sample size of that study ($N = 39$) means that this result should be interpreted with caution.

In contrast to the EBI, which was an established instrument, the MALT was developed by the researcher in the context of the EC programme at MUIC. Although the types of knowledge that the EC programme aspires to develop in the students can be represented by WPA outcomes statement for first-year composition (reported in the introductory section), at the time of the study, these outcomes had not been explicitly applied to the programme. Moreover, as aspirational, they could not be assumed to inform the workday realities of classes in the programme. In consideration of this, the transferable academic literacy statements that became Likert-type items in the MALT were derived from practice and in consultation with instructors in the programme. The items so derived were grouped into categories that were most evident to the instructors: *Reading and research* and *Writing*.

The PCA of the MALT, however, revealed a structure that differed from the initial categories discussed above. Using methods of rotation and indicators of factorial thresholds that were consistent with those of the PCA of the EBI, numerous iterations revealed two dimensions to the academic literacy knowledge represented in the instrument: *critical, evaluative knowledge* (CEK) and *rhetorical knowledge* (RK), each consisting of six items. Items under *critical, evaluative knowledge* involved more judgement and discernment on the part of the learners: for example, distinguishing between fact and opinion, identifying problems in logic, and discerning the most important points in a text. Items grouped under *rhetorical knowledge*, by distinction, were more inclined to relate to surface features of writing, such as writing a thesis statement, organising an essay according to a rhetorical pattern, and following explicit steps in the process of writing.

In relating these dimensions to the overall conceptual framework of the study, it can be argued that *rhetorical knowledge*, by its relatively superficial nature, was closely related to the type of learning that was transferred by means of low-road transfer while *critical, evaluative knowledge* corresponded more closely to the more de-contextualised, metacognitive knowledge that is applied by means of high-road transfer. This idea is developed further in the discussion below.

5.1.2. Transfer of Learning to the Disciplines

The statistical analysis of the MALT indicated that most students agreed that they were transferring learning from the EC programme to the disciplines. This agreement was indicated by both the median value (Mdn = 4; 1 = "strongly disagree"; 5 = "strongly agree") and the mean in every item retained in each of the two dimensions (*rhetorical knowledge*, M = 4.04; *critical, evaluative knowledge*, M = 3.95) following the factorial analysis of the MALT (see Table 11). Agreement, however, was not unanimous; most of the questions displayed a full range of responses from strong disagreement to strong agreement. The theme-based analysis of the open-ended questions and the semi-structured interviews provided insights into the learning that students perceived they had transferred to the disciplines. Some students made comments that exhibited a general awareness of the applicability of the knowledge gained in EC to the disciplines; these students were frequently either unwilling or unable, without prompting, to articulate the specific knowledge that they had found useful, and the contexts in which they had applied it.

However, those students who did specify the types of knowledge they had found useful cited knowledge related to the more superficial aspects of writing, such as writing thesis statements and topic sentences, or using referencing appropriately. This kind of knowledge, which was related to the *rhetorical knowledge* dimension of the MALT, was mentioned more frequently than the more metacognitive aspects of writing, such as planning or reflection, which was more the province of the *critical, evaluative knowledge* dimension. Furthermore, many students perceived transfer was occurring to courses that had essay assignments or presentation requirements that resembled those of the EC classes. The Social Science courses, in addition to certain writing-intensive classes in Business Administration and Tourism Management were frequently mentioned in terms of the usefulness of the *rhetorical knowledge* that students had found useful, while a theme that emerged from the data (despite the focus on academic literacy knowledge of the research framework) was the usefulness of the oral presentation knowledge (from the EC3 course) in courses requiring project presentations, particularly in the Business Administration major.

The nature of the transfer that the data revealed was consistent with much of the literature concerning the transfer of learning. Prominent in the literature was the conceptualisation of Salomon and Perkins (1989), who had examined the reasons for the apparent failure of transfer in many studies, such as that of Scribner and Cole (1981) and Bransford et al. (1986), that had examined the phenomenon. These studies had observed that subjects often failed to transfer learning to new situations, even where they could reasonably be expected to do so.

As discussed in the conceptual development of the current study, Perkins and Salomon, in examining the apparent failure of transfer in many of the pertinent studies, argued that only certain types of transfer—those that required a certain amount of decontextualisation and the abstraction of principles from the learning context—were apt to fail. Transfer in which the surface features of the task of the learning context resembled that of the target context, in contrast, was more likely to succeed.

Salomon and Perkins referred to these two types of transfer as high-road and low-road transfer, respectively. In the current study, low-road transfer, that which involves the transfer of superficial learning to target contexts that resemble the learning context, was more prominent in the responses to the open-ended questions and the interview than the less-readily observed high-road transfer, which involves "deliberate mindful abstraction... from one context for application in another" (Perkins & Salomon, 1988, p. 25).

In relation to the high-road/ low-road model, students expressed the usefulness of rhetorical knowledge, particularly surface features, in contexts that had an immediate resemblance to the learning context. Hence, low-road transfer was more prominent in this study than was high-road. Further to their conceptual development, Perkins and Salomon asserted that the primary reason that high-road transfer was more likely to fail was that instructional strategies did not directly address it. The assumption in education that high-road transfer would occur automatically without such explicit instruction Salomon and Perkins referred to as the "Bo-Peep theory" of education. To address this alleged neglect, they accordingly devised instructional strategies that addressed both types of transfer. To effect low-road transfer, they prescribed *hugging*, which addressed superficial stimuli by, for instance, modelling. To effect the more elusive high-road transfer learners, teachers could elucidate general principles behind certain knowledge, requiring analogical thinking, or coach students in problem-solving, for example. In short, in order to be effected, high-road transfer could not simply be left to its own devices.

The propensity of students in this study to observe the transfer of superficial knowledge to contexts similar to that of the EC programme can be further situated in terms of the model that has been discussed here. While the outcomes framed by the WPA (see Appendix A) were considered to be broadly representative of the aims of the EC programme at the time of the study, and were descriptive of tacit objectives, these outcomes were adopted *explicitly* only subsequent to the collection of data for this study. Following the design of this study and the collection of data, these outcomes came to be expressed in student course outlines and grading rubrics in order to effect the desired transfer to the disciplines. However, as this study focused on current practice prior to this adoption, the MALT was derived from assumptions of customary teaching adopted by instructors in the EC programme at the time. In probability, therefore, it might have been seldom, if ever, that students were expressly exposed to the objectives of transfer as reflected by the WPA outcomes statement as it came to be adopted by the EC programme. It is thus wholly possible, from perspective of the researcher's experience of both an instructor in the programme and its director at the time, that the Bo-Peep theory of education was pervasive in the programme: instructors expected the sought-after transfer without the benefit of the explicit principles or pedagogy that would facilitate such transfer. Therefore, by the terms of the model developed by Perkins and Salomon, the apparent failure of students in this study to perceive the transfer of more metacognitive knowledge is understandable. Such knowledge would accord with high-road transfer, which would only be effected by means of explicit, rather than tacit, instructional strategies.

The apparent failure to transfer the more metacognitive knowledge, might, however, be just that: *apparent*, rather than actual. The subsection addressing students' responses in the interviews revealed that some students, while perceiving the overall relevance of knowledge developed in the EC programme to their other courses, were unable, or unwilling, unless prompted to articulate the specific knowledge that they had used in these contexts. The absence of conscious knowledge, however, does not necessarily equate with the complete absence of knowledge. Hence, while students might have applied, in fact, certain elements of the knowledge complex to their disciplinary courses, they may not have perceived this application. Such a view would accord with that of Carroll (2002), also discussed earlier in the conceptual development of the current study. Carroll, in her longitudinal study of first-year composition at Pepperdine College in the US, observed, firstly, that a facile view of transfer would be that which accounted only for superficial features of transfer—grammar, spelling, references and similar, easily-detectable elements. Literacy, however, could not be characterised either as simple or unitary. In addition, Carroll notes in respect to the composition programme:

> the number of opportunities , outside of composition classes, that students have to practice writing in response to complex literacy tasks is very inconsistent from semester to semester. Students' writing abilities do not develop in a neat linear progression from assignments in general education courses, including first-year composition, on to major projects in upper-division classes. (p. 51)

Very close parallels exist between the courses and conditions Carroll describes in this passage and those of the EC programme at MUIC. MUIC, similarly to Pepperdine, is a liberal-arts college where students progress from general education to their major classes. The composition courses at Pepperdine are also similar in their focus and their aims to the EC programme at MUIC, and similarly, a "neat, linear progression" is not apparent. Students, therefore, may have difficulty in perceiving, beyond the most obvious and superficial features, precise transfer from the programme to the disciplines. This, however, is not to suggest that this transfer is not occurring; it may be doing so in very complex and almost inexplicable ways.

In conclusion, while most students perceived that they were transferring knowledge from the EC programme to their majors, when they were able to articulate this transfer, they mostly reported using surface features of academic literacy in courses that were superficially similar to those of the EC programme. Conceptually, this perception could be explained in either of two ways: firstly, as Perkins and Salomon asserted, the relative deficiency of explicit high-road instruction meant that such transfer was not occurring as frequently as the more readily effected low-road transfer. Alternatively, as Carroll observes, although such transfer may have been occurring, it was not as readily detectable to the students as was the low-road transfer, owing to its greater complexity and the non-uniform progression of literacy-orientated tasks as students moved from general education through to their majors.

5.1.3. The Relationship between Transfer of Learning and Students' Beliefs about Knowledge and Learning

While the parametric Pearson product-moment correlation failed to demonstrate a significant relationship between either the subscales of the MALT and the EBI or the scales as a whole, the non-parametric Spearman correlation found a small-to-moderate, yet significant negative correlation between the scales. This relationship was confirmed by the linear regression model that was subsequently generated, which indicated that the composite EBI scores could significantly predict the MALT scores. The negative correlation that emerged from both analyses suggested that a lower score on the EBI was associated with a higher score on the MALT. As lower scores in the EBI signify more-availing beliefs—in Schommer-Aikins's terms (Schommer, 1990, 1994), more "sophisticated,"—these findings suggested that students who held more availing beliefs tended to perceive a greater amount of transfer from the EC programme to the disciplines.

The findings from the questionnaire data thus indicated that a relationship existed between availing beliefs and perceptions of transfer of learning. Therefore, beliefs that had been hypothesised as availing of learning, in general, could be, more specifically, considered as *availing of transfer of learning* in the context of the study.

The data from the semi-structured interviews was illustrative of the beliefs themselves. The trends that emerged from the *ab initio* themes derived from the PCA and CFA of the EBI could be summed up as follows:

1. *Innate ability:* Students tended to believe that intelligence was innate, but that, nevertheless, effort could ensure academic or other success;

2. *Certain, authoritative knowledge:* Some of the students held non-availing views of the teacher as the ultimate source of knowledge while others recognised that individual students could gain knowledge independently of the teacher. The students' responses often seemed to suggest transmission, rather than constructivist view of knowledge. It was also common for students to have a reified view of knowledge, although at least one student recognised the mutability and uncertainty of knowledge. In relation to authority, students were not prepared to question their parents while, in contrast, they held a more availing, positivist view of the law and more distant authority;

3. *Simple knowledge:* Students tended to prefer fact to theory. They were tolerant of theory only as far as it was instrumental to practical application. None of the responses indicated an appreciation of knowledge abstraction or reflection, although one student expressed an awareness of the complexity of knowledge and had accordingly classified types of knowledge.

The trends reported above should not be taken to suggest that there was no variation in the students' responses. Moreover, the students' beliefs in each of the dimensions could not be placed on either extreme of the continua from availing to non-availing that the comprise each of the dimensions. Thus, a student who expressed more availing beliefs in one statement could equally express non-availing ones in the next.

In addition to the variability of the responses in relation to the dimensions, a strong theme that emerged inductively was a certain ambivalence of beliefs arising from an awareness and comparison of cultural contexts. Students' responses often implied a consciousness that what might be an appropriate belief in one context, such as Thai culture, may not be suitable in another. As much as the belief dimensions might be related to the transfer of learning, this cultural duality might in itself have such an association: students might conceivably only transfer learning from one context to another if they perceived it as culturally appropriate, a view that concurs with that of Pea (1997). Further reflections as to the relationship between culture and beliefs are presented in the next subsection.

The interview data, thus, provided a deeper understanding of the beliefs of the students about knowing and learning while the analysis of the questionnaire data suggested a relationship between these beliefs and students' perceptions of the transfer of learning from the EC programme to the disciplines. It should be recounted, however, that the relationship as suggested by the Pearson correlation, although significant, was low-to-moderate, and that the regression model showed that the EBI scores only accounted for 6.3% of the variability of the MALT scores. The beliefs, therefore, should be considered among the variables that predict transfer of learning. Aspects of epistemic beliefs, it has been argued by Barzilai and Zohar (2014), following the conceptual development of others, such as Buehl and Alexander (2006), can be conceptualised as integral to metacognition; so it may be for related beliefs about learning. Possibly, then, some of the remaining variances in the MALT could be explained be other aspects metacognition of the type, for instance, that the interviews yielded. This would be compatible with the bridging strategies outlined by Perkins and Salomon (1988) in obtaining high-road transfer: these strategies required *mindful* consideration of the possibilities of transfer to new contexts. Along with metacognition and, by no means incompatible with the psychological structures and processes represented in the cultural matrix, attitude and motivation could also account for much of the further variation. Attitude and motivation have been shown to have links to transfer of learning (see, for example, Ngeow, 1998).

If, as the analysis has indicated, beliefs are related to learning, it is possible that the coaching of students in beliefs conducive to transfer, alongside other metacognitive strategies, may avail learners' transfer of learning. These implications are taken up further in this section.

5.1.4. The Relationship between Students' Beliefs about Knowledge and Learning and their Secondary School Backgrounds

Strong conceptual support exists for a relationship between culture and individual beliefs. This includes philosophical or ideological stances, such as those of Hegel and Marx, or social psychological models, such as that of Nisbett (2004) and Fiske et al. (1998). Concerning the relationship between beliefs about knowledge and learning, in particular, and culture, theorising by writers such as Hofer (2008) has provided strong additional support.

The cultural matrix elucidates the mediating role of a society's key institutions (and institutional practices) between broader societal core values and individual psychological processes, a view that finds support in the work of other influential theorists, such as Lave. The immediate role of organisation culture and climate on individual actions, moreover, has been recognised by organisational behaviourists such as Hofstede. The secondary school is undoubtedly a key societal institution that possesses an organisational culture that may have such a relationship with student learning. This view has received empirical support by studies such as that of Ventura et al. (2008), who found that active engagement in secondary schooling had more of an influence than did passive immersion in broader societal culture on psychological processes related to learning. The specific behaviour in the case of the study by Ventura et al. was de-contextualisation, an element germane to the current study because of its theoretical relationship to transfer of learning—particularly high-road transfer.

Despite this conceptual and empirical support in the literature, this study failed to detect, in its analysis of the association between the EBI and demographic details in the questionnaire, a significant relationship between students' secondary school backgrounds and their beliefs about knowledge and learning. Neither did further analytical probing suggest a significant relationship between students' reported primary nationalities and their beliefs.

However, in the context of the strong conceptual support, such findings cannot be assumed to support the absence the relationship. Moreover, the factorial analysis of the EBI, in the variability of the factors extracted from across different cultural contexts, including this one, can be accepted as at least partial support for an association between cultural context and beliefs. Therefore, various explanations for the failure to detect a significant relationship are worth exploring here, as they may lead to the strengthening of potential research that follows this study or to further conceptual development.

The first of these reasons may be the well-documented difficulty in measuring or conceptualising culture or cultural dimensions. Tay, Woo, Klafehn, and Chiu (2010) have highlighted some of these difficulties, including the following questions:

- Whether culture is "a coherent meaning system with a deep structure and organized by such themes as individualism" or "a network of domain-specific symbolic elements with loose inter connections";
- Whether culturally typical responses are "reflections of shared pre-stored and enduring personality or knowledge structures, or... situation-dependent responses evoked in a shared environment; and
- Whether it is feasible to study cultural relativity using a universalistic measures—or as Tay et al. express it, "Can researchers quantitatively arrange or classify cultures according to culture-universal scales, while simultaneously analysing them from a qualitative, idiosyncratic perspective?" (p. 2)

Although the present study, in its conceptual development, has aligned itself with a view of culture as a coherent meaning system that can be characterised by certain themes, such as those of Nisbett and Hofstede, the second and third issues might be ones that confound the discernment of a possible relationship between beliefs and culture. It is possible, in terms of the second question, that the EBI evoked responses that were reflective of the perceptions of the students as to the particular situation (i.e., the context of the EC programme) rather than representative of deeper, more enduring cultural values and beliefs.

In addition to situational influences, individual responses may be unreliable reflections of cultural values. As Rohner (1984) observed, individual behaviour "may or may not be congruent with 'shared' cultural meanings, and personal desires may be incompatible with cultural norms" (p. 124). Rohner also cautioned against assuming that individual beliefs are determined *solely* by cultural beliefs—the cultural determinist fallacy. As Fu et al. (2004) asserted, "the beliefs held by individuals regardless of their cultural backgrounds might ... be among other factors that affect behaviours more directly than cultural values" (p. 285). The mediating effect of individual beliefs, hence, may account for the finding of a significant relationship between these beliefs and perceptions of transfer of learning, but also for the failure to detect any direct relationship between said transfer of learning and culture.

Many other potential variables exist in this study, such as the attrition of core cultural values as a result of time spent away from the secondary school or home environment, the influence of peers and popular culture. By extension, although learner's beliefs may be a significant predictor of cognitive manifestations, such as transfer of learning, high school background, taken alone, may not be a significant predictor of these beliefs, despite the findings of Ventura et al. (2008) that active engagement in the school environment has more of an influence than broader immersion in culture. At the risk of generating a less parsimonious model, rather than isolating high school background as a vector of cultural values and beliefs, perhaps it should be considered as part of a complex, including all the variables suggested in the cultural matrix. Such variables include home background, which, similarly to the school environment, has individuals engaging domestically in cultural practices, such as a parent's routine of reading bedtime stories to children, in a way which is more iterative and immediate than the broad abstract of societal culture. The latter variable would accord with Nisbett's (2009) account of the influence of home culture on intelligence and academic success.

The third question that Tay et al. (2010) raised concerns using universalistic measures to study cultural relativity. This issue has been addressed in direct relation to the EBI and was a major consideration in conducting prior factorial analysis. Nevertheless, from a culturally relativistic stance, it may be mendacious to use a Western paradigm or conceptualisation of epistemology, despite efforts, through the factorial analysis, to validate the constructs of the EBI for the context of this study.

Perhaps a fresh conceptualisation—involving members of the culture in question—is needed that takes into account that dimensions such as *authority*, for instance, are not as prominent as features in the Asian mental landscape as they are in the Western one. Hofstede (2001) commented on a similar concern in collecting data for his influential study. He had "used a questionnaire composed by Western minds":

> If arguments… about the cultural relativity of practices *and* theories are taken seriously, then this restrictive Western input into the research instrument should be a matter of concern. When the surveys were administered, not only Western but also non-Western respondents were confronted with Western questions. They dutifully answered them, but could the results really be supposed to express their values fully? (pp. 351-2)

Similar considerations must guide discussions of the current study and may account for the failure to detect an association between students' reported cultural backgrounds and their scores for the Western-designed EBI.

The interview data present further considerations that may also account for the absence of a significant relationship in the analysis. These considerations may also be conducive to conceptual development of culturally relative beliefs. The development of these ideas follows.

In the demographic section of the questionnaire, students had been asked to report the type of secondary school they had last attended. In the expectation that they would be revealing of variations in personal beliefs, typical respondents were selected as representatives of each of the prominent secondary school classifications—state/ government school in Thailand; international school in Thailand; bilingual school in Thailand; school in North America, Australia, New Zealand, or Europe; or school in Asia other than Thailand. However, in the interviews it transpired that only two of the eight interviewees had had uniform secondary school experiences. All students were of Thai nationality and, in most cases, the students had attended not only two or more different schools, but also two or more different *types* of schools each accompanied, it is assumed, by a different cultural ethos. Implicit in the research question, however, was the assumption that these students had engaged for most of their secondary school careers in a homogeneous high school experience.

In addition to this observation as to the cultural plurality of the interviewees' secondary school experiences was a strong inductive theme that emerged from their responses to questions probing their beliefs within the dimensions that had emerged from the questionnaires. These responses, in addition to instances of awareness of subject context, revealed a high level of cultural consciousness and ambivalence of beliefs. What was appropriate, or expected, behaviour on the part of students or teachers in an international or American school context, for example, was not so in that of a Thai state school. Students, moreover, compared Thai values—or a "mind-set"—implicitly and explicitly to Western ones; this was particularly evident in considering questions of authority. Concerning authority, some of the students interviewed expressed relatively availing views with regard to that of teachers—depending on the cultural context—and the law. At least two of the participants, however, felt that their parents should not be questioned, as this was a tradition, particularly in Thai society.

A possibility is that students—particularly those who have, from young, been exposed to a number of different cultures—are practising a kind of *epistemic-shifting* that is analogous to the code-shifting of multilinguals. The lack of a constant in relation to this would make it difficult for an instrument to detect a relationship between culture and the beliefs of the students.

Variations in students' attitudes to authority at large and that of their Thai parents, moreover, leads one to speculate as to nature of sometimes conflicting beliefs between societal culture, as presented by the home environment, and that evident in learning contexts—particularly Western-orientated classrooms and schools. One may posit, for example, that while the secondary school context may have an immediate association with an individual's beliefs, the beliefs engendered in this way may be more transient than core cultural values, especially where these two spheres do not converge.

Given a situation where students "switch' beliefs between sometimes alien school or classroom cultures, but continue to revert to their Thai upbringing, Hofstede's distinction between the more immediate, yet pliable organisational culture and the more indirect, yet enduring societal culture becomes relevant. While students may adapt their beliefs to suit particular contexts, a certain set of fundamental, base beliefs may continue to exist, even in apparent conflict with the beliefs appropriate in other, more transient settings.

The possibility that students develop culturally-specific beliefs, yet retain and revert to a stock of "home" culture beliefs recalls, furthermore, conceptions of domain-generality and -specificity by Schommer-Aikins (2002), Limón (2006), and Buehl and Alexander (2006). Buehl and Alexander (2006), illustratively, recognise a duality in learner's beliefs: as learners engage increasingly in more discipline-relevant learning, their beliefs become more domain-specific. Nevertheless, the learners simultaneously retain and refer to domain-general beliefs in accessing previous learning.

The co-existence of domain-specific and domain-general beliefs is integrated into the model of Muis, Bendixen and Haerle (see Fig. 1), which accounts, in a similar manner to Buehl and Alexander (2006), for the co-existence of domain-specific and -general beliefs. The model, representing the *theory of integrated domains in epistemology* (TIDE), it may be recalled, comprises a number of interrelated belief strata. The base consists of general beliefs that a student holds before active engagement in an academic context. The intermediate stratum comprises the academic beliefs—beliefs that are still relatively general in nature but are particular to the academic setting. The uppermost layer consists of delineated areas of specific beliefs that are developed and instantiated as the student engages in more discipline-specific enquiry. While the uppermost layer develops last, the beliefs that comprise the lower layers beliefs do not simply dissipate; they remain a stock that can be drawn upon by the learner, depending on the judgements of the learner as to appropriate engagement.

While these conceptions of plurality of beliefs are offered to account for the development of subject-domain epistemology, they may, by analogy, be applied to cultural contexts. Thus, while the students in our case may retain their home culture as an underlying stock of beliefs, their in-depth exposure to multiple cultures has developed in them a further stratum (or even strata) of cultural-specific beliefs from which they become adept at drawing at appropriate times—such as the administration of a questionnaire and interview that is clearly related to the EC programme. The plurality of beliefs expressed in these theories as to domain-generality and -specificity may, therefore, further account for a failure in the EBI to detect beliefs about knowledge and learning significantly related to either secondary culture or nationality.

The TIDE of Buehl and Alexander shares some of its concepts with the cultural matrix, particularly in the way in which it accounts for an integrated system of sociocultural elements. Some of the further concepts developed by Fiske et al. (1998) in their elucidation of the matrix may also apply to the difficulty in detecting an association between culture and beliefs.

One of the mechanisms that Fiske et al. employ to account for the internalisation of cultural influences in the form of individual psychological processes is that of enculturation. As discussed in Section 2.5.1., the process of enculturation entails the development of an individual's primary culture, developed early through proximal influences encountered on a daily basis, such as school and family. In brief, Fiske et al. explain enculturation as a process of interaction between certain proclivities in the individual and guided sociocultural interaction. In their view of these cultural proclivities, they draw an express analogy to the well-known theorising by Chomsky as to first-language acquisition. They extend their analogy of first-language acquisition to speculation as to the existence of a critical period for enculturation.

One of the assumptions of this research, particularly as framed by the cultural matrix, was that the process of enculturation was relevant to the students in the population because it involved the proximal, familial context of schooling, particularly as it was compatible with, and integrated into, the societal culture as a whole. This is the relationship which is represented by the cultural matrix. However, the interview data revealed that this assumption of uniformity was often violated: most students interviewed had varied secondary school backgrounds, and expressed views that were apparently reflective of ambivalent and sometimes conflicting beliefs (see, for example, Gudykunst & Kim, 2003; Kramer, 2012). This situation is arguably representative of the backgrounds and beliefs of many students who have been exposed to multiple cultural contexts through international education—hence the MUIC population. Thus, the assumption of the suitability of enculturation as an explanatory device in this population needs to be questioned.

Acculturation, in contrast to enculturation, because it accounts for individuals learning aspects of a second or third culture, often in order to survive in that culture, may be better equipped to deal with conflict. This view may be supportable if one extends the language acquisition analogy developed by Fiske et al. to culture in terms of the critical period hypothesis: many of the students in this study may have developed a strong home culture, reflective of the broader societal culture, before their secondary school experience. This may have occurred during a critical period during which enculturation was possible; subsequent exposure to second or third cultural contexts may be better explained by acculturation, much in the way that development of a second or additional language in an individual is better explained by learning rather than acquisition. This is not to suggest that enculturation is irrelevant in the present data set: only that both processes may be simultaneously present and lead, thus, to difficulties in discerning a clear relationship.

In sum, the failure of the statistical analysis to find a significant relationship between culture, whether that of the broader society or the secondary school, and learners' beliefs about knowledge and learning does not—particularly in the presence of strong conceptual support—necessarily signify the absence of such a relationship. The failure to find a clear relationship is understandable given the difficulty of conceptualising culture and delineating it, and given the diverse, multicultural backgrounds of the students. While elements relating to multiculturalism can be considered confounding variables, they also provide rich ground for further exploration and conceptual development as to the relationship between culture and individuals' psychological processes.

5.2. Limitations

Some of the limitations of this study have already been presented in previous sections of where they were integral to discussions of the findings. Most of these limitations comprise questions as to the conceptual development of the study, particularly that related to the construct of culture.

Questions include, for example, whether views reflected in the questionnaire and the interview reflect enduring cultural constructs on the part of the participants or whether their responses are influenced by the immediate context of the interview; whether the EBI recorded domain-general or domain-specific beliefs; and whether enculturation or acculturation is better for describing the belief systems of the participants.

The last question, in particular, is pertinent to the validity of the conceptual framework of the research, the cultural matrix, as the model incorporates compatible, integrated components that are aligned with enculturation, rather than the conflicting values of acculturation. The matrix itself is, thus, arguably only relevant to the extent that enculturation is relevant.

One may mitigate this concern, however, by considering that enculturation must play a role in every student's development of, at least, his or her "home," primary culture. It follows, in terms of the conceptualisation of domain-general and domain-specific beliefs discussed previously, that "home" culture is reflective of domain-general beliefs. Domain-general beliefs, according to Limón (2006), are what the EBI and similar instruments purport to measure, as these instruments are not sufficiently sensitive to detect domain-specific beliefs. In sum, if enculturation applies to home culture, and home culture relates to domain-general beliefs, then the beliefs about knowledge and learning measured by the EBI are relevant to the cultural matrix. This argument, however, does not account for the role of secondary school background where such background is not aligned with the home culture. Furthermore, acculturation beliefs may have emerged through probing in the interviews, which may have accounted for the ambivalent and sometimes apparently conflicting beliefs that were expressed by the interviewees.

These questions are limitations only to the extent that no conceptual development is ever complete, and as far as any empirical exploration is ever certain. As in all such cases, however, they do merit further investigation.

Another limitation relates to the self-report nature of both the questionnaire and the interviews. Some of these have been noted in Chapter 3 and include the positivist perspective that participants perceptions do not always accord with objective "reality." The student's perceptions of transfer of learning from the disciplines, accordingly, may not correspond with actual, observable evidence that indicates the extent to which this transfer is, in fact, occurring. While the researcher is aware of these concerns, a counterargument could comprise the interpretive claim that the perception is the reality, an ontological stance that is particularly relevant to research into sociocultural phenomena. From a more pragmatic stance, and in direct relation to the transfer of learning, the use of a self-report instrument in this study was also motivated by Carroll's (2002) observation (discussed earlier) that it is the students themselves who are in the best position to evaluate their own use of the knowledge complex in the disciplines. Furthermore, the aim of this study was to seek the applicability of a general, parsimonious model to the study; a self-report questionnaire, because it allows wider participation, is more conducive to this aim. Despite these justifications, however, the limitations of self-report are valid, and as such, results should be interpreted with caution.

A potential limitation in the data collected from the semi-structured interviews was that the interviews were conducted in English, whereas the first language of all the interview participants, as it so happened, was Thai. One may argue that the use of English might restrict many interpretational nuances from emerging from the data, and this potential deficit was indeed a consideration in the planning of the interviews. However, as detailed in Section 3.5.2, interpretational (e.g., Filep, 2009) and practical considerations favoured the use of English: not all students in the cohort were Thai speakers; moreover, students in an English-medium college that has rigorous admissions standards, including those pertaining to English proficiency, could be assumed to have a satisfactory level of expression in the language. Therefore, while certain subtle distinctions may have been lost, the interview data yielded the relational data that the research questions demanded.

Further limitations are those related to the statistical analysis of the questionnaire data. The sample size, particularly apropos the PCA and CFA of the EBI and MALT, may be a concern, depending on which of the many, sometimes conflicting, guidelines to which one chooses to adhere. Guidelines range between ratios of 5 to 15 respondents per variable; many advise "good" or "comforting" absolute sample sizes of 300 (Comrey & Lee, 1992; Tabachnik & Fidell, 2007). For the remaining 17 items of the final iteration of the PCA of EBI, the sample of 177 produces a ratio of 10.41, which seems reasonable if one follows the ratio rule. The sample size is, however, well below 300, which could be regarded as a limitation. The 11 remaining variables of the final iteration of the PCA of the MALT, with a sample of 166 produce a safe ratio of 15; again, however, the sample is below the ideal. It is, moreover, the absolute sample size that seems more indicative of reliability than the ratio, according to Arrindel and van der Ende (1985, in Field, 2009), and Guadagnoli and Velicer (1988, in Field, 2009). According to Field, Guadagnoli and Velicer found, moreover, that "if a factor has four or more loadings greater than 0.6 then it is reliable, regardless of sample size" (p. 647). Unfortunately, the factor loadings in neither the EBI nor the MALT reached these thresholds.

An alternative indicator of sampling adequacy is the Kaiser-Meyer-Olkin (KMO) measure. As a guideline, .5 is the minimum for acceptability, values of .7 to .8 good, and .8 and higher "great" to "superb." The EBI produced a KMO of .66, (acceptable), and the MALT produced a KMO of .74 (good). In sum, while the KMO indicates adequate to good sampling for the EBI and MALT respectively, the results should be approached with some caution.

A factor in favour of more confidence in the PCA of the EBI is the outcome of the ML analysis conducted in the CFA. The model fit was good in relation to the normed chi-square (x^2/df), 1.2; RMSEA, .03 and the conventional guidelines for the CFI, .90—all of these reported indices minimise the impact of sample size (see Table 5). However, in the case of the MALT, the values were not as satisfactory, with the normed chi-square (x^2/df) at a potentially acceptable 2.6, but RMSEA and CFI both being somewhat below the thresholds at .10 and .79 respectively.

A final limitation that should be listed here concerns the reliability of the subscales emerging from the factorial analysis of the EBI: α = .67 (IA); α = .50 (CAK); α = .52 (SK). In the interpretation of the factors, it became necessary to balance conceptual coherence with statistical reliability. Although the reliability scores for the subscales of the items extracted by the PCA (see Table 2) are not completely unacceptable by conventional guidelines (George & Mallery, 2003; Kline, 1999), they are low in relation to what is desirable in psychometric scales in general. Nevertheless, they are reflective of other analyses of the EBI. Originators of the EBI, Schraw, Bendixen, and Dunkle (2002), for example, reported alpha values of .58 to .68, while a recent study by Cam, Topcu, Sulun, Guven, and Arabacioglu (2012) reported alpha values of .51 to .75. The latter researchers also reflect that in studies of epistemological beliefs studies in general, such as that of Schommer (1990), alpha values have ranged from .51 to .78; they observe that differences in populations, translation discrepancies and cultural differences may account for these relatively low scores.

5.3. Conclusions: Transfer of Learning and the Cultural Matrix

As the research was framed by the cultural matrix of social psychology (Fiske et al., 1998), it is appropriate to consider the research questions discussed above in relation to the model.

The matrix, it will be recalled, presented a system of interrelated elements that flow bi-directionally from (i) core cultural ideas (concerning what is good, what is moral, and what is self) to (ii) the customs, norms, practices and institutions that reflect and promote those core ideas. These elements, in turn, flow into (iii) the recurrent episodes in "local worlds" that personalise the core ideas in (i), which are themselves immediately related to (iv) individuals' psychological structures and processes. These structures and processes then flow into (v) action on the part of individuals.

Taken in reverse order from the above, the phenomenon of *transfer of learning*, the investigation of which provided the initial impetus for this study, comprised, in relation to the matrix, (v), the action of individuals, while *students' beliefs about knowing and learning* were the psychological structures under investigation. The students' *secondary school backgrounds* were the construct examined under (iii), the recurrent episodes that personalised the core ideas. These three elements were the direct focus of the study, while (i) core cultural beliefs and (ii) concomitant customs, norms, practices and institutions provided the broader sociocultural context. The application of the matrix to learning was in agreement with related theorising by Vygotsky, Lave, and others.

The first research question, which investigated the nature of transfer of learning from the EC programme to the disciplines, concerned the action of individuals as manifested by transfer of learning. Both the questionnaire and the interview data indicated that such action was occurring, at least as perceived by most students.

The second research question, which examined the nature of the relationship between students' beliefs about knowledge and learning and transfer of learning, was represented in the matrix as the proximal association between learners' actions and these individuals' psychological structures. Although, owing to limitations relating to sample size, the findings based on the MALT and EBI factors should be interpreted with caution, the non-parametric analysis of correlations between the EBI and the MALT—between students' beliefs and their perceptions of transfer of learning—and the subsequent regression model indicated a moderate relationship between the beliefs and the transfer of learning. The regression model, however, suggested that the beliefs only accounted for 6.3% of the variability in the transfer of learning. This would suggest, in terms of the model, that while the psychological structures (beliefs) were associated with the action (transfer or learning), other variables were present for which the study did not account. These structures, in respect of learning, may include variables such as attitude and motivation—the focus of many other studies in educational psychology. Nevertheless, some support exists for the applicability of the model as far as the relationship between beliefs and transfer of learning are concerned.

The third, and final, research question specified investigation into the relationship between recurrent episodes in an immediate cultural context, as represented in this study by secondary school, and the psychological constructs—students' beliefs about knowledge and learning. Possibility owing to difficulties in conceptualising and measuring culture, however, a significant relationship was not indicated by the statistical analysis. One possible difficulty in terms of conceptualisation was the possibility that acculturation was more closely related with students' beliefs (at least at the time that they completed the questionnaire) than was the enculturation that the matrix assumes. An acculturation model seems at least partly feasible in considering some of the students' ambivalence to questions in the interviews about their beliefs, particularly when one consider, too, their multicultural backgrounds.

In short, the failure of the statistical analysis should not be taken as the absence of a relationship between culture and students' beliefs. Rather, one may speculate, for example, that the conceptual relevance of the matrix *to this particular group of students* could be reconsidered, as these students have all had exposure to diverse international education experiences. The matrix, which assumes enculturation, may be better suited to students who have been more homogeneously schooled, particularly where such schooling aligns with customs and norms that reflect the core values of the "home culture."

In sum, the findings provide some support for the applicability of the cultural matrix to transfer of learning. The particular population in this study—students in an international college, most having multicultural exposure—however, may have introduced acculturation factors that confounded the model in the extent to which it may predict an association between secondary school background and students' beliefs about knowledge and learning.

5.3.1. Implications for Theory

The study outlined the lack of a generally accepted model for the transfer of learning, one that accounts for the components that Baldwin and Ford (1988), for example, considered essential to transfer of learning: the instruction itself, the learning context, and the learner. The cultural matrix of social psychology (Fiske et al. 2002) accounts for all of these concepts. It integrates individual beliefs and transfer of learning—micro-level elements—with organisational and societal culture on the macro level. The cultural matrix, therefore, could be adapted as the kind of "meso-model" that Fu et al. (2004, p. 285) have advocated. In terms of general acceptability, it also integrates both inner psychological structures and processes of the kind conceptualised by the cognitivists with sociocultural elements in a dialectic that accords with Vygotsky's internalisation of the interpersonal.

While the statistical analysis of the questionnaire data found only partial support for the relationships suggested in the cultural matrix—that pertaining to transfer of learning and beliefs about knowledge and learning, this does not necessarily entail wholesale rejection of the model. Strong conceptual and empirical support exists for the discrete relationships that comprise the matrix: between culture and beliefs, and between beliefs and learning. Although a significant relationship between secondary school background and beliefs was not detected, this could be accounted for by the nature of the population: students engaged in international education, most of whom have been exposed to multiple cultural settings.

This study contributes, therefore, partially to the development of a general theory of transfer of learning based on the cultural matrix. Further conceptual development, however, is called for that, without sacrificing the parsimony of the model, could account, for example, for the relationship between both home and school contexts, with their concomitant routines and practices, and psychological processes and structures that include not only learners' beliefs, but also elements such as attitude and motivation. The cultural model accommodates these related variables; the relevant spheres are not limited to a single recurring event context, such as school, or a single psychological construct, such as epistemic beliefs.

Further empirical evidence, perhaps from studies conducted in more homogeneous environments, could also further investigate the applicability of the cultural matrix to a general theory of transfer of learning. This study, furthermore, reveals the need to develop models accounting for the role of acculturation, in contrast to the enculturation assumed by the cultural matrix. Such acculturation models may assume increasing significance as trends towards greater student mobility, often across cultural contexts, continue.

5.3.2. Implications for Practice

If the interrelationship among culture, beliefs and transfer of learning is compatible with the cultural matrix, possible implications are that addressing culture on the institutional level may increase outcomes related to transfer of learning. This may be preferable to ad hoc classroom methods to address transfer of learning (e.g., Salomon & Perkins, 1989) or personal epistemology (Boden et al., 2008) as it is more strategic and less dependent on classroom or subject micro-context.

If the model is accepted, it may increase the justification for existing school-wide projects, such as IDEAS, that focus not only on classroom instruction strategies, but also on institutional culture, and provide motivation for the establishment of similar projects elsewhere. This is not to suggest that instructional strategies such as hugging and bridging be abandoned, only that these should be integrated into initiatives that also address school culture, and all the everyday activities and events that comprise that culture.

At the very least, the findings, although they should be interpreted with caution, suggest a relationship between beliefs about knowing and learning and transfer of learning. If such a relationship exists, it is possible that the explicit instruction that addresses these beliefs as part of a package of general metacognitive strategies, in the manner of Boden (2008), could facilitate greater transfer, particularly high-road.

5.4. Recommendations

Because this project was broad in scope, it contains many areas for future research that may develop the cultural matrix as a model for transfer of learning, one or more components of the model, or alternative models that may apply in different circumstances and contexts. This potential research, drawing from lessons learnt in this study, may take several forms:

- Studies that move beyond self-report and students' perceptions in examining the relationship between culture, beliefs and transfer; these studies would incorporate more objective measures of transfer, such as the examination of artefacts, classroom observations, case studies, or discourse analysis that reveals "culturally resonant metaphors" (Closson, 2013, p. 66);

- Studies that go beyond establishing associations and examine *causal* relationships between elements such as culture and beliefs, or beliefs and transfer of learning;

- Studies that compare the elements in this study not in a single, diverse population, but in discrete, culturally-homogeneous settings that would better facilitate cross-cultural investigation, relatively free of confounding variables;

- Studies that develop and test acculturation models that may account for beliefs and the transfer of learning;

- And studies that examine, in the manner of those that have considered discipline-related domain-generality and -specificity (e.g., Muis et al., 2006), the possibility of analogous domain-generality and -specificity for individuals traversing cultural contexts. Such conceptualisations may be complementary to enquiries into acculturation models.

These potential research areas, while not exhaustive, are illustrative of areas that may lead to further validation of the concepts developed in this study, or to competing conceptualisations that may prove more suitable in certain cultural contexts. All contribute to a relativistic understanding of psychological constructs or phenomena across different cultures.

References

Ailon, G. (2008). Mirror, mirror on the wall: *Culture's Consequences* in a value test of its own design. *The Academy of Management Review, 33*(4), 885–904.

Al-Attas, S. N. (1979). *Aims and objectives of Islamic education*. London: Hodder and Stroughton.

Anderson, J. R. (1982). Acquisition of cognitive skill. *Psychological Review, 89*(4), 369-406.

Arner, D. G. (1972). *Perception, reason, and knowledge: An introduction to epistemology*. Glenview, IL.: Scott, Foresman.

Association of American Colleges and Universities. (2012). What is a 21st century liberal education? Retrieved from http://www.aacu.org/leap/what_is_liberal_education.cfm

Assumption College Thonburi. (n. d.). VDO introduce Assumption College Thonburi (English version) Retrieved from http://swis.act.ac.th/html_edu/cgi-bin/act/main_php/print_news.php?id_news=8170

Ayatollahi, M. A., Rasekh, A. E., & Tavakoli, M. (2012). Learner beliefs, self-regulated learning strategies and L2 academic reading comprehension: A structural equation modeling analysis. *World Applied Sciences Journal, 17*(1), 36-49.

Bagdonavicius, V., Kruopis, J., & Nikulin, M. S. (2011). *Non-parametric tests for complete data*. Hoboken, NJ: Wiley-ISTE.

Baldwin, T. T., & Ford, J. K. (1988). Transfer of training: A review and directions for future research. *Personnel Psychology, 41*, 63–105.

Bandura, A. (1977). Self-efficacy: Toward a unifying theory of behavioral change. *Psychological Review, 84*, 191-215.

Barrows, H. S., & Tamblyn, R. M. (1980). *Problem-based learning: An approach to medical education*. New York, NY: Springer.

Barry, J. (2007). Acculturation. In J. Grusec & P. Hastings (Eds.), *Handbook of socialization: Theory and research* (pp. 543-560). New York, NY: Guilford Press.

Barth, F. (1995). Other knowledge and other ways of knowing. *Journal of Anthropological Research, 51*(1), 65-68.

Barzilai, S., & Zohar, A. (2014). Reconsidering personal epistemology as metacognition: A multifaceted approach to the analysis of epistemic thinking. *Educational Psychologist, 49*(1), 13-35. doi: 10.1080/00461520.2013.863265

Baskerville, R. F. (2003). Hofstede never studied culture. *Accounting, Organizations and Society, 28*(1), 1-14. doi: 10.1016/S0361-3682(01)00048-4

Bazeley, P. (2011). *Qualitative data analysis with NVivo*. London, UK: SAGE Publications.

Bazerman, C., Little, J., Bethel, L., Chavkin, T., Fouquette, D., & Garufis, J. (Eds.) (2005). *Reference guide to Writing Across the Curriculum.* West Lafayette, IN: Parlor Press. Retrieved from http://wac.colostate.edu/books/bazerman_wac/

Belenky, M., Clinchy, B., Goldberger, N., & Tarule, J. (1986). *Women's ways of knowing: The development of self, voice, and mind.* New York, NY: Basic Books.

Bendixen, L. D., & Rule, D. C. (2004). An integrative approach to personal epistemology: A guiding model. *Educational Psychologist, 39*(1), 69–80.

Bendixen, L. D., Schraw, G., & Dunkle, M. E. (1998). Epistemic beliefs and moral reasoning. *The Journal of Psychology, 132*(2), 187-200.

Bertsekas, D. P., & Tsitsiklis, J. N. (2002). *Introduction to probability* (1st ed.). Belmont, MA: Athena Scientific.

Bielaczyc, K., & Collins, A. (1999). Learning communities in classrooms: A reconceptualization of educational practice. In C. M. Reigeluth (Ed.), *Instructional design theories and models* (Vol. 2). Mahwah, NJ: Lawrence Erlbaum Associates.

Biglan, A. (1973). The characteristics of subject matter in different academic areas. *Journal of Applied Psychology, 57*(3), 195-203.

Billing, D. (2007). Teaching for transfer of core/key skills in higher education: Cognitive skills. *Higher Education, 53,* 483-516. doi:10.1007/s10734-005-5628-5

Boden, C. J., Franklin-Guy, S., Gibson, D., Lasker-Scott, T., Scudder, R. R., & Smart, J. T. (2008). Seven methodologies professors use to promote student epistemological development and self-directedness. *International Journal of Learning, 15*(11), 11-21.

Bond, M. (1991). Cultural influences on modes of impression management: Implications for the cultural diverse organization. In R. Giacalone & P. Rosenfeld (Eds.), *Applied impression management: How image-making affects managerial decisions.* Newbury Park, CA: Sage.

Bond, M. H., Wan, K. C., Leung, K., & Giacalone, R. A. (1985). How are responses to verbal insult related to cultural collectivism and power distance? *Journal of Cross-Cultural Psychology, 16,* 111-127.

Borofsky, R., Barth, F., Shweder, R. A., Rodseth, L., & Stolzenberg, N. M. (2001). When: A conversation about culture. *American Anthropologist, 103*(2), 432-446.

Boyatzis, R. E. (1998). *Transforming qualitative information: Thematic analysis and code development.* Thousand Oaks, CA: SAGE Publications.

Brady, P. (2008). Working towards a model of secondary school culture. *Canadian Journal of Educational Administration and Policy, 73*(5), 1-26.

Brand, S., Reimer, T., & Opwis, K. (2007). How do we learn in a negative mood? effects of a negative mood on transfer and learning. *Learning and Instruction, 17.* doi:10.1016/j.learninstruc.2006.11.002

Bransford, J. D., Franks, J. J., Vye, N. J., & Sherwood, R. D. (1986). *New approaches to instruction because wisdom can't be taught*. Paper presented at the Conference on Similarity and Analogy, University of Illinois.

Bransford, J. D., & Schwartz, D. (1999). Rethinking transfer: A simple proposal with multiple implications. *Review of research in education, 24*, 61-100.

Bråten, I., Gil, L., Strømsø, H. I., & Vidal-Abarca, E. (2009). Personal epistemology across cultures: exploring Norwegian and Spanish university students' epistemic beliefs about climate change. *Social Psychology of Education, 12*(4), 529-560. doi: 10.1007/s11218-009-9097-z

Bråten, I., Strømsø, H. I., & Samuelstuen, M. (2008). Are sophisticated students always better? The role of topic-specific personal epistemology in the understanding of multiple expository texts. *Contemporary Educational Psychology, 33*(4), 814-840. doi: 10.1016/j.cedpsych.2008.02.001

Brophy, J. (1997). *Motivating students to learn*. Guilford, CT: McGraw-Hill.

Brown, A. L., & Campione, J. C. (1994). Guided discovery in a community of learners. In K. McGilly (Ed.), *Classroom lessons: Integrating cognitive theory and classroom practice* (pp. 229-272). Cambridge, MA: The MIT Press.

Brown, J. S., Collins, A., & Duguid, P. (1989). Situated cognition and the culture of learning. *Educational Researcher, 18*(1), 32-42.

Bruner, J., Goodnow, J., & Austin, A. (1956). *A study of thinking*. New York, NY: Wiley.

Bryman, A. (2012). *Social research methods* (4th ed.). New York, NY: Oxford University Press.

Buehl, M. M., & Alexander, P. A. (2006). Examining the dual nature of epistemological beliefs. *International Journal of Educational Research, 45*(1–2), 28-42. doi: 10.1016/j.ijer.2006.08.007

Buehl, M. M., Alexander, P. A., & Murphy, P. K. (2002). Beliefs about schooled knowledge: Domain specific or domain general? *Contemporary Educational Psychology, 27*(3), 415-449. Retrieved from http://www.sciencedirect.com/science/article/pii/S0361476X01911038

Burke, V., Jones, I., & Doherty, M. (2005). Analysing student perceptions of transferable skills via undergraduate degree programmes. *Active Learning in Higher Education, 6*(2), 132-144. doi:10.1177/1469787405054238

Butterfield, E. C., & Nelson, G. D. (1989). Theory and practice of teaching for transfer. *Educational Technology Research and Development, 37*(3), 5-38. doi: 10.1007/BF02299054

Butterfield., E. C. (1988). On solving the problem of transfer. In M. M. Grunesberg, P. E. Morris & R. N. Skyes (Eds.), *Practical aspects of memory* (Vol. 2, pp. 377–382). London, UK: Academic Press.

Cam, A., Topcu, M. S., Sulun, Y., Guven, G., & Arabacioglu, S. (2012). Translation and validation of the Epistemic Belief Inventory with Turkish pre-service teachers. *Educational Research and Evaluation: An International Journal on Theory and Practice*. doi:10.1080/13803611.2012.689726

Campbell, M., & Hourigan, N. (2008). Institutional cultures and development education. *Policy & Practice: A Development Education Review, 7*(Autumn), 35-47.

Carroll, L. A. (2002). *Rehearsing new roles: How college students develop as writers*. Carbondale and Edwardsville, IL: Southern Illinois University Press.

Carver, R. P. (1978). The case against statistical significance testing. *Harvard Educational Review, 48*(3), 378-399.

Chan, N.-M., Ho, I. T., & Ku, K. Y. L. (2011). Epistemic beliefs and critical thinking of Chinese students. *Learning and Individual Differences, 21*, 67-77. doi:10.1016/j.lindif.2010.11.001

Changkakoti, N., & Broyon, M. A. (2008). Buddhist education as a challenge to modern schooling. In P. R. Dasen & A. Akkari (Eds.), *Educational theories and practices from the majority world* (pp. 286-304). New Delhi, India: SAGE Publications.

Chase, W. C., & Simon, H. A. (1973). Perception in chess. *Cognitive Psychology, 4*, 55-81.

Cheng, Y. C. (1997). A framework of indicators of education quality in Hong Kong primary schools: Development and application. In H. Meng, Y. Zhou & Y. Fang (Eds.), *School based indicators of effectiveness: Experiences and practices in APEC members* (pp. 207-250). China: Guangxi Normal University Press.

Cheng, Y. C. (1999). Recent education developments in the South East Asia. Special issue of *School Effectiveness and School Improvement: An International Journal of Research, Policy, and Practice, 10*(1), 3-124.

Cheng, Y. C. (2000). Cultural factors in educational effectiveness: A framework for comparative research. *School Leadership and Management: Formerly School Organisation, 20*(2), 207-225. doi: 10.1080/13632430050011434

Chomsky, N. (1959). A review of B. F. Skinner's *Verbal behavior*. *Language, 35*(1), 26-58.

Closson, R. (2013). Racial and cultural factors and learning transfer. *New Directions for Adult and Continuing Education,,137*, 61-69. doi:10.1002/ace.20045

Coffin, C., & Donahue, J. P. (2012). Academic Literacies and systemic functional linguistics: How do they relate? *Journal of English for Academic Purposes, 11*, 64-75. doi: 10.1016/j.jeap.2011.11.004

Comrey, A. L., & Lee, H. B. (1992). *A first course in factor analysis*. Hillsdale, NJ: Erlbaum

Corder, G. W., & Foreman, D. I. (2009). *Nonparametric statistics for non-statisticians: A step-by-step approach*. Hoboken, NJ: Wiley.

Cornelius, L. L., Herrenkohl, L. R., & Wolfstone-Hay, J. (2013). Organizing collaborative experiences around subject matter domains: The importance of aligning social and intellectual structures in instruction. In C. E. Hmelo-Silver (Ed.), *The international handbook of collaborative learning* (pp. 333-350). New York, NY: Routledge.

Costello, A. B., & Osborne, J. W. (2005). Best practices in exploratory factor analysis: Four recommendations for getting the most from your analysis. *Practical Assessment, Research and Evaluation, 10*(7). Retrieved from http://pareonline.net/getvn.asp?v=10&n=7

Council of Writing Program Administators. (2008). WPA outcomes statement for first-year composition. Retrieved from http://www.wpacouncil.org/positions/outcomes.html

Crabtree, B. F., & Miller, W. L. (1999). Using codes and code manuals: A template organizing style of interpretation. In B. F. Crabtree & W. L. Miller (Eds.), *Doing qualitative research* (2nd ed.). Thousand Oaks, CA: SAGE Publications.

Crowther, F., & Andrews, D. (2006, Summer). Power to the profession. *EQ Australia (Education Quarterly)*, 8-10.

Curtis, J., Billingslea, R., & Wilson, J. P. (1988). Personality correlates of moral reasoning and attitudes toward authority. *Psychological Reports, 63*, 947-954.

Damon, W. (1988). *The moral child*. New York, NY: The Free Press.

De Corte, E., & Op 't Eynde, P. (2003). *Students' Mathematics-related beliefs: Where do epistemological beliefs fit in?* Paper presented at the Annual Meeting of the American Educational Research Association, Chicago, IL.

Deal, T. E., & Kennedy, A. A. (1982). *Corporate cultures: The rights and rituals of corporate life*. New York, NY: Perseus.

deBacker, T. K., Crowson, H. M., Beesley, A. D., Thoma, S. J., & Hestevold, N. L. (2008). The challenge of measuring epistemic beliefs: An analysis of three self-report instruments. *The Journal of Experimental Education, 76*(3), 281-312. doi: 10.3200/JEXE.76.3.281-314

Denzin, N. K., & Lincoln, Y. S. (2003). *Collecting and interpreting qualitative materials* (2nd ed.). Thousand Oaks, CA: SAGE Publications.

Detterman, D. K. (1993). The case for the prosecution: Transfer as an epiphenomenon. In D. K. Detterman & R. J. Sternberg (Eds.), *Transfer on trial: Intelligence, cognition, and instruction*. New Jersey, NJ: Alex Publishing Corporation.

Diener, C. I., & Dweck, C. S. (1978). An analysis of learned helplessness: Continuous change in performance, strategy, and achievement cognitions following failure. *Journal of Personality and Social Psychology, 36*, 451-462.

Dimmock, C. (2000). *Designing the learning-centred school: A cross-cultural perspective*. London, UK: Falmer Press.

DiStefano, C., Zhu, M., & Mîndrilă, D. (2009). Understanding and using factor scores: Considerations for the applied researcher. *Practical Assessment, Research and Evaluation, 14*(20), 1-11. Retrieved from http://pareonline.net/getvn.asp?v=14&n=20

Donald, J. G. (1990). University professors' views of knowledge and validation processes. *Journal of Educational Psychology, 82*(2), 242-249.

Dörnyei, Z. (1994). Motivation and motivating in the foreign language classroom. *Modern Language Journal, 78*(3), 273-284.

Dörnyei, Z. (2007). *Research methods in Applied Linguistics: Quantitative, qualitative and mixed methodologies.* Oxford, UK: Oxford University Press.

Dweck, C. S., & Elliott, E. S. (1983). Achievement motivation. In P. Mussen & E. M. Hetherington (Eds.), *Handbook of child psychology.* New York, NY: Wiley.

Elby, A. (2009). Defining personal epistemology: A response to Hofer & Pintrich (1997) and Sandoval (2005). *Journal of the Learning Sciences, 18*(1), 138-149. doi:10.1080/10508400802581684

Estes, D., Chandler, M., Horvath, K. J., & Backus, D. W. (2003). American and British college students' epistemological beliefs about research on psychological and biological development. *Applied Developmental Psychology, 23*(6), 625–642. doi: 10.1016/S0193-3973(03)00002-9

Fafunwa, B. (1982). *A history of education in Nigeria.* London, UK: George Allen and Unwin.

Fereday, J., & Cochran, E. M. (2006). Demonstrating rigor using thematic analysis: A hybrid approach of inductive and deductive coding and theme development. *International Journal of Qualitative Methods,* 5(1), 1-11. Retrieved from http://www.ualberta.ca/~iiqm/backissues/5_1/pdf/fereday.pdf

Field, A. (2009). *Discovering statistics using SPSS* (3rd ed.). London, UK: SAGE Publications.

Filep, B. (2009). Interview and translation strategies: Coping with multilingual settings and data. *Social Geography, 4,* 59-70. Retrieved from http://www.soc-geogr.net/4/59/2009/sg-4-59-2009.pdf

Fiske, A. P., Kitayama, S., Markus, H. R., & Nisbett, R. E. (1998). The cultural matrix of social psychology. In D. T. Gilbert, S. T. Fiske & G. Lindzey (Eds.), *The handbook of social psychology* (4th ed., pp. 915-981). New York: McGraw-Hill.

Fives, H., & Buehl, M. (2012). Spring cleaning for the "messy" construct of teachers' beliefs: What are they? Which have been examined? What can they tell us? In K. R. Harris, S. Graham & T. Urdan (Eds.), *APA Educational Psychology Handbook* (Vol. 2 Individual differences and Cultural and Contextual Factors, pp. 471-499). Washington, MA: American Psychological Association.

Fogarty, R., Perkins, D., & Barell, J. (1992). *How to teach for transfer.* Palatine, IL: Skylight Publishing.

Frost, P., & Stablein, R. (1992). *Doing exemplary research*. Newbury Park, CA: SAGE Publications.

Fu, P. P., Kennedy, J., Tata, J., Yukl, G., Bond, M. H., Peng, T.-K., . . . Cheosakul, A. (2004). The impact of societal cultural values and indivdual social beliefs on the perceived effectivness of managerial influence strategies: A meso approach. *Journal of International Business Studies, 35*, 284-305.

Fujiwara, T. (2007). *Mathematics discipline-specific personal epistemology of Thai university students: Cultural influence on mathematics-related beliefs*, in Enhancing higher education, theory and scholarship. Paper presented at the 30th HERDSA Annual Conference, Adelaide, Australia.

Fujiwara, T., & Phillips, B. (2006). *Personal epistemology of Thai university students: Cultural influence on the development of beliefs about knowledge and knowing*. Paper presented at the 29th HERDSA Annual Conference, Western Australia.

Gagne, R., Briggs, L., & Wager, W. (1992). *Principles of instructional design*. Fort Worth, TX: HBJ College.

Gaziel, H. H. (1997). Impact of school culture on effectiveness of secondary schools with disadvantaged students. *Journal of Educational Research, 90*(5), 310.

Gilbert, N. (1993). *Researching social life*. London, UK: Sage Publications.

Glantz, S. A. (2005). *Primer of biostatistics* (6th ed.). New York, NY: McGraw Hill Professional.

Green, J. H. (2008). EAP: English for Any Purpose? *International Journal of Learning, 15*(7), 63-71.

Green, J. H. (2013). Transfer of learning and its ascendancy in higher education: A cultural critique. *Teaching in Higher Education, 18*(4), 365-376. doi: 10.1080/13562517.2012.719155

Green, J. H. (2015). Teaching for transfer in EAP: Hugging and bridging revisited. *English for Specific Purposes, 37*, 1-12. doi: 10.1016/j.esp.2014.06.003

Greene, J. A., Azevedo, R., & Torney-Purta, J. (2008). Modeling epistemic and ontological cognition: Philosophical perspectives and methodological directions. *Educational Psychologist, 43*(3), 142-160. doi: 10.1080/00461520802178458

Greeno, J. G. (1998). The situativity of knowing, learning, and research. *American Psychologist, 53*(1), 5-26. doi: 10.1037/0003-066X.53.1.5

Gudykunst, W. B., & Kim, Y. Y. (2003). *Communicating with strangers: An approach to intercultural communication* (4th ed.). New York, NY: McGraw-Hill Education.

Hall, E. T. (1976). *Beyond culture*. Garden City, NY: Anchor Press.

Hallinger, P., & Kantamara, P. (2001). Exploring the cultural context of school improvement in Thailand. *School Effectivness and School Improvement: An International Journal of Research, Policy and Practice, 12*(4), 385-408.

Halpern, D. F., & Hakel, M. D. (2003). Applying the science of learning to the university and beyond: Teaching for long-term retention and transfer. *Change, July/ August*, 2-13. doi: 10.1080/00091380309604109

Hammer, D. H., & Elby, A. (2002). On the form of personal epistemology. In B. K. Hofer & P. R. Pintrich (Eds.), *Personal epistemology: The psychology of beliefs about knowledge and knowing* (pp. 169-190). Mahwah, NJ: Erlbaum.

Hammerich, K., & Lewis, R. D. (2013). *Fish can't see water: How national culture can make or break your corporate strategy*. Hoboken, NJ: Wiley.

Harragan, B. L. (1977). *Games mother never taught you: Corporate gamesmanship for women*. New York, NY: Rawson, Wade.

Haskell, R. E. (2001). *Transfer of learning: Cognition, instruction, and reasoning*. San Diego, CA: Academic Press.

Helfenstein, S., & Saariluoma, P. (2006). Mental contents in transfer. *Psychological Research, 70*, 293-303. doi:10.1007/s00426-005-0214-0

Heyward, M. (2002). From international to intercultural: Redefining the international school for a globalised world. *Journal of Research in International Education, 1*(1), 9-32. doi:10.1177/147524090211002

Hirsch, E. D. J. (1987). *Cultural literacy: What every American needs to know*. Boston, MA: Houghton Mifflin.

Hofer, B. K. (2000). Dimensionality and disciplinary differences in personal epistemology. *Contemporary Educational Psychology, 25*(4), 378-405. doi: 10.1006/ceps.1999.1026

Hofer, B. K. (2001). Personal epistemological research: Implications for learning and teaching. *Journal of Educational Psychology Review, 13*(4), 353-383.

Hofer, B. K. (2008). Personal epistemology and culture. In M. S. Khine (Ed.), *Knowing, knowledge and beliefs: Epistemological studies across diverse cultures* (pp. 3-22). New York, NY: Springer.

Hofer, B. K., & Pintrich, P. R. (1997). The development of epistemological theories: Beliefs about knowledge and knowing and their relation to learning. *Review of Educational Research, 67*(1), 85-120.

Hofer, B. K., & Sinatra, G. M. (2010). Epistemology, metacognition, and self-regulation: Musings on an emerging field. *Metacognition and Learning, 5*(1), 113-120.

Hofstede, G. (2001). *Culture's consequences: Comparing values, behaviors, institutions, and organizations across nations* (2nd ed.). Thousand Oaks, CA: SAGE Publications.

Hofstede, G. (2002). Dimensions do not exist: A reply to Brendan McSweeney. *Human Relations, 55*(11), 1355-1361. doi: 10.1177/00187267025511004

Hofstede, G. (2003). What is culture? A reply to Baskerville. *Accounting, Organizations and Society, 28*(7–8), 811-813. doi: 10.1016/S0361-3682(03)00018-7

Hofstede, G., Hofstede, G. J., & Minkov, M. (2010). *Cultures and organizations: Software of the mind*. New York, NY: McGraw-Hill.

Holton, E. F., Bates, R. A., & Ruona, W. E. A. (2000). Development of a generalized learning transfer system inventory. Human Resource Development Quarterly, 11(4), 333-360. doi: 10.1002/1532-1096(200024)11:4<333::AID-HRDQ2>3.0.CO;2-P

Hooper, D., Coughlan, J., & Mullen, M. R. (2008). Structural equation modelling: Guidelines for determining model fit. *Electronic Journal of Business Research Methods, 6*(1), 53-60. Retrieved from www.ejbrm.com

Inhelder, B., & Piaget, J. (1958). *The growth of logical thinking from childhood to adoloescence*. New York, NY: Basic Books.

James, M. A. (2006). Teaching for transfer in ELT. *ELT Journal, 60*(2), 151-159. doi:10.1093/elt/cci102

Jehng, J.-C. J., Johnson, S. D., & Anderson, R. C. (1993). Schooling and students' epistemological beliefs about learning. *Contemporary Educational Psychology, 18*, 23-35.

Jordan, R. R. (1997). *English for Academic Purposes: A guide and resource book for teachers*. Cambridge, UK: Cambridge University Press.

Kanter, R. M. (1984). *The change masters: Innovation and entrepreneurship in the American corporation*. New York, NY: Simon and Schuster.

Kardash, C. M., & Scholes, R. J. (1996). Effects of preexisting beliefs, epistemological beliefs, and need for cognition on interpretation of controversial issues. *Journal of Educational Psychology, 88*, 260–271.

Kasintorn Academy. (2014). Retrieved May 10, 2014, from http://www.kasintorn.com/en/aboutschool.asp

Kidder, T. (1981). *The soul of a new machine*. Boston, MA: Little Brown.

Kilmann, R. H., Saxton, M. J., & Serpa, R. (1985). Introduction: Five key issues in understanding and changing culture. In R. H. Kilmann, M. J. Saxton & R. Serpa (Eds.), *Gaining control of the corporate culture*. Hoboken, NJ: Jossey-Bass.

Kirakowski, J. (1997). *Questionnaires in usability engineering: A list of frequently asked questions*. Retrieved from http://www.ucc.ie/hfrg/resources/gfaql.html

Kowitwanij, W. (2008). Catholic schools in Thailand, places of excellence and inter-faith dialogue. *AsiaNews.it*. Retrieved from http://www.asianews.it/news-en/Catholic-schools-in-Thailand,-places-of-excellence-and-inter-faith-dialogue-13351.html

Kozulin, A. (1998). *Psychological tools: A sociocultural approach to education*. Cambridge, MA: Harvard University Press.

Kramer, E. M. (2012). Dimensional accrual and dissociation: An introduction. In J. Grace (Ed.), *Comparative Cultures and Civilizations* (Vol. 3). Cresskill, NJ: Hampton.

Krashen, S. (1981). *Second language acquisition and second language learning*. Oxford, UK: Pergamon Press.

Kraska-Miller, M. (2014). *Nonparametric statistics for social and behavioral sciences*. Boca Raton, FL: CRC Press.

Kroeber, A. L., Kluckhohn, C.: . (1952). Culture: A critical review of concepts and definitions. *The Museum, 47*(1), 223

Larkin, J. H. (1983). The role of problem representation in Physics. In D. Gentner & A. L. Stevens (Eds.), *Mental models*. Hillsdale, NJ: Lawrence Erlbaum Associates.

Larsen-Freeman, D. (2013). Transfer of learning transformed. *Language Learning, 63*, 107-129. doi: 10.1111/j.1467-9922.2012.00740.x

Lave, J. (1988). *Cognition in practice: Mind, Mathematics and culture in everyday life*. Cambridge, UK: Cambridge University Press.

Lawrence, D. P. (1993). Quantitative versus qualitative evaluation: A false dichotomy? *Environmental Impact Assessment Review, 13*(1), 3-11. doi:10.1016/0195-9255(93)90025-7

Limón, M. (2006). The domain generality–specificity of epistemological beliefs: A theoretical problem, a methodological problem or both? *International Journal of Educational Research, 45*(1–2), 7-27. doi: 10.1016/j.ijer.2006.08.002

Lising, L., & Elby, A. (2005). The impact of epistemology on learning: A case study from introductory physics. *American Journal of Physics, 73*(4). doi:10.1119/1.1848115

Lobato, J. (2006). Alternative perspectives on the transfer of learning: History, issues, and challenges for future research. *Journal of the Learning Sciences, 15*(4), 431-449. doi: 10.1207/s15327809jls1504_1

Louca, F. (2007). The demise of Critical Theory in Economics. In B. Santos (Ed.), *Cognitive justice in a global world* (pp. 315-336). Lanham, MD: Rowman & Littlefield.

Louca, L., Elby, A., Hammer, D., & Kagey, T. (2004). Epistemological resources: Applying a new epistemological framework to science instruction. *Educational Psychologist, 39*(1), 57-68.

Macaulay, C., & Cree, V. E. (1999). Transfer of learning: Concept and process. *Social Work Education, 18*(2), 183-194. doi: 10.1080/02615479911220181

Macionis, J., & Gerber, L. (2010). *Sociology* (7th ed.).

Marini, A., & Genereux, R. (1995). The challenge of teaching for transfer. In A. McKeough, J. Lupart & A. Marini (Eds.), *Teaching for transfer: Fostering generalization in learning* (pp. 1-20). Mahwah, NJ: Lawrence Erlbaum Associates.

Marmarelis, V. Z., Shin, D. C., Zhang, Y., Kautzky-Willer, A., Pacini, G., & D'Argenio, D. Z. (2013). Analysis of intravenous glucose tolerance test data using parametric and nonparametric modeling: Application to a population at risk for diabetes. *Journal of Diabetes Science Technology, 7*(4), 952-962.

Matthayom Watnairong English Program School. (2015). About. Retrieved December 14, 2015, from http://nairong.ac.th/about/

Mayer, R. E., & Wittrock, M. C. (1996). Problem-solving transfer. In D. C. Berliner & R. C. Calfee (Eds.), *Handbook of educational psychology* (pp. 47-62). New York, NY: MacMillan.

McAlpine, L., Eriks–Brophy, A., & Crago, M. (1996). Teaching beliefs in Mohawk classrooms: Issues of language and culture. *Anthropology & Education Quarterly,* 27(3), 390-413. doi: 10.1525/aeq.1996.27.3.04x0355q

McGeoch, J. A. (1942). *The psychology of human learning.* New York, NY: Longmans, Green.

McSweeney, B. (2002). Hofstede's model of national cultural differences and their consequences: A triumph of faith – a failure of analysis. *Human Relations,* 55, 89–118.

Mori, Y. (1999). Epistemological beliefs and language learning beliefs: What do language learners believe about their learning? *Language Learning,* 49(3), 377-415.

Moser, C. A., & Kalton, G. (1979). *Survey methods in social investigation.* Aldershot, England: Gower Publishing Company.

Muis, K. R. (2004). Personal epistemology and mathematics: A critical review and synthesis of research. *Review of Educational Research,* 74(3), 317-377. doi: 10.3102/00346543074003317

Muis, K. R., Bendixen, L. D., & Haerle, F. C. (2006). Domain-generality and domain-specificity in personal epistemology research: Philosophical and empirical reflections in the development of a theoretical framework. *Educational Psychology Review,* 18(1), 3-54. doi:10.1007/s10648-006-9003-6

Muis, K. R., & Franco, G. (2009). Epistemic beliefs and metacognition: Support for a consistency hypothesis. *Metacognition and Learning,* 5(1), 27-45. doi: 10.1007/s11409-009-9041-9

Muis, K. R., & Sinatra, G. M. (2008). University cultures and epistemic beliefs: Examining differences between two academic environments. In M. S. Khine (Ed.), *Knowing, knowledge and beliefs: Epistemological studies across diverse cultures.* New York, NY: Springer.

Mü ller, S., Rebmann, K., & Liebsch, E. (2008). Trainers' beliefs about knowledge and learning: A pilot study. *European Journal of Vocational Training,* 45(3), 90-108.

Ngeow, K. Y.-H. (1998). Motivation and transfer in language learning. *ERIC Clearinghouse on Reading, English, and Communication, 138.* Retrieved from http://www.ericdigests.org/1999-4/motivation.htm

Nisbett, R. E. (2004). *The geography of thought: How Asians and Westerners think differently... and why.* New York, NY: Free Press.

Nisbett, R. E. (2009). *Intelligence and how to get it: Why schools and cultures count* (1st ed.). New York, NY: W. W. Norton & Co.

Nishimura, S., Nevgi, A., & Tella, S. (2008). *Communication style and cultural features in high/low context communication cultures: A case study of Finland, Japan and India.* Retrieved from www.helsinki.fi/~tella/nishimuranevgitella299.pdf

Nussbaum, E. M., & Bendixen, L. D. (2003). Approaching and avoiding arguments: The role of epistemic beliefs, need for cognition, and extroverted personality traits. *Contemporary Educational Psychology,* 28, 573-595. doi:10.1016/S0361-476X(02)00062-0

O' Connor, B. P. (2000). SPSS and SAS programs for determining the number of components using parallel analysis and Velicer's MAP test. *Behavior Research Methods, Instrumentation, and Computers, 32*, 396-402.

Onwuegbuzie, A. J., & Leech, N. L. (2005). On becoming a pragmatic researcher: The importance of combining quantitative and qualitative research methodologies. *International Journal of Social Research Methodology, 8*(5), 375-387. doi:10.1080/13645570500402447

Opfer, J. E., & Thompson, C. A. (2008). The trouble with transfer: Insights from microgenetic changes in the representation of numerical magnitude. *Child Development, 79*(3), 788-804. doi: 10.1111/j.1467-8624.2008.01158.x.

Osborne, J. W., & Overbay, A. (2004). The power of outliers (and why researchers should always check for them). *Practical Assessment, Research & Evaluation, 9*(6), 1 - 12.

Osgood, C. E. (1949). The similarity paradox in human learning: a resolution. *Psychological Review, 56*(3), 132-143.

Östman, & Wickman. (2014). A pragmatic approach on epistemology, teaching, and learning. *Science Education, 98*(3), 375-382. doi:10.1002/sce.21105

Ouchi, W. (1981). *Theory Z*. New York, NY: Addison-Wesley.

Owens, R. G. (2001). *Organizational behavior in education: Instructional leadership and school reform* (7th ed.). Boston, MA: Allyn and Bacon.

Packer, M. J., & Addison, R. B. (Eds.). (1989). *Entering the circle: Hermeneutic investigation in psychology*. Albany, NY: State University of New York Press.

Pagram, P., & Pagram, J. (2006). Issues in e-learning: A Thai case study. *Electronic Journal on Information Systems in Developing Countries, 26*(6), 1-8. Retrieved from http://www.ejisdc.org

Pajares, M. F. (1992). Teachers' beliefs and educational research: Cleaning up a messy construct. *Review of Educational Research, 62*(3), 307-332.

Paris, S. G., Lipson, M. Y., & Wixson, K. K. (1983). Becoming a strategic reader. *Contemporary Educational Psychology, 8*, 293-316.

Paulsen, M. B., & Wells, C. T. (1998). Domain differences in the epistemological beliefs of college students. *Research in Higher Education, 39*(4), 365-384.

Pea, R. D. (1987). Socializing the knowledge transfer problem. *International Journal of Educational Research, 11*(6), 639-663. doi: 10.1016/0883-0355(87)90007-3

Pennington, N., Nicolich, R., & Rahm, I. (1995). Transfer of training between cognitive subskills: Is knowledge use specific? *Cognitive Psychology, 28*, 175-224.

Perkins, D. N., & Salomon, G. (1988). Teaching for transfer. *Educational Leadership, 46*(1), 22-32.

Pernet, C. R., Wilcox, R., & Rousselet, G. A. (2012). Robust correlation analyses: False positive and power validation using a new open source

Matlab toolbox. *Fromtiers in Psychology,* 3(606). doi:10.3389/fpsyg.2012.00606

Perry, W. G. J. (1970). *Forms of intellectual and ethical development in the college years: A scheme.* New York, NY: Holt, Rinehart and Winston.

Piaget, J. (1952). *The origins of intelligence in children.* New York, NY: International University Press.

Pilkington, K., & Lock, G. (2013). Innovative designs for enhancing achievements in schools: The Western Australian experience. *Leading and Managing, 19*(1), 89-102. Retrieved from http://ro.ecu.edu.au/ecuworks2013/572/

Plato. (1993). *Plato's Republic* (R. Waterfield, Trans.). Oxford, UK: Oxford University Press.

Platt, J. (1998). *A history of sociological research methods in America, 1920-1960.* Cambridge, UK: Cambridge University Press.

Poore, P. (2005). School culture: The space between the bars; the silence between the notes. *Journal of Research in International Education, 4*(3), 351-361. doi:10.1177/1475240905057815

Prathumarach, M. (2011). *A professional development model for teacher leaders of Catholic schools in Thailand.* (Doctor of Philosophy dissertation), Assumption University of Thailand.

Presley, S. L. (1985). Moral judgment and attitudes toward authority of political resisters. *Journal of Research in Personality, 19*, 135–151.

Ralston, F. (1995). *Hidden dynamics: How emotions affect business performance and how you can harness their power for positive results.* New York, NY: American Management Association.

Ravindran, B., Greene, B. A., & deBacker, T. K. (2005). The role of achievement goals and epistemological beliefs in the prediction of pre-service teachers' cognitive engagement and learning. *Journal of Educational Research, 98*(4), 222-233.

Rebello, N. S. (2007). *Consolidating traditional and contemporary perspectives of transfer of learning: A framework and implications.* Paper presented at the NARST 2007 Annual Meeting, New Orleans, LA.

Richardson, V. (1996). The role of attitudes and beliefs in learning to teach. In J. Sikula (Ed.), *Handbook of research on teacher education.* New York, NY: Macmillan.

Richter, T., & Schmid, S. (2010). Epistemological beliefs and epistemic strategies in self-regulated learning. *Metacognition and Learning, 5*(1), 47-65. doi: 10.1007/s11409-009-9038-4

Robertson, S. I. (2001). *Problem solving.* Philadelphia, PA: Psychology Press / Taylor & Francis.

Robinson, E. S. (1927). The "similarity" factor in retroaction. *American Journal of Psychology, 39*, 297-312.

Rogers, C. (1959). A theory of therapy, personality and interpersonal relationships as developed in the client-centered framework. In S. Koch (Ed.), *Psychology: A study of a science* (Vol. 3: Formulations of the person and the social context). New York: McGraw Hill.

Rogoff, B. (1990). *Apprenticeship in thinking: Cognitive development in social context*. New York, NY: Oxford University Press.

Rogoff, B. (1994). Developing understanding of the idea of communities of learners. *Mind, Culture, and Activity, 1*(4), 209-229.

Rohner, R. P. (1984). Toward a conception of culture for cross-cultural psychology. *Journal of Cross-Cultural Psychology, 15*(2), 111-138. doi: 10.1177/0022002184015002002

Rousson, V., Gasser, T., & Seifert, B. (2002). Assessing intrarater, interrater and test-retest reliability of continuous measurements. *Statistics in Medicine, 21*(22), 3431-3446. doi:10.1002/sim.1253

Royce, J. R. (1978). Three ways of knowing and the scientific world view. *Methodology and Science, 11*, 146-164.

Royce, J. R., & Mos, L. P. (1980). *Manual: Psycho-epistemological profile*. Alberta, Canada: Center for Advanced Study in Theoretical Psychology, University of Alberta.

Rutter, M., Maughan, B., Mortimore, P., & Ouston, J. (1979). *Fifteen thousand hours: Secondary schools and their effects on children*. Cambridge, MA: Harvard University Press.

Salomon, G., & Perkins, D. N. (1989). Rocky roads to transfer: Rethinking mechanisms of a neglected phenomenon. *Educational Psychologist, 24*(2), 113-142. doi: 10.1207/s15326985ep2402_1

Sam, D. L., & Berry, J. W. (2010). Acculturation: When individuals and groups of different cultural backgrounds meet. *Perspectives on Psychological Science, 5*(4), 472-481. doi: 10.1177/1745691610373075.

Sandoval, W. A. (2005). Understanding students' practical epistemologies and their influence of learning through inquiry. *Science Education, 89*, 634-656.

Sardar, Z. (1994). *Introducing cultural studies*. London, UK: Totem Books.

Schein, E. H. (1992). *Organizational culture and leadership* (2nd ed.). San Francisco, CA: Jossey-Bass.

Schoenfeld, A. H. (1988). When good teaching leads to bad results: The disasters of "well-taught" mathematics courses. *Educational Psychologist, 23*(2), 145-166.

Schommer, M., Crouse, A., & Rhodes, N. (1992). Epistemological beliefs and mathematical text comprehension: Believing it is simple does not make it so. *Journal of Educational Psychology, 84*, 435–443.

Schommer, M. A. (1990). Effects of beliefs about the nature of knowledge on comprehension. *Journal of Educational Psychology, 82*(3), 498-504.

Schommer, M. A. (1993). Epistemological development and academic performance among secondary schools. *Journal of Educational Psychology, 85*(3), 406-411.

Schommer, M. A. (1994). Synthesizing epistemological belief research: Tentative understandings and provocative confusions. *Educational Psychology Review, 6*(4), 293-319.

Schommer, M. A., & Walker, K. (1995). Are epistemological beliefs similar across domains? *Journal of Educational Psychology, 87*(3), 424-432.
Schommer-Aikins, M., & Duell, O. K. (2013). Domain specific and general epistemological beliefs: Their effects on mathematics. *Revista de Investigació n Educativa, 31*(2), 317-330. doi: 10.6018/rie.31.2.170911
Schön, D. A. (1983). *The reflective practitioner: How professionals think in action.* New York, NY: Basic Books.
Schraw, G., Bendixen, L. D., & Dunkle, M. E. (2002). Development and validation of the Epistemic Belief Inventory (EBI). In B. K. Hofer (Ed.), *Personal epistemology: The psychology of beliefs about knowledge and knowing* (pp. 261-275). Mahwah, NJ: Lawrence Erlbaum Associates.
Scribner, S., & Cole, M. (1981). *The psychology of literacy.* Cambridge, MA: Harvard University Press.
Senge, P. M. (1990). The leader's new work: Building learning organisations. *Sloan Management Review, Fall,* 7-23.
Shernoff, D. J. (2013). *Optimal learning environments to promote sudent engagement.* New York, NY: Springer.
Sirikanchana, P. (1998). Buddhism and education: The Thai experience. In B. Saraswati (Ed.), *The cultural dimension of education.* New Delhi: Indira Gandhi National Centre for the Arts.
Soloway, E., & Ehrlich, K. (1984). Empirical studies of programming knowledge. *IEEE Transactions on Software Engineering, SE-10*(5), 595-609.
Son, J. Y., & Goldstone, R. L. (2009). Contextualization in perspective. *Cognition and Instruction, 27*(1), 51-89. doi: 10.1080/07370000802584539
Soudien, C. (2011). *A pedagogy of care: No "ifs" and "buts".* Paper presented at the Nineteenth International Conference on Learning, Mauritius.
Spector, P. E. (1994). Using self-report questionnaires in OB research: A comment on the use of a controversial method. *Journal of Organizational Behaviour, 15*(5), 385-392. http://www.jstor.org
Spivak, G. C. (1988). Can the subaltern speak? In C. Nelson & L. Grossberg (Eds.), *Marxism and the interpretation of culture.* London, UK: Macmillan.
Spradley, J. P. (1977). Foreword. In R. S. Weppner (Ed.), *Street ethnography: Selected studies of crime and drug use in natural settings* (pp. 13-16).
Stahl, E., & Bromme, R. (2007). The CAEB: An instrument for measuring connotative aspects of epistemological beliefs. *Learning and Instruction, 17*(6), 773-785. doi: 10.1016/j.learninstruc.2007.09.016
Sternberg, R. J. (1989). Domain-generality versus domain-specificity: The life and impending death of a false dichotomy. *Merrill-Palmer Quarterly, 35,* 115-130.

Sternglass, M. S. (1997). *Time to know them: A longitudinal study of writing and learning at the college level.* Mahwah, NJ: Lawrence Erlbaum Associates.

Stoneham, N. (2004, April 20). Teaching traditional values. *Bangkok Post.*

Sulimma, M. (2009). Relations between epistemological beliefs and culture classifications. *Multicultural Education & Technology Journal, 3*(1), 74-89.

Tabachnik, B. G., & Fidell, L. S. (2012). *Using multivariate statistics* (6th ed.). Boston, MA: Pearson.

Tagiuri, R. (1968). The concept of organizational climate. In R. Tagiuri & G. H. Litwin (Eds.), *Organizational Climate: Exploration of a Concept.* Boston, MA: Harvard University, Division of Research, Graduate School of Business Administration.

Tay, L., Woo, S. E., Klafehn, J., & Chiu, C.-y. (2010). *10 Conceptualizing and Measuring Culture: Problems and Solutions. The SAGE Handbook of Measurement.* London, UK: SAGE Publications.

The Hofstede Centre. (2014). Cultural tools: Country comparison. Retrieved 15 April, 2014, from http://geert-hofstede.com

Thomas, R., Anderson, L., Getahun, L., & Cooke, B. (1992). *Teaching for transfer of learning* (pp. 1-93). Washington, DC.: Office of Vocational and Adult Education.

Thomas, W. P., & Collier, V. (1997). School effectiveness for language minority students. *National Clearinghouse for Bilingual Education Resource Collection Series* (Vol. 9). Washington, DC.

Thorndike, E. L., & Woodworth, R. S. (1901a). The influence of improvement in one mental function upon the efficiency of other functions. (I). *Psychological Review, 8*(3), 247-261.

Thorndike, E. L., & Woodworth, R. S. (1901b). The influence of improvement in one mental function upon the efficiency of other functions. II. The estimation of magnitudes. *Psychological Review, 8*(4), 384-395. doi: 10.1037/h0071280

Ventura, P., Pattamadilok, C., Fernandes, T., Klein, O., Morais, J., & Kolinsky, R. (2008). Schooling in Western culture promotes context-free processing. *Journal of Experimental Child Psychology*(100), 79-88. doi: 10.1016/j.jecp.2008.02.001

von Glasersfeld, E. (1995). A constructivist approach to teaching. In P. L. Steffe & J. Gale (Eds.), *Constructivism in education.* Hillsdale, NJ: Lawrence Erlbaum Associates.

Vongvipanond, P. (1994). *Linguistic perspectives of Thai culture.* Paper presented at the Workshop of Teachers of Social Science, University of New Orleans.

Vygotsky, L. S. (1962). *Thought and language.* Cambridge, MA: MIT.

Walker, M. G., & Shi, J. (2014). Non-parametric tests. *Statistics Consulting: Biostatistics and bioinformatics for Pharmaceutical and Biotechnical Research and Development.* Retrieved from http://www.walkerbioscience.com

Wang, X., Zhang, Z., Zhang, X., & Dadong. (2013). Validation of the Chinese version of the Epistemic Beliefs Inventory using confirmatory factor analysis. *International Education Studies, 6*(8), 98-111. doi: 10.5539/ies.v6n8p98

Welch, A. G., & Roy, C. M. (2012). A preliminary report of the psychometric properties of the Epistemic Beliefs Inventory. *The European Journal of Social and Behavioural Sciences, 2*(2), 278-303. doi: 10.15405/FutureAcademy/ejsbs(2301-2218).2012.2.12

Wilcox, R. (2012). *Introduction to robust estimation and hypothesis testing* (3rd ed.). Waltham, MA: Academic Press.

Wilkins, A. L., & Patterson, K. J. (1985). You can't get from there to here: What will make culture projects fail. In R. H. Kilmann, M. J. Saxton & R. Serpa (Eds.), *Gaining control of the corporate culture*. Hoboken, NJ: Jossey-Bass.

Wood, P., & Kardash, C. (2002). Critical elements in the design and analysis of studies of epistemology. In B. K. Hofer & P. R. Pintrich (Eds.), *Personal epistemology: The psychology of beliefs about knowledge and knowing* (pp. 231-260). Mahwah, NJ: Erlbaum.

Wyatt, D. K. (2003). *Thailand: A short history* (2nd ed.). New Haven, CT: Yale University Press.

Wylie, H. H. (1919). An experimental study of transfer of response in the white rat. *Behavioral Monographs, 3*(16).

Youn, I., Yang, K.-M., & Choi, I.-J. (2000). An analysis of the nature of epistemic beliefs: Investigating factors affecting the epistemological development of South Korean high school students. *Asian Pacific Education Review, 2*(1), 10-21.

Appendices

Appendix A: Excerpt from Outcomes Statement for First-Year Composition from Council of Writing Program Administrators (2008)

Rhetorical Knowledge

By the end of first year composition, students should:

- Focus on a purpose
- Respond to the needs of different audiences
- Respond appropriately to different kinds of rhetorical situations
- Use conventions of format and structure appropriate to the rhetorical situation
- Adopt appropriate voice, tone, and level of formality
- Understand how genres shape reading and writing
- Write in several genres

Critical Thinking, Reading, and Writing

By the end of first year composition, students should:

- Use writing and reading for inquiry, learning, thinking, and communicating
- Understand a writing assignment as a series of tasks, including finding, evaluating, analyzing, and synthesizing appropriate primary and secondary sources
- Integrate their own ideas with those of others
- Understand the relationships among language, knowledge, and power

Processes

By the end of first year composition, students should:

- Be aware that it usually takes multiple drafts to create and complete a successful text
- Develop flexible strategies for generating, revising, editing, and proof-reading
- Understand writing as an open process that permits writers to use later invention and re- thinking to revise their work
- Understand the collaborative and social aspects of writing processes
- Learn to critique their own and others' works
- Learn to balance the advantages of relying on others with the responsibility of doing their part
- Use a variety of technologies to address a range of audiences

Knowledge of Conventions

By the end of first year composition, students should:

- Learn common formats for different kinds of texts
- Develop knowledge of genre conventions ranging from structure and paragraphing to tone and mechanics
- Practice appropriate means of documenting their work
- Control such surface features as syntax, grammar, punctuation, and spelling

Composing in Electronic Environments

By the end of first year composition, students should:

- Use electronic environments for drafting, reviewing, revising, editing, and sharing texts
- Locate, evaluate, organize, and use research material collected from electronic sources, including scholarly library databases; other official databases (e.g., federal government databases); and informal electronic networks and internet sources

Appendix B: Part One of Questionnaire[1]

PART 1: EPISTEMIC BELIEFS INVENTORY (EBI)

Please indicate how strongly you agree or disagree with each of the statements listed below. Please circle the number that best corresponds to the strength of your belief.

กรุณาระบุว่าคุณเห็นด้วยหรือไม่เห็นด้วยอย่างไรกับแต่ละข้อความดังต่อไปนี้
กรุณาวงกลมตัวเลขที่สอดคล้องกับระดับความเชื่อของคุณมากที่สุด

1. It bothers me when instructors don't tell students the answers to complicated problems.
   มันทำให้ฉันรู้สึกรำคาญเมื่ออาจารย์ไม่เฉลยคำตอบกับปัญหาที่ซับซ้อนแก่นักศึกษา

   Strongly disagree / ไม่เห็นด้วยอย่างยิ่ง   1   2   3   4   5   Strongly agree / เห็นด้วยอย่างยิ่ง

2. Truth means different things to different people.
   ความจริงมีความหมายแตกต่างกันไปตามแต่ละบุคคล

   Strongly disagree / ไม่เห็นด้วยอย่างยิ่ง   1   2   3   4   5   Strongly agree / เห็นด้วยอย่างยิ่ง

3. Students who learn things quickly are the most successful.
   นักศึกษาที่เรียนรู้ได้เร็วคือคนที่ประสบความสำเร็จที่สุด

   Strongly disagree / ไม่เห็นด้วยอย่างยิ่ง   1   2   3   4   5   Strongly agree / เห็นด้วยอย่างยิ่ง

4. People should always obey the law.
   ประชาชนควรเคารพกฎหมายเสมอ

   Strongly disagree / ไม่เห็นด้วยอย่างยิ่ง   1   2   3   4   5   Strongly agree / เห็นด้วยอย่างยิ่ง

5. Some people will never be smart no matter how hard they work.
   บางคนไม่มีวันฉลาดเลยไม่ว่าเขาจะขยันแค่ไหนก็ตาม

   Strongly disagree / ไม่เห็นด้วยอย่างยิ่ง   1   2   3   4   5   Strongly agree / เห็นด้วยอย่างยิ่ง

6. Absolute moral truth does not exist.
   ความจริงแห่งคุณธรรมที่แท้จริงไม่มี

   Strongly disagree / ไม่เห็นด้วยอย่างยิ่ง   1   2   3   4   5   Strongly agree / เห็นด้วยอย่างยิ่ง

7. Parents should teach their children all there is to know about life.
   พ่อแม่ควรสอนลูกทุกอย่างที่จำเป็นต้องรู้เกี่ยวกับชีวิต

   Strongly disagree / ไม่เห็นด้วยอย่างยิ่ง   1   2   3   4   5   Strongly agree / เห็นด้วยอย่างยิ่ง

EBI (English/ Thai) revised 28 May 2011   Original instrument: Schraw, Bendixen, & Dunkle (2002)
Thai translation: Tawatchai Mongkolsakulrit (March, 2011)
Thai translation revised: Arpaporn Iemubol (May, 2011)

---

[1] The original English language version of EBI is used with the kind permission of Prof. Gregory Schraw, University of Nevada (personal communication, June 3, 2011).

8. Really smart students don't have to work as hard to do well in school.
   นักศึกษาที่ฉลาดจริงๆไม่จำเป็นต้องขยันเพื่อให้ได้คะแนนดี

   Strongly disagree / ไม่เห็นด้วยอย่างยิ่ง   1   2   3   4   5   Strongly agree / เห็นด้วยอย่างยิ่ง

9. If a person tries too hard to understand a problem, they will most likely end up being confused.
   ถ้าคนเราพยายามทำความเข้าใจกับปัญหามากเกินไป มักจะเกิดความสับสนในที่สุด

   Strongly disagree / ไม่เห็นด้วยอย่างยิ่ง   1   2   3   4   5   Strongly agree / เห็นด้วยอย่างยิ่ง

10. Too many theories just complicate things.
    ทฤษฎีมากเกินไปมีแต่ทำให้เรื่องราวซับซ้อนยิ่งขึ้น

    Strongly disagree / ไม่เห็นด้วยอย่างยิ่ง   1   2   3   4   5   Strongly agree / เห็นด้วยอย่างยิ่ง

11. The best ideas are often the most simple.
    ความคิดที่ดีที่สุดมักเป็นความคิดที่ง่ายที่สุด

    Strongly disagree / ไม่เห็นด้วยอย่างยิ่ง   1   2   3   4   5   Strongly agree / เห็นด้วยอย่างยิ่ง

12. People can't do too much about how smart they are.
    คนเราไม่สามารถทำอะไรเกี่ยวกับความฉลาดของเขาได้มากนัก

    Strongly disagree / ไม่เห็นด้วยอย่างยิ่ง   1   2   3   4   5   Strongly agree / เห็นด้วยอย่างยิ่ง

13. Instructors should focus on facts instead of theories.
    อาจารย์ควรมุ่งเน้นความจริงมากกว่าทฤษฎี

    Strongly disagree / ไม่เห็นด้วยอย่างยิ่ง   1   2   3   4   5   Strongly agree / เห็นด้วยอย่างยิ่ง

14. I like teachers who present several competing theories and let their students decide which is best.
    ฉันชอบคุณครูที่นำเสนอหลายๆทฤษฎีแข่งกัน และให้นักเรียนตัดสินว่าอันไหนดีที่สุด

    Strongly disagree / ไม่เห็นด้วยอย่างยิ่ง   1   2   3   4   5   Strongly agree / เห็นด้วยอย่างยิ่ง

15. How well you do in school depends on how smart you are.
    ผลการเรียนคุณดีแค่ไหนขึ้นอยู่กับว่าคุณฉลาดแค่ไหน

    Strongly disagree / ไม่เห็นด้วยอย่างยิ่ง   1   2   3   4   5   Strongly agree / เห็นด้วยอย่างยิ่ง

16. If you don't learn something quickly, you won't ever learn it.
    ถ้าคุณไม่เรียนรู้บางอย่างอย่างรวดเร็ว คุณก็จะไม่มีวันเรียนรู้มัน

    Strongly disagree   1   2   3   4   5   Strongly agree
    ไม่เห็นด้วยอย่างยิ่ง   เห็นด้วยอย่างยิ่ง

17. Some people just have a knack for learning and others don't.
    บางคนมีความสามารถพิเศษในการเรียนรู้และบางคนไม่มี

    Strongly disagree   1   2   3   4   5   Strongly agree
    ไม่เห็นด้วยอย่างยิ่ง   เห็นด้วยอย่างยิ่ง

18. Things are simpler than most professors would have you believe.
    เรื่องราวต่างๆง่ายกว่าที่อาจารย์ส่วนใหญ่อยากให้คุณเชื่อ

    Strongly disagree   1   2   3   4   5   Strongly agree
    ไม่เห็นด้วยอย่างยิ่ง   เห็นด้วยอย่างยิ่ง

19. If two people are arguing about something, at least one of them must be wrong.
    ถ้าคนสองคนถกเถียงกัน อย่างน้อยจะต้องมีคนหนึ่งที่ผิด

    Strongly disagree   1   2   3   4   5   Strongly agree
    ไม่เห็นด้วยอย่างยิ่ง   เห็นด้วยอย่างยิ่ง

20. Children should be allowed to question their parents' authority.
    เด็กๆควรได้รับอนุญาตให้ตั้งข้อสงสัยเกี่ยวกับอำนาจของพ่อแม่

    Strongly disagree   1   2   3   4   5   Strongly agree
    ไม่เห็นด้วยอย่างยิ่ง   เห็นด้วยอย่างยิ่ง

21. If you haven't understood a chapter the first time through, going back over it won't help.
    ถ้าคุณไม่เข้าใจบทเรียนในหนังสือตั้งแต่แรก การย้อนกลับไปก็ไม่ช่วยอะไร

    Strongly disagree   1   2   3   4   5   Strongly agree
    ไม่เห็นด้วยอย่างยิ่ง   เห็นด้วยอย่างยิ่ง

22. Science is easy to understand because it contains so many facts.
    วิทยาศาสตร์เป็นสิ่งที่เข้าใจง่าย เนื่องจากประกอบด้วยข้อเท็จจริงมากมาย

    Strongly disagree   1   2   3   4   5   Strongly agree
    ไม่เห็นด้วยอย่างยิ่ง   เห็นด้วยอย่างยิ่ง

23. The moral rules I live by apply to everyone.
    กฎคุณธรรมที่ฉันปฏิบัติอยู่นำไปใช้กับทุกๆคน

    Strongly disagree   1   2   3   4   5   Strongly agree
    ไม่เห็นด้วยอย่างยิ่ง   เห็นด้วยอย่างยิ่ง

24. The more you know about a topic, the more there is to know.
    คุณยิ่งรู้เกี่ยวกับหัวข้อมากเท่าไร ยิ่งมีสิ่งที่ต้องรู้มากขึ้น

    Strongly disagree   1   2   3   4   5   Strongly agree
    ไม่เห็นด้วยอย่างยิ่ง   เห็นด้วยอย่างยิ่ง

EBI (English/ Thai) revised 28 May 2011

Original instrument: Schraw, Bendixen, & Dunkle (2002)
Thai translation: Tawatchai Mongkolsakulrit (March, 2011)
Thai translation revised: Arpaporn Iemubol (May, 2011)

25. What is true today will be true tomorrow.
สิ่งที่เป็นจริงในวันนี้จะต้องเป็นจริงในวันหน้า

   Strongly disagree 1 2 3 4 5 Strongly agree
   ไม่เห็นด้วยอย่างยิ่ง   เห็นด้วยอย่างยิ่ง

26. Smart people are born that way.
คนที่ฉลาดเป็นมาตั้งแต่เกิด

   Strongly disagree 1 2 3 4 5 Strongly agree
   ไม่เห็นด้วยอย่างยิ่ง   เห็นด้วยอย่างยิ่ง

27. When someone in authority tells me what to do, I usually do it.
เมื่อคนที่มีอำนาจบอกให้ฉันทำอะไร ฉันมักจะทำตาม

   Strongly disagree 1 2 3 4 5 Strongly agree
   ไม่เห็นด้วยอย่างยิ่ง   เห็นด้วยอย่างยิ่ง

28. People who question authority are troublemakers.
คนที่สงสัยในอำนาจคือผู้ก่อความเดือดร้อน

   Strongly disagree 1 2 3 4 5 Strongly agree
   ไม่เห็นด้วยอย่างยิ่ง   เห็นด้วยอย่างยิ่ง

29. Working on a problem with no quick solution is a waste of time.
การแก้ไขปัญหาโดยไม่มีทางแก้ที่รวดเร็วนั้นเป็นการเสียเวลา

   Strongly disagree 1 2 3 4 5 Strongly agree
   ไม่เห็นด้วยอย่างยิ่ง   เห็นด้วยอย่างยิ่ง

30. You can study something for years and still not really understand it.
คุณสามารถศึกษาบางอย่างเป็นแรมปีและยังคงไม่เข้าใจอยู่ดี

   Strongly disagree 1 2 3 4 5 Strongly agree
   ไม่เห็นด้วยอย่างยิ่ง   เห็นด้วยอย่างยิ่ง

31. Sometimes there are no right answers to life's big problems.
บางครั้งปัญหาที่ยิ่งใหญ่ของชีวิตก็ไม่มีคำตอบที่ถูกต้อง

   Strongly disagree 1 2 3 4 5 Strongly agree
   ไม่เห็นด้วยอย่างยิ่ง   เห็นด้วยอย่างยิ่ง

32. Some people are born with special gifts and talents.
บางคนเกิดมาพร้อมพรสวรรค์และความสามารถพิเศษ

   Strongly disagree 1 2 3 4 5 Strongly agree
   ไม่เห็นด้วยอย่างยิ่ง   เห็นด้วยอย่างยิ่ง

Appendix C: Part Two of Questionnaire

PART 2: MEASURE OF ACADEMIC LITERACY TRANSFER (MALT)

A. Reading and Research

Please indicate your agreement to the following statements, which are about your courses OTHER THAN ENGLISH. **Circle** the appropriate number.

In **other courses**, I use what I have learnt in the English Communication (EC) classes to...

1. tell the difference between fact and opinion in a reading text.

    Strongly disagree   1   2   3   4   5   Strongly agree
    ไม่เห็นด้วยอย่างยิ่ง   เห็นด้วยอย่างยิ่ง

2. find the main idea of a reading text.

    Strongly disagree   1   2   3   4   5   Strongly agree
    ไม่เห็นด้วยอย่างยิ่ง   เห็นด้วยอย่างยิ่ง

3. find problems in the reasoning (logic) of an argument.

    Strongly disagree   1   2   3   4   5   Strongly agree
    ไม่เห็นด้วยอย่างยิ่ง   เห็นด้วยอย่างยิ่ง

4. find problems in the support (evidence) of an argument.

    Strongly disagree   1   2   3   4   5   Strongly agree
    ไม่เห็นด้วยอย่างยิ่ง   เห็นด้วยอย่างยิ่ง

5. decide which sources (books, websites, articles, etc.) will be useful for a research assignment.

    Strongly disagree   1   2   3   4   5   Strongly agree
    ไม่เห็นด้วยอย่างยิ่ง   เห็นด้วยอย่างยิ่ง

6. tell the difference between a reliable source (book, website, article, etc.) and an unreliable one.

    Strongly disagree   1   2   3   4   5   Strongly agree
    ไม่เห็นด้วยอย่างยิ่ง   เห็นด้วยอย่างยิ่ง

7. avoid plagiarism (using citation and referencing).

    Strongly disagree   1   2   3   4   5   Strongly agree
    ไม่เห็นด้วยอย่างยิ่ง   เห็นด้วยอย่างยิ่ง

8. In which course(s), **other than EC**, do you most use the reading and/ or research skills listed above?

_____
_____

9. In what other ways, if any, have your EC reading and/ or research skills helped you **in other courses?**

_____
_____
_____

MALT Original version: Green (2008)

B. Writing

Please indicate your agreement to the following statements, which are about your courses OTHER THAN ENGLISH. **Circle** the appropriate number.

In **other courses**, I use what I have learnt in the English Communication (EC) classes to...

10. write information from texts in my own words (paraphrase).

    Strongly disagree / ไม่เห็นด้วยอย่างยิ่ง   1   2   3   4   5   Strongly agree / เห็นด้วยอย่างยิ่ง

11. back up statements with specific support (examples, expert opinion, facts, statistics).

    Strongly disagree / ไม่เห็นด้วยอย่างยิ่ง   1   2   3   4   5   Strongly agree / เห็นด้วยอย่างยิ่ง

12. plan and organize my writing (outlines, drafts etc.).

    Strongly disagree / ไม่เห็นด้วยอย่างยิ่ง   1   2   3   4   5   Strongly agree / เห็นด้วยอย่างยิ่ง

13. write a thesis statement for written assignments.

    Strongly disagree / ไม่เห็นด้วยอย่างยิ่ง   1   2   3   4   5   Strongly agree / เห็นด้วยอย่างยิ่ง

14. write topic sentences to start paragraphs.

    Strongly disagree / ไม่เห็นด้วยอย่างยิ่ง   1   2   3   4   5   Strongly agree / เห็นด้วยอย่างยิ่ง

15. structure my writing according to a pattern (compare/ contrast, classification, cause/ effect etc.)

    Strongly disagree / ไม่เห็นด้วยอย่างยิ่ง   1   2   3   4   5   Strongly agree / เห็นด้วยอย่างยิ่ง

16. take care to use correct grammar and spelling.

    Strongly disagree / ไม่เห็นด้วยอย่างยิ่ง   1   2   3   4   5   Strongly agree / เห็นด้วยอย่างยิ่ง

17. In which course(s), **other than EC**, did you most use the writing skills listed above?

    _____
    _____
    _____

18. In what other ways, if any, have EC writing skills been useful **in other courses**?

    _____
    _____
    _____

MALT Original version: Green (2008)

Appendix D: Part Three of Questionnaire

PART 3: DEMOGRAPHIC SURVEY

Please tick the applicable box (☑) in each category. Fill in information where required.

Gender:	☐ Male ☐ Female	**Age:**	☐ 16-18 ☐ 19-21 ☐ 22-25 ☐ 26-30 ☐ 30+
Primary nationality *(if you have multiple nationalities, with which do you most identify yourself?):*	☐ Thai, Malaysian, Laotian or other Southeast Asian ☐ Chinese, Japanese, Korean or other East Asian ☐ Indian, Pakistani, other subcontinental Asian, or Middle Eastern ☐ European, North American, Australian, New Zealand ☐ Other (please specify): _____	**Type of high school last attended** *(excluding exchange programs)*	☐ State/ Government School in Thailand ☐ Bilingual School in Thailand ☐ International School in Thailand ☐ School Abroad in Southeast Asia ☐ School Abroad in other Asia (please specify: _____ ☐ School abroad in North America, Europe, Australia or New Zealand ☐ Other (please specify):
		Time spent at last high school *(excluding exchange programs)*	☐ 5 years or more ☐ 4 years ☐ 3 years ☐ 2 years ☐ 1 year ☐ **less than** 1 year
High School GPA *(on a 4-point scale; if applicable):*	☐ 0-2.0 ☐ 2.0-2.25 ☐ 2.26-2.5 ☐ 2.51-3.0 ☐ 3.10-3.5 ☐ 3.6-4.00	Did you participate in a student exchange program during high school:	☐ Yes ☐ No If yes, to which country: _____ For how long: _____
Current Trimester at MUIC:	☐ 1st ☐ 2nd ☐ 3rd ☐ 4th ☐ 5th ☐ 6th ☐ 7th ☐ other (specify): _____	**Current College GPA** *(on a 4-point scale):*	☐ 0-2.0 ☐ 2.0-2.25 ☐ 2.26-2.5 ☐ 2.51-3.0 ☐ 3.10-3.5 ☐ 3.6-4.00

Appendix E: Matrix for Semi-Structured Interviews

Matrix for Semi-Structured Interviews

Introduction: purpose of research, tape recorder/confidentiality, conduct of interview.

Overarching Themes (from Research Framework)	Questions	Possible Probes (Follow-up Questions)
Secondary Schooling Background	Please can you tell me about the high school/ secondary school that you attended?	What did you like/ dislike about the school? Where were the teachers from? What were they like?
	Can you tell me about a typical class session in the school you attended?	What kind of activities did you do? Why do you think you did these activities?
About Knowledge and Knowing	How do you feel when students question the teachers' authority in class? (1)	Why do you feel this way?
	Do you agree that true knowledge stays the same over time (2)	(If yes) Why? (If no) What changes can happen? How?
	Some people believe that it's better to learn things slowly, over time. To what extent do you agree with this? (3)	How do you feel when you can't immediately understand what you read in textbooks or hear in lectures?
	How do you feel about courses that offer a lot of theories instead of facts?	Why do you feel this way?
	What kind of students do you believe are the most successful in college? (5)	Why do you think these students are successful?
Perceptions of Transfer from English Communications Classes	Why do you think students' are required to study the English Communications (EC) courses at MUIC?	Are these objectives being met? Why/ why not?
	In what ways, if any, have the EC courses been useful to you personally in your studies?	What skills or knowledge from EC do you use in your other courses? In which courses do you use the skills or knowledge from EC?

Conclusion: gratitude, reassurance of confidentiality and right to withdraw, further information on research findings, grievance procedures

DEEP UNIVERSITY PRESS
SCIENTIFIC BOARD MEMBERS

Dr. Araceli Alonso, Global Health Institute, Department of Gender and Women's Studies, University of Wisconsin-Madison, USA

Dr. Ronald C. Arnett, Chair and Professor, Department of Communication & Rhetorical Studies, Duquesne University

Dr. Gilles Baillat, Rector, ex-Director of CDIUFM Conference of French Teacher Education Directors, University of Reims, France

Dr. Niels Brouwer, Graduate School of Education, Radboud Universiteit Nijmegen, The Netherlands

Dr. Jianlin Chen, Shanghai International Studies University, China

Dr. Yuangshan Chuang, President of APAMALL, NETPAW Director, Tajen University, Taiwan, ROC

Dr. Enrique Correa Molina, Professor and Vice-Dean, Faculty of Education, University of Sherbrooke, Canada

Dr. José Correia, Dean of Education, University of Porto, Portugal

Dr. Muhammet Demirbilek, Head, Educational Science Department, Suleyman Demirel University, Isparta, Turkey

Dr. Ángel Díaz-Barriga Casales, Professor, Autonomous National University of México UNAM (Mexico)

Dr. Isabelle C. Druc, Department of Anthropology, University of Wisconsin-Madison, USA

Bertha Du-Babcock, Professor, Department of English for Business, City University of Hong Kong, Hong Kong, China

Dr. W. John Coletta , Professor, University of Wisconsin-Stevens Point, USA

Marc Durand, Professor, Faculty of Psychology and Education, University of Geneva, Switzerland

Dr. Paul Durning, Doctoral School, French National Observatory, EUSARF, University of Paris X Nanterre, Paris, France

Dr. Manuel Fernandez Cruz, Professor, University of Granada, Spain

Dr. Stephanie Fonvielle, Associate Professor, Teacher Education University Institute, University of Aix-Marseille, France

Dr. Elliot Gaines, Professor, Wright State University, President of the Semiotic Society of America, Internat. Communicology Institute

Dr. Mingle Gao, Dean, College of Education, Beijing Language and Culture University (BLCU), Beijing, China

Dr. Mercedes González Sanmamed, Professor at the University of Coruña, Spain

Dr. Gabriela Hernández Vega, Professor, University of Nariño, Colombia

Dr. Xiang Long, Guilin University of Electronic Technology, China

Dr. Maria Masucci, Drew University, New Jersey, USA

Dr. Liliana Morandi, Associate Professor, National University of Rio Cuarto, Cordoba, Argentina

Dr. Joëlle Morrissette, Professor, Department of Educational Psychology, Université of Montreal, Quebec, Canada

Dr. Martha Murzi Vivas, Professor, University of Los Andes, Venezuela

Dr. Thi Cuc Phuong Nguyen, Vice Rector, Hanoi University, Vietnam

Dr. Shirley O'Neill, Associate Professor, President of the International Society for leadership in Pedagogies and Learning, University of Southern Queensland, Australia

Dr. José-Luis Ortega, Professor, Foreign Language Education, Faculty of Education, University of Granada, Spain

Dr. Surendra Pathak, Head and Professor, Department of Value Education, IASE University of Gandhi Viday Mandir, India

Dr. Charls Pearson, Logic, Semiotics, Philosophy of Science, Peirce Studies, Director of Research, Semiotics Research Institute

Dr. Luis Porta Vázquez, Professor at the National University of Mar del Plata CONICET (Argentina)

Dr. Shen Qi, Associate Professor, Shanghai Foreign Studies University (SHISU), Shanghai, China

Dr. Timothy Reagan, Professor and Dean of the College of Education at Zayed University in Abu Dhabi/Dubai, Saudi Arabia

Dr. Antonia Schleicher, Professor, NARLC Director, NCTOLCTL Exec. Director, ACTFL Board, Indiana University-Bloomington, USA

Dr. Farouk Y. Seif, Exec. Director of the Semiotic Society of America, Center for Creative Change, Antioch University Seattle, Washington

Dr. Gary Shank, Professor, Educational Foundations and Leadership, Duquesne University, Pittsburgh, Pennsylvania

Dr. Kemal Silay, Professor, Flagship Program Director, Department of Central Eurasia, Indiana University-Bloomington, USA

Dr. José Tejada Fernández, Professor at the Autonomous University of Barcelona, Spain

Dr. François Victor Tochon, Professor, University of Wisconsin-Madison, President of the International Network for Language Education Policy Studies, USA

Dr. Brooke Williams Deely, Women, Culture and Society Program, Philosophy Department, University of St. Thomas, Houston

Dr. Jianfang Xiao, Associate Professor at School of English and Education, Guangdong University of Foreign Studies, China

Dr. Ronghui Zhao, Director, Institute of Linguistic Studies, Shanghai Foreign Studies University, Shanghai, China

Other referees may be contacted depending the Book Series or the nature and topic of the manuscript proposed.

Contact: publisher@deepuniversity.net

Deep Language Learning Book Series

Language learning needs to be reconceptualized in two ways: first, as an expression of dynamic planning prototypes that can be activated through self-directed projects. Second, integrating structure and agency to meet deeper, humane aims. The dynamism of human exchange is meaning- producing through multiple connected intentions among language task domains.

Language-learning tasks have a cross-cultural purpose which then become meaningful within broader projects that meet higher values and aims such as deep ecology, deep culture, deep politics and deep humane economics. Applied semiotics will be a tool beyond the linguistic in favor of value-loaded projects that are chosen in order to revolutionize the current state of affairs, in increasing our sense of responsibility for our actions as humans vis-à-vis our fellow humans and our home planet. In this respect, deep instructional planning offers a grammar for action. Understanding adaptive and complex cross-cultural situations is the prime focus of such a hermeneutic inquiry.

For more, see here:

http://deepuniversity.com/deeplanguage.html

Language Education Policy Book Series

Language Education Policy (LEP) is the process through which the ideals, goals, and contents of a language policy can be realized in education practices. Language policies express ideological processes. Their analysis reveals the perceptions of realities proper to certain sociocultural contexts. LEPs further their ideologies by defining and disseminating the values of policymakers. Because Language Education Policies are related to status, ideology, and vision of what society should be and traditions of thoughts, such issues are complex, quickly evolving, submitted to trends and political views, and they need to be studied calmly. The way to approach them is to get comparative information on what has been done in many settings, which are working or not, which are their flaws and merits, and try to grasp the contextual variables that might apply in specific locations, without generalizing too fast.

Policy discourses and curricula reveal the ideological framing of the constructs that they encode and create, project, enact, and enforce aspects such as language status, power and rights through projective texts generated to forward and describe the contexts of their enactments. Policy documents are therefore socially transformative through their evaluative function that frames and guides action in order to achieve language reforms. While temperance and reflection are required to address such complex issues, because moving to fast may create trouble, nonetheless the absence of action in this domain may lead to systemic intolerance, injustice, inequity, mass discrimination and even, genocidal crimes.

http://deepuniversity.com/lep.html

Science Teachers Who Draw: The *Red* Is Always There

Dr. Merrie Koester
Project Draw for Science
Center for Science Education
University of South Carolina

This book documents the ways in which science teacher researchers used drawing to construct semiotic spaces inside which students acquired significant aesthetic capital and agency. Many previously failing students brokered this new capital into improved academic achievement and a sense of felt freedom.

Science Teachers Who Draw: The Red is Always There is a book which asks, "What happens when science teachers adopt an *aesthetic* approach to inquiry, using drawing to communicate deep understanding?" This narrative inquiry was driven by quantitative studies which reveal a robust positive correlation between students' test scores in reading and science, beginning at the middle school level. When the data are disaggregated, there exists a vast achievement gap for low income and English language learners. Science teachers are faced with a semiotic nightmare. Often possessing inadequate pedagogical content knowledge themselves, science teachers must somehow symbolically *communicate* often highly abstract knowledge in ways that can be not only be decoded by their students' but later used to construct deeper, more differentiated knowledge, which can be applied to make sense of and adapt successfully to life on Planet Earth.

An invaluable resource for teachers, teacher educators, and qualitative researchers.

http://www.deepuniversity.net/koester.html

Out of Havana:
Memoirs of Ordinary Life in Cuba

Dr. Araceli Alonso
University of Wisconsin-Madison

Out of Havana provides an uncommon ordinary woman's insight into the last half century of Cuba's tumultuous recent history. More powerfully than an academic study or historical account, it allows us intimately to grasp the enthusiasm, commitment and sense of promise that defined many average Cubans' experience of the 1959 Revolution and the first triumphant decades of the Castro regime. As the story shifts into the final decades of the last century (the 1980s Mariel Boatlift, the so-called "special period in time of peace" [from 1991 to the end of the decade], and the 1994 Balseros or Rafters Crisis), it starts gradually to reveal, with understated yet relentless eloquence, an ultimately insuperable rift between the high-flown official rhetoric of uncompromising struggle and revolutionary sacrifice and the harsh conditions and cruelly absurd situations that the protagonist, along with the majority of Cubans, begin routinely to live out. It is a rare and important document, a unique personal chronicle of an everyday Cuban reality that most Americans continue to know only fragmentarily.

Dr. Araceli Alonso is a 2013 United Nations Award Winner for her activism on women's health and women right. Associate Faculty at the University of Wisconsin-Madison in the Department of Gender and Women's Studies and in the School of Medicine and Public Health, she is the Founder and Director of the award-winning non-profit organization Health by Motorbike.

http://www.deepuniversity.net/ara.html

Formación Y Desarrollo De Profesionales De La Educación: Un enfoque profundo

Manuel Fernández Cruz
Universidad de Granada

El libro contiene herramientas prácticas para la intervención formativa. Se plantea la formación desde la perspectiva del desarrollo profesional y se adopta un enfoque profundo novedoso que integra los ámbitos racionales, emocionales y vivenciales que requiere el aprendizaje y la actualización permanente en las profesiones educativas: la docencia, la pedagogía, la psicología, o la formación de formadores.

- El estudiante universitario va a contar con un manual teórico-práctico de referencia para dominar el ámbito de la formación y el desarrollo profesional.
- El educador va a encontrar en el texto herramientas provechosas para encarar su propio proceso de desarrollo y perfeccionamiento.
- El formador de formadores va a disponer de referencias teóricas y actividades prácticas que facilitarán su intervención.

Dr. Manuel Fernández Cruz, Licenciado en Pedagogía y Doctor en Ciencias de la Educación, es profesor de la Universidad de Granada desde 1992. Actualmente es Director del Departamento de Didáctica y Organización Escolar y Coordinador General del Consorcio Internacional MUNDUSFOR (Formación de Profesionales de la Formación).

http://www.deepuniversity.net/book5.html

Guide to Authors

What our Publishing Team can offer:

- An international editorial team, in more than 20 universities around the world.
- Dedicated and experienced topic editors who will review and provide feedback on your initial proposal.
- A specific format that will speed up the production of your book and its publication.
- Higher royalties than most publishers and a discount on the initial batch orders of 100 copies.
- Global distribution and marketing in the U.S., UK, Europe, Australia, Brazil, China, Mexico, Russia, and Asian countries.
- Fast recognition of your work in your area of specialization.
- Quality design and affordable sales pricing. Using the latest technology, our books are produced efficiently, quickly and attractively.
- A global marketing plan, including electronic and web marketing on social networks and review mailing.
- Book Series: Deep Education; Deep Language Learning; Semiotic Depth; Language Education Policy; Deep Professional Development; Deep Activism.

http://www.deepuniversitypress.com/universitypress.html

- Contact : publisher@deepuniversity.net

Deep University Online !

For updates and more resources
Visit the Deep University Website:

www.deepuniversity.net

www.deepuniversitypress.org

Contact : **publisher@deepuniversity.net**

❖ Facebook group on Deep Language Learning :
https://www.facebook.com/groups/deep.approach/

❖ Twitter: http://twitter.com/Deep_Approach

Correspondence

Dr. Jonathan H. Green

jonohgreen@gmail.com

CPSIA information can be obtained at www.ICGtesting.com
Printed in the USA
LVOW06s2035100815
449580LV00025B/96/P